Provincial Royal Commissions and Commissions of Inquiry, 1867-1982:
A Selective Bibliography

Commissions royales provinciales et commissions d'enquête, 1867-1982 :
bibliographie sélective

Compiled by / Préparée par Lise Maillet

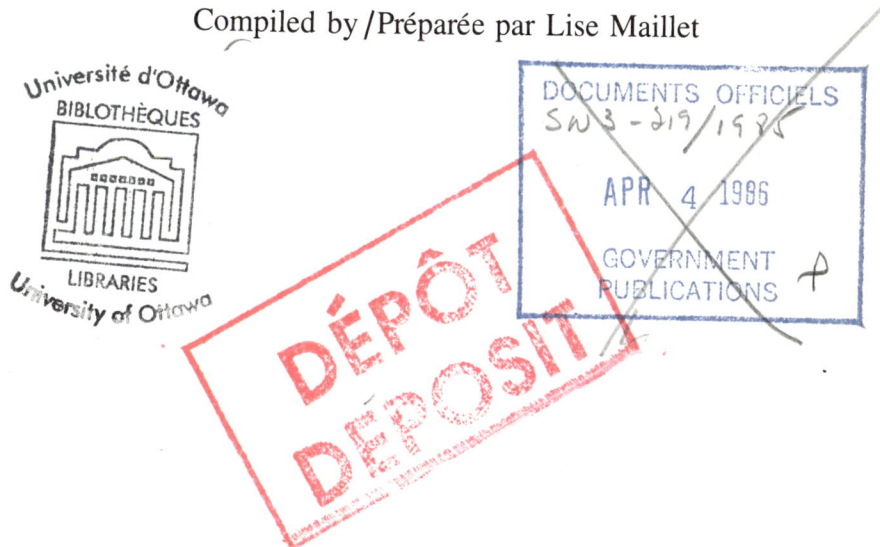

 National Library of Canada — Bibliothèque nationale du Canada

OTTAWA
1986

Canadian Cataloguing in Publication Data

Maillet, Lise
   Provincial royal commissions and commissions of inquiry, 1867-1982 = Commissions royales provinciales et commissions d'enquête, 1867-1982

Text in English and French.
Includes index.
ISBN 0-660-53123-2
DSS Cat. no SN3-219/1985

1. Government investigations--Canada--Provinces. I. National Library of Canada II. Title. III. Title: Commissions royales provinciales et commissions d'enquête, 1867-1982.

Z1373.3.M34 1986   016.3547109'3   C86-090026-6E

Cover Design: Map from the Department of Energy, Mines and Resources

Données de catalogage avant publication (Canada)

Maillet, Lise
   Provincial royal commissions and commissions of inquiry, 1867-1982 = Commissions royales provinciales et commissions d'enquête, 1867-1982

Texte en anglais et en français.
Comprend un index.
ISBN 0-660-53123-2
Cat. MAS no SN3-219/1985

1. Enquêtes publiques--Canada--Provinces.
I. Bibliothèque nationale du Canada II. Titre.
III. Titre: Commissions royales provinciales et commissions d'enquête, 1867-1982.

Z1373.3.M34 1986   016.3547109'3   C86-090026-6F

Couverture: Carte provenant du ministère de l'Énergie, des Mines et des Ressources

© Minister of Supply and Services Canada 1985

Available in Canada through

Authorized Bookstore Agents
and other bookstores

or by mail from

Canadian Government Publishing Centre
Supply and Services Canada
Ottawa, Canada, K1A 0S9

Catalogue No. SN3-219/1985   Canada: $15.00
ISBN 0-660-53123-2   Other countries: $18.00

Price subject to change without notice.

© Ministre des Approvisionnements et Services Canada 1985

En vente au Canada par l'entremise de nos agents libraires agréés
et autres librairies

ou par la poste auprès du:

Centre d'édition du gouvernement du Canada
Approvisionnements et Services Canada
Ottawa, (Canada) K1A 0S9

No de catalogue SN3-219/1985   au Canada: $15.00
ISBN 0-660-53123-2   à l'étranger: $18.00

Prix sujet à changement sans préavis.

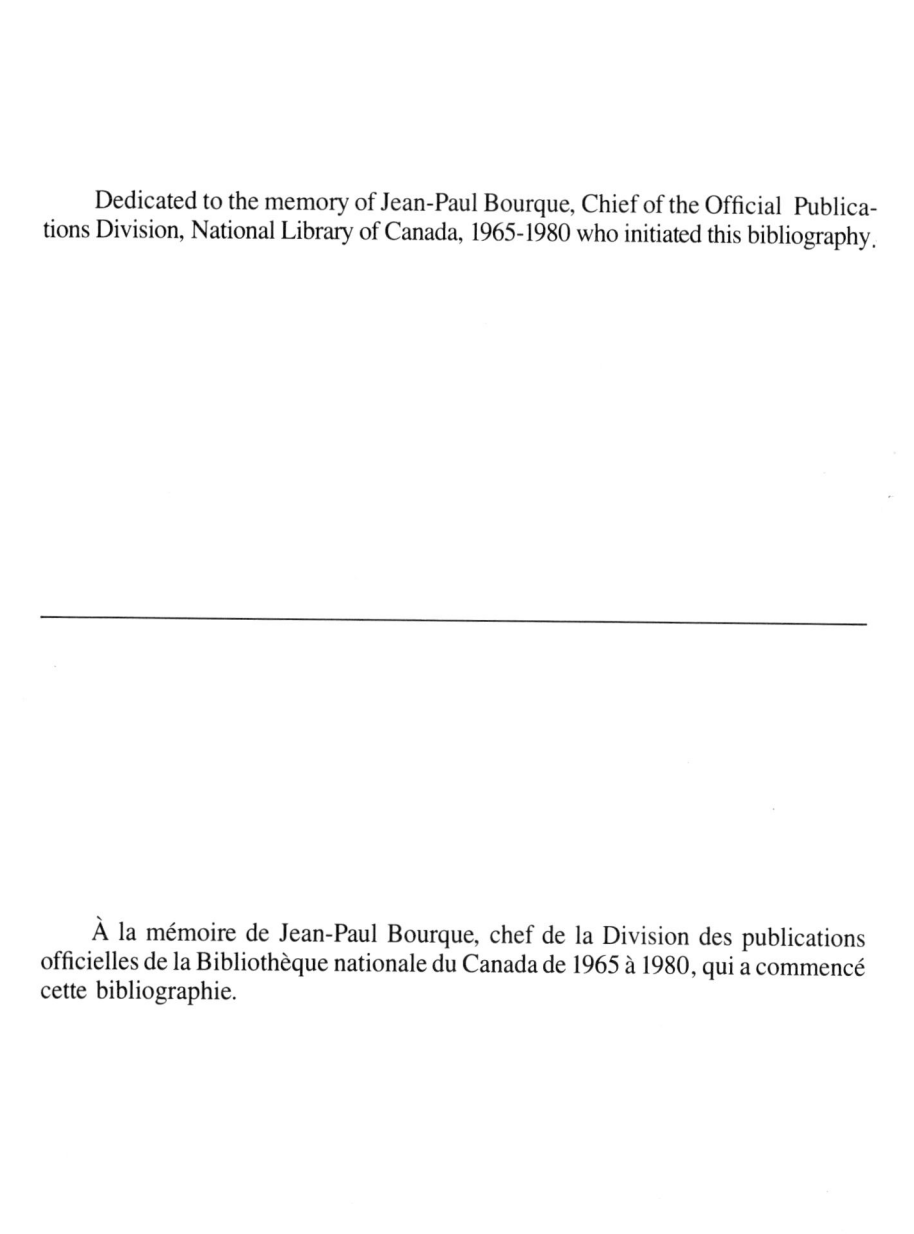

Dedicated to the memory of Jean-Paul Bourque, Chief of the Official Publications Division, National Library of Canada, 1965-1980 who initiated this bibliography.

À la mémoire de Jean-Paul Bourque, chef de la Division des publications officielles de la Bibliothèque nationale du Canada de 1965 à 1980, qui a commencé cette bibliographie.

PREFACE

Provincial Royal Commissions and Commissions of Inquiry, 1867-1982: A Selective Bibliography is the product of a cooperative effort on the part of the National Library of Canada and all ten provinces. It is intended as a national reference tool through which students and researchers may be made aware of the range and diversity of documentation resulting from investigations into political, cultural, economic, and social issues in provincial jurisdictions from both an historical and contemporary viewpoint. The National Library of Canada has prepared and published this bibliography as a support to Canadian studies.

Marianne Scott

National Librarian

PRÉFACE

Commissions royales provinciales et commissions d'enquêtes, 1867-1982: bibliographie sélective est le fruit d'un effort collectif de la Bibliothèque nationale du Canada et des dix provinces. Il s'agit d'un ouvrage de référence national grâce auquel étudiants et chercheurs peuvent se rendre compte de l'étendue et de la diversité de la documentation issue d'enquêtes sur des questions politiques, culturelles, économiques et sociales dans les provinces. La Bibliothèque nationale a préparé et publié cette bibliographie pour appuyer les études canadiennes.

Le directeur général,

Marianne Scott

CONTENTS / TABLE DES MATIÈRES

Page

Preface / Préface.. v
Introduction ix
New Brunswick / Nouveau-Brunswick 1
Nova Scotia / Nouvelle-Écosse 13
Ontario 32
Québec 81
Manitoba 117
British Columbia / Colombie-Britannique 138
Prince Edward Island / Île-du-Prince-Édouard 182
Alberta 187
Saskatchewan 203
Newfoundland / Terre-Neuve 216
Index to Chairmen and Commissioners / 229
  Index des présidents et commissaires
Subject Index / Index des sujets 243

INTRODUCTION

Since Confederation, provincial royal commissions and commissions of inquiry have been established by provincial governments to examine important political, cultural, economic, or social problems in their jurisdiction. More specifically, a royal commission is a body set up by a province's Cabinet via an Order-in-Council, whose purpose it is to carry out an investigation of a specified subject, and to make recommendations for the government's consideration. Commissions of inquiry address themselves to broad issues of government policy by either gathering information relevant to an issue and advising the government, or by investigating the facts of a particular alleged problem usually associated with the functioning of government. Many inquiries both advise and investigate.

The mechanism for creating these commissions varies from province to province, but usually emanates from an Order-in-Council issued by the provincial Cabinet, which cites that province's Public Inquiries Act as the authorizing statute; in some cases, most notably in those commissions set up in the Province of Quebec, a commission may be created under the authority of a special act that may cite the Public Inquiries Act or its equivalent to describe the wide range of powers these special commissions are granted by a government.

The term "royal" as applied to a commission is loosely defined, but usually it is applied to reflect the executive nature of the appointment of the commission; as is

---

INTRODUCTION

Depuis la Confédération, des commissions royales et des commissions d'enquêtes ont été créées par des gouvernements provinciaux pour étudier d'importantes questions politiques, culturelles, économiques ou sociales. Plus précisément, une commission royale provinciale est instituée par un décret du Conseil des ministres de la province dans le but d'enquêter sur une question spécifique et de faire des recommandations au gouvernement. Les commissions d'enquêtes abordent de grandes questions de politique gouvernementale soit en recueillant de l'information sur un sujet donné pour conseiller le gouvernement, soit en enquêtant sur un problème particulier habituellement associé au fonctionnement de l'appareil gouvernemental. Bon nombre de commissions sont à la fois chargées de conseiller et d'enquêter.

Le mécanisme de création de ces commissions varie d'une province à l'autre, mais les commissions sont normalement issues d'un décret du Conseil des ministres émis en vertu de la Loi sur les enquêtes publiques, qui constitue l'instrument d'autorisation. Dans certains cas, notamment au Québec, une commission peut être créée en vertu d'une loi spéciale qui peut invoquer la Loi sur les enquêtes publiques ou une loi équivalente pour décrire l'étendue des pouvoirs conférés à ces commissions spéciales par un gouvernement.

Le terme "royale" appliqué à une commission est plutôt vague, mais traduit le fait que c'est le pouvoir exécutif qui nomme une commission. Comme en fait foi

evident in this bibliography, not all commissions prefer to designate themselves as royal — even some particularly controversial or topical judicial enquiries can technically call themselves royal commissions. Chairpersons of commissions, who are appointed by a government because of their qualifications which may relate to their knowledge of a subject, may decide to call their commissions "royal commissions."

These commissions must submit a written report to the government, usually with specific recommendations as to policy changes or courses of action. Governments are in no sense bound to enact legislatively any or all of the recommendations presented by a royal commission in its report(s). With the presentation of a final report to a government, a royal commission ceases to exist, thus reflecting the *ad hoc* nature of the body and its purpose.

---

cette bibliographie, ce ne sont pas toutes les commissions qui veulent se faire appeler "commission royale"; même certaines enquêtes particulièrement controversées ou certaines enquêtes judiciaires sur des questions d'actualité peuvent en théorie s'appeler "commission royale". Les présidents de commissions nommés par un gouvernement en raison de leurs compétences relatives à un sujet donné peuvent aussi opter pour la désignation "commission royale".

Les commissions doivent soumettre au gouvernement un rapport écrit qui comprend généralement des recommandations spécifiques relativement aux changements qui s'imposent au niveau des politiques ou aux mesures à adopter. Les gouvernements ne sont pas liés par les recommandations que formule une commission royale dans son(ses) rapport(s) et n'ont pas à adopter de lois en conséquence. La commission royale est dissoute à la présentation de son rapport final au gouvernement, reflétant ainsi le caractère provisoire de son mandat.

Organization of the Bibliography

Provincial royal commissions and commissions of inquiry are arranged chronologically by a province's date of entry into Confederation:

1867 — New Brunswick
        Nova Scotia
        Ontario
        Québec

1870 — Manitoba

1871 — British Columbia

1873 — Prince Edward Island

1905 — Alberta
        Saskatchewan

1949 — Newfoundland

Classement de la bibliographie

Les commissions royales provinciales et les commissions d'enquêtes sont classées par ordre chronologique suivant la date d'entrée des provinces dans la Confédération:

1867 — Nouveau-Brunswick
        Nouvelle-Écosse
        Ontario
        Québec

1870 — Manitoba

1871 — Colombie-Britannique

1873 — Île-du-Prince-Édouard

1905 — Alberta
        Saskatchewan

1949 — Terre-Neuve

Printed or published reports of the commissions for each province are arranged chronologically by the date of the report; if two or more reports are published within the same year, the reports are listed in alphabetical order. All reports are numbered sequentially throughout the bibliography. When known, the popular name of a commission has been given: for example, the commission named, Commission Appointed Respecting the General Election of the Legislative Assembly of the Province of Ontario Held on the 19th Day of June, 1934, is also listed with its more popular name, Elections Inquiry Commission.

Bibliographic Entries

Bibliographic entries follow the bibliographic style which is outlined in the "National Library of Canada Bibliographic Style Manual" — to be published in late 1986 or early 1987. In essence, this style is based on those outlined in the documents *ISO/DIS 690, AACR2*, and the *Chicago Manual of Style* (13th ed.). The aim in presenting bibliographic entries is consistency and clarity, with sensitivity to the Canadian context. All entries are taken from either the original document or from a photocopy of the title page. Entries are not translated; where commissions present reports that are bilingual, the English is listed first if it appears first on the original document, and the French follows; the reverse is true, particularly in bilingual documents originating in Québec, where the French comes first and the

---

Les rapports imprimés ou publiés des commissions de chaque province sont classés d'après la date du rapport et par ordre alphabétique si plus d'un rapport est publié la même année. Tous les rapports sont numérotés consécutivement dans la bibliographie. Le nom populaire d'une commission est mentionné lorsqu'il est connu: ainsi, la commission intitulée "Commission Appointed Respecting the General Election of the Legislative Assembly of the Province of Ontario, Held on the 19th Day of June, 1934", est aussi répertoriée sous le nom qu'on lui donnait communément, à savoir "Elections Inquiry Commission".

Notices bibliographiques

Les notices sont conformes au style préconisé dans le "Manuel de présentation bibliographique de la Bibliothèque nationale du Canada" qui sera publié à la fin de 1986 ou au début de 1987. Ce manuel s'inspire essentiellement de trois documents, *ISO/DIS 690, RCAA2* et le *Chicago Manual of Style* (13e édition). La clarté et l'uniformité des notices bibliographiques sont deux qualités essentielles, de même que l'adaptation au contexte canadien. Toutes les rubriques proviennent de l'original ou d'une photocopie de la page titre. Les rubriques ne sont pas traduites. Pour ce qui est des rapports bilingues, l'anglais figure en premier s'il est inscrit en premier sur l'original, suivi du français, et vice versa, particulièrement dans le cas des documents bilingues émanant du Québec, où le français a préséance

English second. Regarding punctuation of bibliographic entries, the ISBD (International Standard Bibliographic Description) rules for punctuation were employed. Chairpersons of commissions are listed as a separate element from commissioners, where evident. Commissioners are listed in alphabetical order.

Scope of the Bibliography

Most of the provincial royal commissions and commissions of inquiry included in this selective bibliography were established as commissions by a provincial Cabinet's issuance of an Order-in-Council naming a province's Public Inquiries Act or its equivalent as the authorizing statute. The title of the Public Inquiries Act not only varies from province to province, but also has varied throughout a province's legislative history; for example, Manitoba's Public Inquiry Act is called the Manitoba Evidence Act. As mentioned in the Introduction, a number of commissions were established by special acts, some of which cite a province's Public Inquiries Act as the authorizing statute; these commissions have been included in this bibliography. In cases where it can be determined that a commission's authorizing statute is a departmental statute with limited powers and with no connection to a special act or a Public Inquiries Act, then that commission is not included in this bibliography. The only other circumstance where a commis-

---

sur l'anglais. Pour ce qui est de la ponctuation, ce sont les règles de l'ISBD (Description bibliographique internationale normalisée) qui ont été utilisées. Les présidents de commissions et les commissaires sont énumérés séparément, lorsque la distinction existant entre eux est évidente. Les commissaires sont énumérés par ordre alphabétique.

Portée de la bibliographie

Les commissions royales provinciales et les commissions d'enquêtes répertoriées dans cette bibliographie sélective ont presque toutes été établies par un décret du Conseil des ministres invoquant la Loi sur les enquêtes publiques d'une province ou une loi équivalente à titre d'instrument d'autorisation. La Loi sur les enquêtes publiques peut s'intituler différemment d'une province à l'autre, et même avoir eu plusieurs appellations dans l'histoire d'une province donnée. Au Manitoba, par exemple, la Loi sur les enquêtes publiques s'appelle "Loi sur la preuve au Manitoba". Comme nous l'avons dit dans l'introduction, un certain nombre de commissions ont été établies en vertu de lois spéciales, dont certaines invoquent la Loi sur les enquêtes publiques comme instrument d'autorisation; ces commissions sont comprises dans cette bibliographie. Les commissions n'ont pas été retenues lorsque l'instrument d'autorisation est un statut ministériel ayant des pouvoirs limités et n'ayant aucun rapport avec une loi spéciale ou avec une Loi sur les

sion is judged to be ineligible for inclusion is one where it has proven impossible to reasonably determine the status of the authorizing statute.

Selection has been limited to an attempt to eliminate the departmental commissions. The aim has been to include as many commissions as possible, thereby providing the user with as comprehensive a research tool as possible. Further information regarding scope parameters is as follows:

1. Chronological coverage 1867-1982;
2. Including only those commissions that have a Public Inquiries Act as their authorizing statute;
3. Including only the relevant reports of a commission, such as interim and final reports unless other documents, such as studies and evidence, are bound with the reports;
4. Including commission reports which can be identified and located.

Location Information

Location symbols are presented in alphabetical order as the last element in each bibliographic entry. Users of this bibliography should refer to the National Library's *Symbols of Canadian Libraries*, 11th ed. (Ottawa: National Library of Canada, 1985). Location information was found in the following sources: the

---

enquêtes publiques. Le seul autre motif d'inadmissibilité est lorsqu'on n'a pu raisonnablement déterminer la nature et la provenance de l'instrument d'autorisation.

La sélection reflète une volonté de ne pas retenir les travaux des commissions ministérielles. Les rédacteurs se sont efforcés d'y inclure le plus grand nombre possible de commissions pour que l'usager puisse disposer d'un instrument de recherche suffisamment exhaustif. Les critères de sélection qui ont été retenus sont les suivants:

1. La période visée s'étend de 1867 à 1982 (inclusivement).
2. Les commissions doivent avoir une Loi sur les enquêtes publiques pour instrument d'autorisation.
3. Seuls les rapports pertinents d'une commission, tels que ses rapports provisoires et finals, ont été inclus, d'autres documents tels que des études et des dépositions ne l'ayant été que s'ils faisaient partie des rapports.
4. Il doit s'agir de rapports de commissions qu'on peut identifier et localiser.

Localisations

Les sigles des bibliothèques employés pour indiquer les localisations des documents sont disposés par ordre alphabétique et constituent le dernier élément des notices bibliographiques. Pour l'explication de ces sigles, les utilisateurs de

Canadian Official Publications Collection of the National Library including Sessional Papers, DOBIS, the National Library's automated cataloguing system; the Canadian Union Catalogue, and the provincial royal commission and commissions of inquiry bibliographies produced by the provinces of Nova Scotia, Québec, Ontario, Alberta, and British Columbia. Many of the older reports of commissions exist only in manuscript format — others are typescripts of the original handwritten reports; in these cases, the original document was not perused because usually only one copy exists in a provincial archive or legislative library and it is not available for interlibrary loan.

Indexes

All chairpersons of commissions and commissioners are listed in alphabetical order in a distinct index. As well, a subject index has been provided to facilitate access to items in the bibliography: keywords were taken from individual bibliographic entries and used as subject headings and from indexes published in existing bibliographies prepared by several provinces.

---

cette bibliographie devraient consulter les *Sigles des bibliothèques canadiennes*, 11e édition (Ottawa: Bibliothèque nationale du Canada, 1985). Des données de localisation ont été trouvées dans les sources suivantes: la collection des publications officielles canadiennes de la Bibliothèque nationale (incluant les documents de la session), le DOBIS, système de catalogage automatisé de la Bibliothèque nationale du Canada, le Catalogue collectif canadien ainsi que les bibliographies de commissions royales provinciales et de commissions d'enquêtes de diverses provinces, notamment la Nouvelle-Écosse, le Québec, l'Ontario, l'Alberta et la Colombie-Britannique. De nombreux rapports de commissions plus anciennes n'existent qu'en version manuscrite alors que d'autres sont des transcriptions dactylographiées de manuscrits originaux; en pareil cas, le document original n'a pas été consulté et il n'existe habituellement qu'un seul exemplaire du document dans un établissement d'archives provincial ou dans la bibliothèque d'une assemblée législative, exemplaire qui ne peut faire l'objet d'un prêt entre bibliothèques.

Index

Tous les présidents de commissions et les commissaires figurent en ordre alphabétique dans un index distinct. De plus, un index-sujets facilite l'accès aux documents répertoriés: les mots clés ont été tirés de notices bibliographiques individuelles et employés comme vedettes-matières ou proviennent d'index faisant partie de bibliographies déjà publiées dans plusieurs provinces.

Acknowledgements

The compilation of this bibliography owes much to the following published checklists of five provinces:

Nova Scotia Royal Commissions and Commissions of Inquiry, 1849-1984: A Checklist. 3rd ed. Halifax: The Legislative Library, 1984.

Ontario Royal Commissions and Commissions of Inquiry, 1867-1978: A Checklist of Reports. Compiled by Susan Waintman and Ana Tampold. Toronto: Legislative Library, Research and Information Services, 1980. (with a 1984 update).

Commissions et comités d'enquêtes au Québec depuis 1867. Québec: Assemblée nationale, Bibliothèque de la législature, 1972.

Royal Commissions and Commissions of Inquiry Under the "Public Inquiries Act" in British Columbia, 1872-1942: A Checklist. By Marjorie C. Holmes. Victoria: Provincial Library, 1942.

Royal Commissions and Commissions of Inquiry Under the "Public Inquiries Act" in British Columbia, 1943-1980: A Checklist. By Judith Antonik Bennett. Victoria: Legislative Library, 1982.

Royal Commissions and Commissions of Inquiry in Alberta, 1905-1976. Compiled by Christine E. Backhaus. Edmonton: Legislative Library, 1977.

Remerciements

Les listes de contrôle suivantes, provenant de cinq provinces, ont été grandement mises à contribution lors de la préparation de cette bibliographie:

Nova Scotia Royal Commissions and Commissions of Inquiry, 1849-1984: A Checklist. 3e éd. Halifax: The Legislative Library, 1984.

Ontario Royal Commissions and Commissions of Inquiry, 1867-1978: A Checklist of Reports. Préparée par Susan Waintman et Ana Tampold. Toronto: Legislative Library, Research and Information Services, 1980. (Mise à jour en 1984.)

Commissions et comités d'enquêtes au Québec depuis 1867. Québec: Assemblée nationale, Bibliothèque de la législature, 1972.

Royal Commissions and Commissions of Inquiry Under the "Public Inquiries Act" in British Columbia, 1872-1942: A Checklist. Par Marjorie C. Holmes. Victoria: Provincial Library, 1942.

Royal Commissions and Commissions of Inquiry Under the "Public Inquiries Act" in British Columbia, 1943-1980: A Checklist. Par Judith Antonik Bennett. Victoria: Legislative Library, 1982.

Royal Commissions and Commissions of Inquiry in Alberta, 1905-1976. Préparé par Christine E. Backhaus. Edmonton: Legislative Library, 1977.

We are also very grateful to numerous individuals from various provincial legislative libraries and provincial libraries and archives, who generously provided photocopies of reports, in their entirety or in part, and who supplied much general information without which this bibliography would not be as complete and accurate as it is.

Les rédacteurs tiennent à remercier le personnel des diverses bibliothèques d'assemblées législatives et des bibliothèques et établissements d'archives provinciaux qui leur ont gracieusement fourni des photocopies de rapports partiels ou complets et quantité de renseignements généraux sans lesquels cette bibliographie ne serait pas complète et manquerait de précision.

NEW BRUNSWICK / NOUVEAU-BRUNSWICK

1 **1893**

Commission to Investigate and Report upon the Best Method of Administering the Crown Timber Lands of the Province.
Report. In New Brunswick. Legislative Assembly. *Journals*. 1st Session. Fredericton: G.E. Fenety, Printer to the Queen's Most Excellent Majesty, 1893. p. D1-D8. (Appendix D)

Commissioners/Commissaires: A.F. Randolph, A. Ritchie, F. Todd.

Loc.: AEP, BVAU, BVIP, MWP, NBFL, NBFU, NBMOU, NBS, NBSAM, NFSM, NSHL, OONL, OWTU, QMM, QMU, QQL, SRL

2 **1894**

Commission of Inquiry upon Charges Relating to the Bathurst Schools and Other Schools in Gloucester County.
Report. [Fredericton] 1894. 72 p.

Commissioner/Commissaire: J.J. Fraser.

Loc.: NBFL

3 **Commission upon Civic and Municipal Taxation.**
Report. In New Brunswick. Legislative Assembly. *Journals*. 2nd Session. Fredericton: G.E. Fenety, Printer to the Queen's Most Excellent Majesty, 1894. p. 58-62. (Supplementary appendix)

Chairman/Président: A.R. McClelan.

Commissioner/Commissaire: W.E. Vroom.

Loc.: AEP, BVAU, MWP, NBFL, NBFU, NBS, NSHL, OONL, OWTU, QMM, QQL, SRL

4 **1905**

Commission Appointed to Enquire into and Investigate as to the Necessity of a Factory Act in the Province of New Brunswick.
Report. In New Brunswick. Legislative Assembly. *Journals*. 4th Legislative Assembly, 3rd Session. Fredericton, 1905. p. 137-153. (Supplementary appendix)

Chairman/Président: J. Palmer.

Commissioners/Commissaires: E.S. Fiske, M.J. Kelly, C. McDonald, K. Shives.

Loc.: AEP, BVAU, MWP, NBFL, NBFU, NBMOU, NBSAM, NFSM, OONL, OTMCL, OWTU, QMM, QQL, SRL

5 **1906**

Royal Commission to Investigate Certain Charges Made Against the Restigouche Boom Company.
Report. [Fredericton, 1906] 23 *l.* (typescript)

Chairman/Président: F.E. Barker.

Commissioners/Commissaires: J. Kilburn, O.P. King.

Loc.: NBFA

6 **1909**

Commission Appointed by Government to Examine into the Affairs of the Central Railway in the Province of New Brunswick.
Report. Moncton, N.B., 1909. 80 p.

Commissioners/Commissaires: P.A. Landry, F. Macdougall, A.I. Teed.

Loc.: NBFL, NSHPL, OONL

7 **1915**

Royal Commission Concerning St. John and Quebec Railway Company Charges.
Report. In New Brunswick. Legislative Assembly. *Journals.* 6th Legislative Assembly, 3rd Session. Fredericton, 1915. p. 116-146. (Supplementary appendix)

Chairman/Président: H.A. McKeown.

Commissioners/Commissaires: W.S. Fisher, W.W. Wells.

Loc.: ACU, MWP, NBFL, NBS, NBSAM, NFSM, OONL, OTMCL, QQL, SRL, SSU

8 **Royal Commission Concerning Timber Limit Charges.**
Report. In New Brunswick. Legislative Assembly. *Journals.* 6th Legislative Assembly, 3rd Session. Fredericton, 1915. p. 95-115. (Supplementary appendix)

Chairman/Président: H.A. McKeown.

Commissioners/Commissaires: W.S. Fisher, W.W. Wells.

Loc.: ACU, MWP, NBFL, NBS, NBSAM, NFSM, OONL, OTMCL, QQL, SRL, SSU

9 **1919**

Commission Appointed under an Act of the Legislative Assembly of the Province of New Brunswick, Chapter 46 of the Acts 8 George V, 1918, to Hold an Investigation and Inquiry into Matters Relating to the New Brunswick Power Company.
Report. [Fredericton, 1919] 11 p.

Chairman/Président: G.W. Currier.

Commissioners/Commissaires: H. Holgate, A.S. Richey.

Loc.: NBFA

10 **Patriotic Potato Inquiry.**
Report. In New Brunswick. Legislative Assembly. *Journals.* 7th Legislative Assembly, 3rd Session. Fredericton, 1919. 45 p. (Appendix)

Commissioner/Commissaire: J. McQueen.

Loc.: MWP, NBFL, NBFU, NFSM, OONL, QMM, QQL, SRL

11 **1922**

Commission to Investigate and Enquire into the Matter of the Execution of Bennie Swim and the Conduct of Officials Taken Part Therein.
Report. [Fredericton, 1922?] 9 *l.* (typescript)

Commissioner/Commissaire: J.B. Dickson.

Loc.: NBFA, NBFL

12 **1926**

Commission re Minto Coal Company, Ltd.
Report. In New Brunswick. Legislative Assembly. *Journal*. 9th Legislative Assembly, 1st Session. Fredericton, 1926. p. 63-74. (Appendix)

Chairman/Président: E.R. Teed.

Commissioners/Commissaires: L.S. Morrison, G.A. Stone.

Loc.: AEP, BVAU, BVIP, MWP, NBFL, NBFU, NBMOU, NBS, NBSAM, NSHL, OONL, OTMCL, OTU, OWTU, QMM, QQL, SRL, SSU

13 **1927**

Royal Commission to Investigate Working of Compensation Act in Respect to Lumber Industry.
Report. In New Brunswick. Legislative Assembly. *Journals*. 9th Legislature, 2nd Session. Fredericton, 1927. p. 4-10. (Supplementary appendix).

Commissioners/Commissaires: F.C. Beatteay, W.C.H. Grimmer, G.A. Stone.

Loc.: ACU, BVAU, MWP, NBFL, NBFU, NBS, NSHL, OONL, OTMCL, QMM, SRL, SSU

14 **1928**

Royal Commission Appointed to Enquire into the Taxation by Cities, Towns and Municipalities of Non-Residents.
Report. In New Brunswick. Legislative Assembly. *Journals*. 9th Legislative Assembly, 3rd Session. Fredericton, 1928. p. [3]-28. (Supplementary appendix)

Commissioners/Commissaires: O.S. Crocket, W.C. Kierstead, E.R. McDonald.

Loc.: AEP, BVAU, BVIP, MWP, NBFL, NBFU, NBMOU, NBS, NBSAM, NSHL, OONL, OTMCL, OWTU, QMM, SRL, SSU

15 **1930**

Commission Appointed to Consider Old Age Pensions.
Interim report. [Fredericton] 1930. 39 *l.* (typescript)

———.
Final report. [Fredericton, 1930] 26 p.

Chairman/Président: W.C.H. Grimmer.

Commissioners/Commissaires: J.B. Chouinard, O.J. Dick, H.F. MacLeod, G.A. Stone.

Loc.: NBFL, OONH, OOS

16 **Commission Appointed to Consider the Payment of Mothers' Allowances.**
Report. [Fredericton, 1930] 23 p.

Chairman/Président: W.C.H. Grimmer.

Commissioners/Commissaires: J.B. Chouinard, O.J. Dick, H.F. MacLeod, G.A. Stone.

Loc.: NBFL, OOL, OONH, OOS

17 **1945**

Royal Commission Inquiry into the Provincial Hospital.
Report. Saint John, N.B., 1945. 62 p.

Chairman/Président: J.B.M. Baxter.

Commissioners/Commissaires: L.M. Pepperdence, E.B. Sweeney.

Loc.: BVAU, MWP, NBFL, NBSM, OONL, OTU

18 **1951**

Commission on Gaol System of New Brunswick.
Report. [Fredericton, 1951] 30 *l.* (typescript)

Commissioner/Commissaire: J.B. Dickson.

Loc.: BVA, NBFL, OONL, OOP, OOSG, OTU, OTYL, QMML

19 **Royal Commission on Rates and Taxes Act.**
Report. Fredericton, 1951. 72 p.

Chairman/Président: R.J. Love.

Commissioners/Commissaires: L.A. Mersereau, L.P.A. Robichaud.

Loc.: NBFL, NBFU, OOB, OOF, OOS, OTCT, OTLS, QQLA, SRL

20 **1952**

Commission Holding Inquiry on the Project of the Reconstruction of the Broad Road from Finnegan Hill to Oromocto.
Report. [Fredericton?] 1952. 29 *l.* (typescript)

Commissioner/Commissaire: G.F.G. Bridges.

Loc.: NBFA

21 **1954**

Commission on Silicosis (Compensation and Control).
Report. [Fredericton, 1954] 10 *l.* (typescript)

Chairman/Président: W.F. Lane.

Members/Membres: C.L. Gass, C. Hicks, C.I. Mills.

Loc.: NBFL, OONL

22 **1955**

Royal Commission on the Financing of Schools in New Brunswick.
Report. Fredericton, 1955. xv, 129 p.

Chairman/Président: W.H. MacKenzie.

Members/Membres: J.-A. Levesque, R.D. Stewart.

Loc.: AEU, BVA, BVAU, MWU, NBFL, NBS, NFSM, NSHPL, OKQ, OLU, OOL, OONL, OTER, OTP, OTU, QMM, QQL, SRU, SSU

23 **1960**

Royal Commission on the New Brunswick Coal Mining Industry.
Final report. Fredericton, 1960. 115, 38, 6 *l.* (typescript)

Chairman/Président: W.Y. Smith.

Members/Membres: A. Tooke, M. Wuhr.

Loc.: AEU, MWP, NBFL, NSHPL, OOB, OOF, OOFF, OONL, OOP, OTMCL, OTYL, QQL

24 **1961**

New Brunswick Liquor Inquiry Commission.
Report. [Fredericton, 1961] 56 p.

Chairman/Président: G.F.G. Bridges.

Commissioners/Commissaires: J.B. Dickson, L.A. LeBel, A.P.N. McLaughlin, J.A. Whitebone.

Loc.: AEU, BVIV, MWP, NBFL, NSHPL, OONL, OORD, OOS, OTY

25 **1962**

Commission royale d'enquête sur l'enseignement supérieur au Nouveau-Brunswick.
Rapport. Fredericton, 1962. 122 p. (publié aussi en anglais)

Président/Chairman: J.J. Deutsch.

Membres/Commissioners: A.-J. Cormier, R.W. Maxwell.

Loc.: NBFL, OONL, OOP

Royal Commission on Higher Education in New Brunswick.
Report. Fredericton, 1962. 118 p. (issued also in French)

Chairman/Président: J.J. Deutsch.

Commissioners/Membres: A.-J. Cormier, R.W. Maxwell.

Loc.: AEU, BVAU, MWP, NBFL, NBS, NBSAM, NBSU, NFSM, NSHPL, OKQM, OOCC, OOCU, OONL, OOP, OOSS, OOTC, OPET, OTER, OTLS, OTU, QMM, SSU

26 **Royal Commission on the New Brunswick Potato Industry.**
Report. Fredericton, 1962. xv, 239 p.

Chairman/Président: H. Whalen.

Commissioners/Commissaires: E. Christensen, F. Hatfield, H. Kilpatrick, E. King.

Loc.: BVAU, BVIV, MWP, NBFL, NBS, NSHPL, OOAG, OOFF, OONL, OOP, OOTC, OTU

27 **1963**

La Commission royale sur la finance et la taxation municipale au Nouveau-Brunswick.
Rapport. Fredericton, 1963. pagination variée (publié aussi en anglais)

Président/Chairman: E.G. Byrne.

Membres/Members: A.E. Andrews, A.J. Boudreau, U. Nadeau, C.N. Wilson.

Loc.: NBFL, OONL, OOP, OOU, OOUD, OTYL

The New Brunswick Royal Commission on Finance and Municipal Taxation.
Report. Fredericton, 1963. various pagings (issued also in French)

Chairman/Président: E.G. Byrne.

Members/Membres: A.E. Andrews, A.J. Boudreau, U. Nadeau, C.N. Wilson.

Loc.: ACU, AEU, BVA, BVAU, MWP, NBFL, NBS, NBSAM, NFSM, OKQ, OONL, OOP, OOU, OPET, OTER, OTLS, OTU, OTY, OWAL, QMG, QMM, QQL, SRL, SSU

28 **The Royal Commission on Metropolitan Saint John.**
Report. [Fredericton, 1963] xi, 48 p.

Commissioner/Commissaire: H.C. Goldenberg.

Loc.: AEU, BVAU, NBFL, NSHPL, OONL, OOP, OTLS, OTMCL, OWA, QQL, QQLA, SRL

29 **1964**

Royal Commission on Primary Forest Products in New Brunswick.
Report. Fredericton, 1964. 95 p.

Commissioner/Commissaire: L.R. Seheult.

Loc.: AEU, BVA, MWP, NBFU, NBFL, NBS, OKF, OOCC, OONL, OOP, OPAL, OTP, OTU, OWA, QQL, QQLA, SRL

30 **1966**

Commission to Inquire into and Concerning all Negotiations and Transactions between the Province and Coastal Industries Limited and St. Regis Paper Company (Canada) Ltd., between January 1, 1964 and December 31, 1965.
Report. [Fredericton] 1966. 51 *l*. (typescript)

Commissioner/Commissaire: R.V. Limerick.

Loc.: MWP, NBFL, OONL, OOP, QMML, SRL

31 **1967**

Commission royale sur les relations employeurs-employés dans les services publics du Nouveau-Brunswick.
Rapport. [Fredericton] 1967. 110 p. (publié aussi en anglais)

Commissaire/Commissioner: S.J. Frankel.

Loc.: NBFL, OOF, OONL, OOP, OOU, OTY, QMU, QQL, QSHERU

Royal Commission on Employer-Employee Relations in the Public Services of New Brunswick.
Report. [Fredericton], 1967. 103 p. (issued also in French)

Commissioner/Commissaire: S.J. Frankel.

Loc.: AEU, BVA, BVAU, MWP, NBFL, NBS, NFSM, NSHPL, OKQM, OLU, OONL, OTLS, OOP, OOU, OTY, OWAL, QMM, QQL, SRL

32 **1971**

La Commission royale d'enquête sur l'agglomération frederictonienne.
Rapport. [Fredericton] 1971. x, 96 p. (publié aussi en anglais)

Commissaire/Commissioner: H.C. Goldenberg.

Loc.: MWU, NBFL, OONL

The Royal Commission on the Greater Fredericton Area.
Report. [Fredericton] 1971. ix, 58 p. (issued also in French)

Commissioner/Commissaire: H.C. Goldenberg.

Loc.: AEU, BVA, BVAU, NBFL, NBFU, NBS, NBSU, OLU, OONL, OOP, OTMCL, OTY, OWA, QMG, QMU

33 **La Commission royale d'enquête sur l'agglomération monctonienne.**
Rapport. [Fredericton] 1971. vii, 114 p. (publié aussi en anglais)

Commissaire/Commissioner: H.C. Goldenberg.

Loc.: NBFL, OONL, OOP, QMU

The Royal Commission on the Greater Moncton Area.
Report. [Fredericton] 1971. viii, 63 p. (issued also in French)

Commissioner/Commissaire: H.C. Goldenberg.

Loc.: BVAS, NBFL, NBFU, NBS, NBSU, NSHPL, OLU, OONL, OOP, OTY, OWA, QMG

34 **La Commission royale d'enquête sur l'industrie laitière au Nouveau-Brunswick.**
Rapport. [Fredericton, 1971] iv, 2-297 p. (manuscrit dactylographié) (publié aussi en anglais)

Président/Chairman: R.L. MacDougall.

Membres/Members: J.E. McArthur, H.R. Scovil.

Loc.: NBFL, OONL

Royal Commission on the Milk Industry in New Brunswick.
Report. [Fredericton, 1971] 198 p. (issued also in French)

Chairman/Président: R.L. MacDougall.

Members/Membres: J.E. McArthur, H.R. Scovil.

Loc.: MWP, NBFL, NBS, OOAG, OONL, OOP, OTMCL, OWA, QQL, QSHERU, SRL

35 1974-1975

Commission d'enquête sur la représentation et sur les lignes de démarcation des circonscriptions électorales.
Rapport/Report. [Fredericton] 1974. 29, 24 *l.* (texte tête-bêche en français et en anglais) (manuscript dactylographié)

Loc.: BVAS, BVAU, BVIV, NBS, NFSM, OONL, OOP

———.
Recommandations et considérations additionnelles/Further consid erations and recommendations. [Fredericton] 1975. ix, 66, 57, viii *l.* (texte tête-bêche en français et en anglais) (manuscrit dactylographié)

Président/Chairman: G.E. Graham.

Commissaires/Commissioners: B. Cloutier, W.W.B. Dick, H.N. Jonah, L. Lanteigne.

Loc.: MWP, NBSU, NFSM, OONL, OOP, QQL, SRL

Representation and Electoral Districts Boundaries Commission.
Report/Rapport. [Fredericton] 1974. 24, 29 *l.* (text in English and French on inverted pages) (typescript)

Loc.: BVAS, BVAU, BVIV, NBS, NFSM, OONL, OOP

———.
Further considerations and recommendations/Recommandations et considérations additionnelles. [Fredericton] 1975. viii, 57, 66, ix *l.* (text in English and French on inverted pages) (typescript)

Chairman/Président: G.E. Graham.

Commissioners/Commissaires: B. Cloutier, W.W.B. Dick, H.N. Jonah, L. Lanteigne.

Loc.: MWP, NBSU, NFSM, OONL, OOP, QQL, SRL

36 1978

Commission d'enquête de l'affaire relative au Ministère de la justice et à la Gendarmerie royale du Canada.
Rapport. [Fredericton] 1978. 128 p. (manuscrit dactylographié) (publié aussi en anglais)

Commissaire/Commissioner: C.J.A. Hughes.

Loc.: NBFL, OONL

Commission of Inquiry into Matters Relating to the Department of Justice and the Royal Canadian Mounted Police.
Report. [Fredericton] 1978. 128 p. (typescript) (issued also in French)

Commissioner/Commissaire: C.J.A. Hughes.

Loc.: NBFL, NBS, OLU, OONL, OOSC

NOVA SCOTIA / NOUVELLE-ÉCOSSE

37 **1878**

Commission Appointed to Investigate the Condition and General Management of the Provincial Hospital for the Insane.
Hospital for insane : report. In Nova Scotia. House of Assembly. *Journal and proceedings.* 26th General Assembly, 4th Session. Halifax: C.C. Blackadar, Queen's Printer, 1878. 12 p. (Appendix no. 10)

Commissioners/Commissaires: C. Campbell, P.C. Hill, D. MacDonald, W.B. Slayter, S. Tobin.

Loc.: BVIP, OONL, OTL, OWA, QQL, SSU

38 **Commission Appointed to Investigate the Expenditure in Connexion with the Road and Bridge Service in County of Kings.**
Kings County expenditure : report. In Nova Scotia. House of Assembly. *Journal and proceedings.* 26th General Assembly, 4th Session. Halifax: C.C. Blackadar, Queen's Printer, 1878. 102 p. (Appendix no. 13)

Commissioners/Commissaires: C.C. Hamilton, P. Lynch, W. Smith.

Loc.: BVIP, NSHL, OONL, OTL, OWA, QQL, SSU

39 **1886**

Commission in the Matter of Certain Charges Affecting the Treatment of the Poor in the County of Digby.
Report. In Nova Scotia. House of Assembly. *Journal and proceedings.* 28th General Assembly, 4th Session. Halifax: Commissioner of Public Works and Mines, Queen's Printer, 1886. 48 p. (Appendix no. 10)

Commissioner/Commissaire: F.H. Bell.

Loc.: BVAU, BVIP, NSHL, OLUL, OONL, OTL, OWA, QQL, SRL

40 **1896**

Commission to Enquire Into the Cause, History, and Effects of Fires in Pictou Coal Mines.
Fires in Pictou mines : report. [Halifax, 1896] 104 p.

Chairman/Président: E. Gilpin, Jr.

Commissioners/Commissaires: A. Dick, W. Madden, Jr., H. Mitchell.

Loc.: NSHPL, OOG, OONL

41 **1908**

Commission Appointed under Chapter 16, Acts 1907, Entitled: "An Act Respecting Old Age Pensions and Miners' Relief Societies".
Report. In Nova Scotia. Legislative Council. *Journal and proceedings.* 34th General Assembly, 2nd Session. Halifax: Commissioner of Public Works and Mines, King's Printer, 1908. 16 p. (Appendix no. 15)

Chairman/Président: W. Crowe.

Commissioners/Commissaires: R. Drummond, W. Hodge, S.B. McNeil.

Loc.: AEP, NSHL, OONL

42 **1910**

Commission on Hours of Labour.
Report. Halifax: Commissioner of Public Works and Mines, King's Printer, 1910. 136 p.

Chairman/Président: R. Magill.

Commissioners/Commissaires: H. MacDonald, D.W. Robb.

Also known as/Également connue sous le nom de: Eight-Hour Day Commission.

Loc.: NSHPL, OOCC, OOL, OONL, OOP

43 **1911**

Commission Appointed for the Purpose of Investigating the Best Methods of Teaching English in the Schools Situate in the French-Speaking Districts of the Province.
Report. In Nova Scotia. Laws, statutes, etc. *Manual of the public instruction acts and regulations of the Council of Public Instruction of Nova Scotia.* Halifax: Commissioner of Public Works, King's Printer, 1911. p. 303-306.

Chairman/Président: W.E. Maclellan.

Commissioners/Commissaires: A.H. Comeau, P.M. Dagnaud, M.J. Doucet, W.M. Leblanc, A.G. MacDonald, A. McKay, A.E. Mombourquette.

Also known as/Également connue sous le nom de: The Acadian Commission.

Loc.: NSHPL, OKQ, OTYL

44 **1914**

Commission Respecting the Halifax and South Western Railway Company's Lands Released from a Mortgage to the Government.
Report. [Halifax, 1914] 14 p.

Chairman/Président: W. Graham.

Commissioners/Commissaires: B. Russell, W.B. Wallace.

Also known as/Également connue sous le nom de: Halifax and South Western Railway Company's Land Enquiry.

Loc.: NSHPL, OONL

45 **1915**

Commission on the Use of Electricity in Mines.
Report. In Nova Scotia. House of Assembly. *Journal and proceedings.* Part 2. Halifax: Commissioner of Public Works and Mines, King's Printer, 1915. 15 p. (Appendix no. 17)

Chairman/Président: G. Patterson.

Commissioners/Commissaires: T.J. Brown, V. McFadden, J. Moffatt, H. Perrin.

Loc.: BVIP, NFSM, OLUL, OONL, OOU, OTL, OTY, OWA, QQL, SRL

46 **1916**

Commission Respecting the Discontinuance of Mining Operations at the Vale Colliery, Pictou County, Nova Scotia.
Report. In Nova Scotia. House of Assembly. *Journals and proceedings.* Part 2. Halifax: Commissioner Public Works and Mines, King's Printer, 1916. 4 p. (Appendix no. 31)

Chairman/Président: G.B. Burchell.

Commissioners/Commissaires: T. Hale, H.A. MacLeod.

Also known as/Également connue sous le nom de: Vale Colliery Commission.

Loc.: BVIP, NSHPL, OONL, OOU, OTL, OTY, OWA, QQL, SRL

47 **1918**

Commission Respecting Feeble Minded in Nova Scotia.
Report. In Nova Scotia. House of Assembly. *Journals and proceedings.* Part 2. Halifax: Commissioner of Public Works and Mines, King's Printer, 1918. unpaged (Appendix 33 [A])

Commissioners/Commissaires: E.H. Blois, W.H. Hattie, A.H. MacKay.

Loc.: BVIP, OONL, OOU, OTL, OTY, OWA, QQL, SRL

48 **1920**

Commission on the Hours of Labour, Wages and Working Conditions of Women Employed in Industrial Occupations.
Report. Halifax: Commissioner of Public Works and Mines, King's Printer, 1920. 31 p.

Chairman/Président: J. McKeen.

Commissioners/Commissaires: E.H. Blois, J.B. Wisdom.

Loc.: NSHPL, OOL, OONL

49 **1921**

Commission on Mothers' Allowances.
Report. Halifax, 1921. 55 p.

Chairman/Président: J. McKeen.

Commissioners/Commissaires: E.H. Blois, J.B. Wisdom.

Loc.: NSHPL, OKQ, OONL

50 **Royal Commission Respecting the Expenditure in Connection with the Construction of Certain Federal Aid Roads by the Provincial Highway Board and of the Purchase of Machinery.**
Report. Halifax: Commissioner of Public Works and Mines, King's Printer, 1921. 20 p.

Chairman/Président: H. Mellish.

Commissioners/Commissaires: F.W.W. Doane, A. MacDonald.

Loc.: NSHPL, OONL

51 **1926**

Agricultural Enquiry Committee, 1926.
Report. Halifax: Minister of Public Works and Mines, King's Printer, 1926. 35 p.

Chairman/Président: D.G. McKenzie.

Commissioners/Commissaires: R.A. Douglas, J.F. Fraser, J.L.P. Robicheau.

Loc.: NSHPL, OOA, OOAG, OONL

52 **Royal Commission Respecting the Coal Mines of the Province of Nova Scotia, 1925.**
Report. Halifax: Minister of Public Works and Mines, King's Printer, 1926. 64 p.

Chairman/Président: A.R. Duncan.

Commissioners/Commissaires: H. Cronyn, H.P. MacPherson.

Also known as/Également connue sous le nom de: Duncan Commission on Coal.

Loc.: BVIV, NSHPL, OKQ, OOA, OOG, OOL, OONL, OTP, OWA, QMG

53 **1927**

Royal Commission Concerning Mentally Deficient Persons in Nova Scotia, 1927.
Report. Halifax, 1927. 46 p.

Chairman/Président: W.L. Hall.

Commissioners/Commissaires: M. Baxter, J.W. McKay, G.H. Murphy, S.H. Prince.

Loc.: AEP, NSHPL, OONL, OOP, SRL

54 **Royal Commission on Ratings of the Lunenburg Fishing Fleet and the Lumber Industry as Applied by the Workmen's Compensation Board.**
Report. Halifax: Minister of Public Works and Mines, King's Printer, 1927. 42 p.

Commissioner/Commissaire: C.D. Dennis.

Loc.: NSHPL, OOA, OOL, OONL, OOP

55 **1929-1930**
The Commission Appointed to Consider Old Age Pensions.
Interim report. Halifax: Minister of Public Works and Mines, King's Printer, 1929. 20 p.

———.

Report. Halifax: Minister of Public Works and Mines, King's Printer, 1930. 24 p.

Commissioner/Commissaire: H.E. Mahon.

Loc.: NSHPL, OOL, OONL, OOP, OTP

56 **1930**

Royal Commission Investigating the Apple Industry of the Province of Nova Scotia.
Report. Halifax: Minister of Public Works and Mines, King's Printer, 1930. 71 p.

Loc.: NSHPL, NSKR, OOA, OOAG, OON, OONL, OOP, OTY

———.

Supplementary report. [Halifax?] 1930. 52 p. (typescript)

Chairman/Président: H.M. Tory.

Commissioners/Commissaires: U.W. Boulter, H.P. MacPherson, H.W. Phinney, F.W. Swindells.

Loc.: OOA, OOAG, OONL

57 **1932**

Royal Commission Respecting the Coal Mines of Nova Scotia, 1932.
Report. Halifax: Minister of Public Works & Mines, King's Printer, 1932. 32 p.

Chairman/Président: A.R. Duncan.

Commissioners/Commissaires: J.W. MacMillan, H.P. MacPherson.

Also known as/Également connue sous le nom de: Duncan Commission on Coal.

Loc.: NSHPL, OOA, OOB, OOF, OOG, OONL, OOP, OTP, OWTU, SRL

58 **1933**

Royal Commission Concerning Jails.
Report. Halifax: Minister of Public Works and Mines, King's Printer, 1933. 115 p.

Chairman/Président: A.J.C. Campbell.

Commissioners/Commissaires: A.D. Campbell, C.F. Curran, S.H. Prince, S.W. Williamson.

Loc.: BVAU, NSHPL, OKQL, OONH, OONL, OTP, OTYL

59 **1934**

Inquiry Nova Scotia Franchise.
Report. Halifax: Provincial Secretary, King's Printer, 1934. 92 p.

Commissioner/Commissaire: H. Ross.

Loc.: NSHPL, OONL

60 **Royal Commission, Provincial Economic Inquiry.**
Report. Halifax: Provincial Secretary, King's Printer, 1934. 236 p.

Chairman/Président: J.H. Jones.

Commissioners/Commissaires: H.A. Innis, A.S. Johnston.

Loc.: AEU, BVA, BVAU, MWU, NBFU, NBSAM, NSHPL, OH, OKQ, OOAG, OOCC, OOF, OOG, OONL, OOP, OPET, OTP, OTU, OWAL, OWTU, QMU, QQL, SRL, SSU

61 **1935**

Commission Appointed to Inquire into the Distribution and Consumption of Milk and Cream in Halifax.
Report. Halifax: Provincial Secretary, King's Printer, 1935. 24 p.

Chairman/Président: A.B. Balcom.

Commissioners/Commissaires: W.J. Bird, A.D. MacKay.

Loc.: NSHPL, OOAE, OONL, OTP

62 **1936**

Royal Commission on Transportation.
Report. Halifax: Provincial Secretary, King's Printer, 1936. 19 p.

Commissioner/Commissaire: I.P. Macnab.

Loc.: NSHPL, OOA, OOAG, OONL, OS, OTU

63 **1937**

Workmen's Compensation Commission.
Report. Halifax: Provincial Secretary, King's Printer, 1937. 21 p.

Chairman/Président: J.A. Hanway.

Commissioners/Commissaires: J.H. Cunningham, W.D. Forrest.
Loc.: NSHPL, OOL, OONL

64 **1939**

Royal Commission on Acadia Coal Company, 1937-1938.
Report. Halifax: Provincial Secretary, King's Printer, 1939. 113 p.

Chairman/Président: W.F. Carroll.

Commissioners/Commissaires: A.S. McKenzie, F.H. Sexton.

Loc.: NSHPL, OOB, OOL, OONL, OTP

65 **Royal Commission on the Queen Hotel Fire, Hollis Street, Halifax, 2nd March, 1939.**
Report. Halifax: Provincial Secretary, King's Printer, 1939. 28 p.

Commissioner/Commissaire: M.B. Archibald.

Loc.: NSHPL, OONL

66 **1944**

Commission on Trenton Steel Works.
Report. Halifax: Provincial Secretary, King's Printer, 1944. 63 p.

Commissioner/Commissaire: W.F. Carroll.

Loc.: NSHPL, OKQ, OONL, OWA

67 **Royal Commission on Provincial Development and Rehabilitation.**
Report. Halifax: King's Printer, 1944. 2 v.

Loc.: AEU, BVA, BVAS, BVAU, MWP, MWU, NBSAM, NBSM, NFSM, NSHPL, OHM, OKQ, OLU, OOA, OOB, OOCI, OOF, OOL, OONL, OOP, OTP, OTU, QMU, SRL, SSU

———.
Report on the Civil Service. Halifax: King's Printer, 1944. 28 p.

Commissioner/Commissaire: R.M. Dawson.

Loc.: OOF, OOL, OONL, OOP

68 **1954**

Royal Commission on National Thrift Corporation and Associate Companies.
Report. Halifax: Queen's Printer, 1954. 96 p.

Commissioner/Commissaire: J.G.A. Robertson.

Loc.: NSHPL, MWP, OOCI, OOIN, OONL, QQL

69 **Royal Commission on Public School Finance in Nova Scotia.**
Report. [Halifax] 1954. xi, 147 p.

Commissioner/Commissaire: V.J. Pottier.

Loc.: BVA, BVAU, BVIV, MWP, MWU, NBFL, NFSM, NSHPL, OKQM, OOA, OOB, OONL, OOP, OPET, OTCT, OTER, OTP, OTU, OTYL, QQL, QQLA, SRL, SRU

70 **1957**

The Royal Commission Appointed to Inquire into the Explosion and Fire in No. 4 Mine at Springhill, N.S.
Report. Halifax: Queen's Printer, 1957. 46 p.

Chairman/Président: D. McInnes.

Commissioners/Commissaires: F.E. Griffith, G.A. Vissac.

Loc.: NSHPL, OONL, OTP

71 **Royal Commission on Automobile Insurance.**
Report. [Halifax, 1957] 2 v.

Chairman/Président: H.E. Read.

Commissioners/Commissaires: W. Berman, R.F. McLellan.

Loc.: BVAU, NSHDL, NSHPL, OKQL, OOIN, OONL, OTU, OTYL

72 **Royal Commission on Rural Credit.**
Report. [Halifax] 1957 xi, 91 p.

Chairman/Président: C.G. Hawkins.

Commissioners/Commissaires: A. Brosha, R.F. Newcombe.

Loc.: NSHPL, OOB, OOCC, OOF, OONL, OTLS, OTU, OTYL, OWA

73 **Royal Commission on the Administration and Operation of Public Cold Storage Plants in Relation to the Annapolis Valley Apple Industry.**
Report. [Halifax, 1957] unpaged

Commissioner/Commissaire: J.A. Walker.

Loc.: NSHPL

74 **Royal Commission on the Cape Breton Hospital.**
Report. [Halifax] 1957. 145 *l.* (typescript)

Commissioners/Commissaires: J.H. MacCallum, J.J. MacRitchie, V.J. Pottier.

Loc.: BVAU, MWP, NSHDL, NSHPL, OKQ, OONL, OTYL

75 **1958**

    Royal Commission on Richmond County Highway Investigation.
Report. Halifax: Queen's Printer, 1958. 38 p.

    Commissioners/Commissaires: I.M. MacKeigan, A.C. Milner.

    Loc.: NSHPL, OONL, OOP, OTLS, OWA

76 **Royal Commission on School Construction in Nova Scotia.**
Report. Halifax, 1958. various pagings

    Chairman/Président: I.P. Macnab.

    Commissioners/Commissaires: F. Musgrave, D.B. Wright.

    Loc.: BVAS, NSHPL, OONL, OTER

77 **Workmen's Compensation Commission.**
Report. Halifax, 1958. 1 v.

    Commissioner/Commissaire: A.H. McKinnon.

    Loc.: BVAS, NSHPL, OTLS, QQL

78 **1959**

    Royal Commission Appointed Pursuant to the Rentals Act, 1959.
Report. [Halifax, 1959] 41 *l.* (typescript)

    Commissioner/Commissaire: G.M. Morrison.

    Loc.: AEU, NSHDL, NSHPL, OKQ, OONL, OWTU

79 **The Royal Commission Appointed to Inquire into the Upheaval or Fall or other Disturbance Sometimes Referred to as a Bump in no. 2 Mine at Springhill, in the County of Cumberland, Province of Nova Scotia, Operated by the Cumberland Railway and Coal Company, on the 23rd Day of October, A.D. 1958.**
Report. [Halifax, 1959] various pagings

    Chairman/Président: D. McInnes.

    Commissioners/Commissaires: T. McLachlan, H. Wilton-Clark.

    Loc.: NSHDL, NSHPL, OONL, OOP, OTP

80 **1960**

Commission to Inquire into and Concerning the Allegations Relating to the Administration of the Municipality of the County of Halifax.
Report. Halifax, 1960. 101 p. (typescript)

Commissioner/Commissaire: G.M. Morrison.

Loc.: NSHDL, NSHPL

81 **1960-1961**

The Royal Commission on Provincial Elections.
Interim report. [Kentville, N.S.] 1960. 84 *l*. (typescript)

Loc.: NSHPL, OONL, OTU, QMML

―――――.
Final report. [Kentville, N.S.] 1961. 2 v. (typescript)

Chairman/Président: R.V. Shaw.

Commissioners/Commissaires: A.J. Meagher, T.P. Slaven.

Loc.: BVAS, MWP, NSHPL, OOCC, OONL, OOP, OTLS, OTU

82 **1961**

Royal Commission Appointed to Enquire into the Application of Nova Scotia Light and Power Company Limited to Develop the Gold River for the Generation of Hydro Electric Energy.
Report. [Halifax, 1961] 73 *l*. (typescript)

Commissioner/Commissaire: R. McInnes.

Loc.: NSA, NSHPL

83 **Royal Commission on Nova Scotia Liquor Laws.**
Report. Halifax, [1961] 64 p.

Chairman/Président: F. Rowe.

Commissioners/Commissaires: G.W. Guptill, H.J. MacDonnell, A.D. Muggah, P. Ronayne, J.C. Wickwire.

Loc.: AEU, BVAS, NSHPL, OONL, OOP, OTLS, OTU, OTYL, QMML

84 **1962**

Commission Appointed to Make Inquiry into Certain Matters Pertaining to the Victoria General Hospital.
Report. Halifax, [1962] 57, 3,2 *l.* (typescript)

Commissioner/Commissaire: F. Rowe.

Loc.: NSHPL, OONL.

85 **Fact-Finding Body re Labour Legislation.**
Report. Antigonish, N.S., 1962. 163 p. (typescript)

Commissioner/Commissaire: A.H. McKinnon.

Loc.: BVA, NSHPL, OOL, OONL, OTP, OTU, OTYL

86 **1963**

Commission on Municipal Boundaries and Municipal Representation.
Report on municipal boundaries and municipal representation and the effectiveness of existing law in relation to changes in boundaries and representation in the light of changing populations and the need for municipal services. [Halifax] 1963. 95 p.

Commissioner/Commissaire: W.D. Outhit.

Loc.: AEU, BVAU, MWP, NSHPL, OKQ, OONL, OOP, OTLS, SRL

87 **Commission to Inquire into What Irregularities, if Any, May Have Occurred in Respect to the Use of Equipment, Furnishing, Chemicals or Supplies in the Department of Agriculture's Laboratory at Bible Hill in the County of Colchester During the Period from 1951 to 1962.**
Report. [Halifax, 1963] 36 *l.* (typescript)

Commissioner/Commissaire: R.E. Inglis.

Loc.: NSHPL

88 **1964**

Commission Appointed under the Provisions of the Public Inquiries Act of the Province of Nova Scotia to Inquire into the Safe Transportation of School Pupils, etc.
Report. Yarmouth, N.S., 1964. various pagings (typescript)

Commissioner/Commissaire: C.R. Rand.

Also known as/Également connue sous le nom de: The School Bus Inquiry.

Loc.: BVAS, MWP, NSHPL, OONL, OOP, OTYL, QQL, SRL

89 **Royal Commission on Prices of Pulpwood and Forest Products.**
Report. [Halifax] 1964. 32 *l.* (typescript)

Commissioner/Commissaire: R.J. MacSween.

Loc.: BVA, BVIV, NBFU, NSHPL, OOCI, OONL, OTLS

90 **1964-1965**

Royal Commission on the Cost of Borrowing Money, the Cost of Credit and Related Matters in the Province of Nova Scotia.
Interim report. [Halifax, 1964] 29 *l.* (typescript)

Loc.: BVAS, BVAU, BVIV, MWP, NSHPL, OONL, OOP, OTU, OTYL, QQL, SRL

———.

Final report. [Halifax, 1965] 3 v. (typescript)

Commissioner/Commissaire: A.R. Moreira.

Loc.: AEU, BVA, BVAU, MWP, MWU, NSHPL, OKQL, OLU, OOP, OOCI, OOF, OONL, OOP, OPET, OTCT, OTYL, OWAL, QMU, SRL, SSU

91 **1967**

Nova Scotia Milk Industry Inquiry Committee.
Report. [Halifax, 1967] iv, 175 p.

Commissioners/Commissaires: J.E. McArthur, R.L. MacDougall, H.A. Renouf, B.M. Trenholm.

Loc.: MWA, NSHPL, OGU, OOAG, OONL, OWA, OWTU

92 **1968**

Medical Care Insurance Advisory Commission.
Report. [Halifax, 1968?] various pagings (typescript)

Chairman/Président: R.M. Black.

Members/Membres: J.H. Delaney, T.W. Gorman, S.S. Jacobson, J.C. Wickwire.

Loc.: BVAU, NSHPL, NSWA, OTY

93 **1968-1970**

Royal Commission on Halifax County Hospital at Cole Harbour.
Interim report. Kentville, N.S., 1968. 56 *l.* (typescript)

Loc.: NSHPL

———.
Second interim report. Kentville, N.S., 1969. Various pagings (typescript)

Loc.: NSHPL, OONL, OOP

———.
Report. [Kentville, N.S., 1970] vi, 272 p. (typescript)

Commissioner/Commissaire: H.P. MacKeen.

Loc.: NSHDM, NSHPL, OONL, OOP

94 **Royal Commission on the Price Structure of Gasoline and Diesel Oil in Nova Scotia.**
Report. [Halifax, 1968] v, 157 p. (typescript)

Commissioner/Commissaire: H.A. Renouf.

Loc.: NSHPL, OOCI, OOEC, OONL, OTY, OTYL

95 **Workmen's Compensation Inquiry (Part III).**
Report. Truro, N.S., 1968. 134 *l.* (typescript)

Commissioner/Commissaire: L.O. Clarke.

Loc.: NSHPL, OTY

96 **1969**

Royal Commission, Election Expenses and Associated Matters.
Report. [Middleton, N.S.] 1969. various pagings (typescript)

Chairman/Président: M.G. Green.

Commissioners/Commissaires: S.R. Balcom, J.H. Delaney, C.F. Kennedy, L.R. Shaw.

Loc.: BVA, BVAS, MWP, NFSM, NSHPL, OONL, OOP, OWA, OWAL, OTYL

97 **Royal Commission on Section 3 of the Expired Collective Agreement between the Sydney School Board and the Nova Scotia Teachers' Union Sydney Local.**
Report. [Halifax, 1969] 43 *l.* (typescript)

Commissioner/Commissaire: A.R. Moreira.

Loc.: NSHPL

98 **1970**

Royal Commission on the Town of Bridgewater Police Department.
Report. [Kentville, N.S., 1970] 34 *l.* (typescript)

Commissioner/Commaissaire: H.B. Dickey.

Loc.: NSHPL, OONL, OTYL

99 **1971**

Royal Commission on the Sackville Land Assembly.
Report. [Halifax, 1971] xiii, 70 p. (typescript)

Commissioner/Commissaire: W.C. Dunlop.

Loc.: NSHPL, OONL, OOP, OTYL

100 **1973**

Royal Commission on Automobile Insurance.
Report. [Halifax] 1973 281 p. (typescript)

Chairman/Président: A.I. Barrow.

Commissioners/Commissaires: I.W. Akerley, V.A. Campbell.

Loc.: AEU, BVAU, MWU, NSHPL, OLU, OOCI, OONL, OOP, OOUD, OTU, OTY, OWAL, SRL, SSU

101 **1974**

> **Commission of Inquiry, Legislative Salaries and Allowances.**
> *Report.* [Halifax] 1974. iii, 106 p. (typescript)
>
> **Chairman/Président:** W.A. MacKay.
>
> **Commissioners/Commissaires:** H. Dowell, J.R. Lynk.
>
> Loc.: AEU, BVAU, MWP, NFSM, NSHPL, OLU, OONL, OOP, OTMCL, QMML, QQL, SRL

102 **Royal Commission on Education, Public Services and Provincial-Municipal Relations.**
> *Summary and recommendations.* Halifax: Queen's Printer, 1974. xiv, 301 p. (Report of the Royal Commission on Education, Public Services and Provincial-Municipal Relations; v. 1)
>
> ⸻.
> *Municipal government and the Province.* Halifax: Queen's Printer, 1974. 5 pts (Report of the Royal Commission on Education, Public Services and Provincial-Municipal Relations; v. 2)
>
> ⸻.
> *Education.* Halifax: Queen's Printer, 1974. 3 pts. (Report of the Royal Commission on Education, Public Services and Provincial-Municipal Relations; v. 3)
>
> ⸻.
> *Appendices.* Halifax: Queen's Printer, 1974. various pagings (Report of the Royal Commission on Education, Public Services and Provincial-Municipal Relations; v. 4)
>
> **Chairman/Président:** J.G. Graham.
>
> **Commissioners/Commissaires:** E.C. Harris, C.E. Walters.
>
> Also known as/Également connue sous le nom de: Graham Commission.
>
> Loc.: AEU, BVA, BVAS, BVIV, MWP, MWU, NBFU, NBS, NBSU, NFSG, NFSM, NSHDL, NSHPL, OKF, OKQM, OOMI, OONL, OOP, OOSC, OOSS, OOU, OPET, OTER, OTMCL, OTY, OWA, QQL, QMU, SRU, SSU, SSUL

103 **1976**

> **Commission in the Matter of the Board of School Commissioners for the Town of Mulgrave.**
> *Report.* [Dartmouth, N.S.] 1976. 94 *l.* (typescript)

Commissioner/Commissaire: W.E. Moseley.

Loc.: NSHPL

104 **1977**

Commission of Inquiry into Matters Related to Employment of Insulators from the United Kingdom at the Heavy Water Plant at Glace Bay.
Report. [Halifax, 1977] iii, 107 *l.* (typescript)

Commissioner/Commissaire: W.A. MacKay.

Loc.: NSHPL

105 **1979**

Commission of Inquiry into the Appropriate Form of Local Government for the Sackville Area.
Report. [Halifax] 1979. 31, 2 *l.*

Commissioner/Commissaire: H.M. Nason.

Loc.: NHSPL

106 **Commission to Inquire into the Complaints of Donald Ross MacInnis, a Medical Doctor.**
Report. [Sydney, N.S., 1979] 76 *l.* (typescript)

Commissioner/Commissaire: L.M. McIntyre.

Loc.: NSHPL

107 **Royal Commission on Renumeration of Elected Provincial Officials.**
Report. [Truro, N.S.] 1979. iii, 103 p. (typescript)

Chairman/Président: W.A. MacKay.

Commissioners/Commissaires: C.H. Dowell, J.R. Link.

Loc.: NSHPL, OONL

108 **1980**

Commission in the Matter of the Fund Administered by the Canada Permanent Trust Company as Agent for the Dominion Coal Workers' Relief Association.
Report. [Sydney, N.S., 1980?] 12 *l.* (typescript)

Commissioner/Commissaire: H.R. MacEwan.

Loc.: OONL, OOP

109 **1981**

Commission to Review the Police Act & Regulations.
Report. [Halifax] 1981. 96, 26, 36 p.

Commissioner/Commissaire: N. Green.

Loc.: NSHPL, OOP

110 **1982**

Commission of Inquiry on Remuneration of Elected Provincial Officials.
Report. [Truro, N.S.] 1982. 85 *l.*

Commissioner/Commissaire: W.A. MacKay.

Loc.: NSHPL

ONTARIO

111 **1873**

Commission to Enquire into and Concerning the Ill Treatment or Extortion Alleged to be Practised upon Visitors or Others at Niagara Falls or in the Neighbourhood.
Report. [Brantford, Ont., 1873] 6 *l.* (manuscript copy)

Commissioner/Commissaire: E.B. Wood.

Loc.: OTAR

112 **1877**

Commission to Enquire into the Financial Affairs of the Corporation of the Town of Belleville and Things Connected Therewith.
Report. [Toronto, 1877] 30, 8 *l.* (manuscript copy)

Commissioners/Commissaires: J. McKibbin, A.R. Morden.

Loc.: OTAR

113 **Royal Commission Appointed to Inquire into the Value of the Central Prison Labour.**
Report. Toronto: Hunter, Rose & Co., 1877. 310 p.

Chairman/Président: W.P. Howland.

Commissioners/Commissaires: Z.R. Brockway, J. Noxon.

Also known as/Également connue sous le nom de: Central Prison Labour Commission.

Loc.: OTAR, OTL

114 **1878**

Central Committee Inquiry of Examiners of the Education Department.
Report. Toronto: Hunter, Rose & Co., 1878. 254 p.

Commissioner/Commissaire: C.S. Patterson.

Loc.: OONL, OTAR, OTC, OTL, OTP

115 **1881**

Ontario Agricultural Commission.
Report. Toronto: C. Robinson, 1881. 4 v.

Chairman/Président: S.C. Wood.

Commissioners/Commissaires: J.B. Aylsworth, T. Ballantyne, W. Brown, E. Byrne, J. Dryden, A.H. Dymond, R. Gibson, E.H. Hilbourn, J. McMillan, F. Malcolm, W. Saunders, E. Stock, T. Stock, J. Watson, W. Whitelaw, A. Wilson, J.P. Wiser.

Loc.: BVAU, NBSAM, OKQ, OOAG, OONL, OOP, OTAR, OTL, OTP, OTY, QMBN, SSU

116 **1884**

Commission to Enquire into Certain Misconduct at the Agricultural College, Guelph.
Report. [Toronto, 1884] 5 *l.* (manuscript copy)

Commissioner/Commissaire: J. Winchester.

Loc.: OTAR

117 **1885**

Commission Appointed to Inquire into and Investigate Certain Charges of a Conspiracy to Corrupt and of Attempts to Bribe Certain Members of the Legislature.
Report. Toronto: "Grip" Printing and Pub., 1885. xiii, 425, 441 p.

Chairman/Président: W. Proudfoot.

Commissioners/Commissaires: A.F. Scott, E.J. Senkler.

Also known as/Également connue sous le nom de: Bribery Commission.

Loc.: OONL, OTAR, OTL, OTMCL, OTP, OWA, QMBM, SRL

118 **1886**

Royal Commission Appointed to Enquire into Certain Charges Against the Warden of the Central Prison and into the Management of the Said Prison.
Central prison investigation: report. Toronto: Warwick & Sons, 1886. 63 p.

Chairman/Président: J.S. Sinclair.

Commissioners/Commissaires: J.W. Langmuir, D.A. O'Sullivan.

Also known as/Également connue sous le nom de: Central Prison Commission.

Loc.: OONL, OTAR, OTL, OTMCL

119 **1888-1889**

The Commission on Municipal Institutions.
First Report. Toronto: Warwick & Sons, 1888. 96 p.

———.
Second Report. Toronto: Warwick & Sons, 1889. 233, xxxiii p.

Commissioners/Commissaires: T.W. Anglin, W. Houston, E.F.B. Johnston.

Loc.: OONL, OOP, OTAR, OTL, OTP, OTYL

120 **1890**

Royal Commission on the Mineral Resources of Ontario and Measures for their Development.
Report. Toronto: Warwick & Sons, 1890. xxiv, 566 p.

Chairman/Président: J. Charlton.

Commissioners/Commissaires: R. Bell, A. Blue, W. Coe, W.H. Merritt.

Loc.: AE, BVA, OKQ, OLU, OOG, OOM, OONL, OTAR, OTL, QMU, QQL, SSU

121 **1891**

Commission Appointed to Enquire into the Prison and Reformatory System of Ontario.
Report. Toronto: Warwick & Sons, 1891. 799 p.

Chairman/Président: J.W. Langmuir.

Commissioners/Commissaires: T.W. Anglin, C. Drury, A.F. Jury, A.M. Rosebrugh.

Also known as/Également connue sous le nom de: Ontario Prison Reform Commission.

Loc.: AEU, BVA, BVAU, OKQ, OOA, OONL, OOS, OTAR, OTE, OTL, OTY, OTYL, OWTU, QMML

1892

122 **Commission Appointed to Enquire into the Claims Made by the Township of Proton to Certain Sums of Money Payable as Alleged to that Municipality under the Act 16 Vict. cap. 159, Sec. 14.**
Report. Toronto: Warwick & Sons, 1892. 25 p.

Commissioners/Commissaires: T.W. Anglin, A. Irving.

Loc.: OONL, OTAR, OTL

123 **Ontario Commission on the Dehorning of Cattle.**
Report. Toronto: Warwick & Sons, 1892. 127 p.

Chairman/Président: C. Drury.

Commissioners/Commissaires: R. Gibson, H. Glendinning, J.J. Kelso, D.M. Macpherson, A. Smith.

Loc.: OONL, OTAR, OTL

124 **Ontario Game and Fish Commission.**
Report. Toronto: Warwick & Sons, 1892. 483 p.

Chairman/Président: G.A. MacCullum.

Commissioners/Commissaires: R.G. Hervey, R.A. Lucas, J. Mitchell, W.S. Pulford, H.K. Smith, A.D. Stewart, A.H. Taylor, E.W. Thompson, J.H. Wilmott.

Loc.: AE, BVAU, NBFU, NSHPL, OH, OKQ, OOC, OOFI, OOG, OONL, OTAR, OTL, OTP, OW, QMBM

1893

125 **Commission of Inquiry as to the Ontario Agricultural College and Experimental Farm.**
Report. Toronto: Warwick & Sons, 1893. 156 p.

Chairman/Président: J. Winchester.

Commissioners/Commissaires: J.S. Pearce, J. Watterworth.

Loc.: OONL, OTAR, OTL, OTP

126 **Commission on Municipal Taxation.**
Report. Toronto: Warwick & Sons, 1893. 86 p.

Chairman/Président: J.R. Cartwright.

Commissioners/Commissaires: T.W. Anglin, E. Saunders.

Loc.: OOF, OONL, OTAR, OTL, OTP, OTYL, OWA, SSU

127 **Drainage Commission for the Province of Ontario.**
Report. Toronto: Warwick & Sons, 1893. 135 p.

Chairman/Président: J.B. Rankin.

Commissioners/Commissaires: R. Lamarsh, W.G. McGeorge, A. McIntyre.

Loc.: OOGB, OONL, OTAR, OTL

128 **Royal Commission on Forest Reservation and National Park.**
Report. Toronto: Warwick & Sons, 1893. 40 p.

Chairman/Président: A. Kirkwood.

Commissioners/Commissaires: A. Blue, J. Dickson, T.W. Gibson, R.W. Phipps, A. White.

Loc.: BVAU, OOAG, OOGB, OONL, OLU, OTAR, OTL, OTMCL, OTU, SRU

129 **1895**

Commission Appointed to Inquire Concerning the Mode of Appointing and Remunerating Certain Provincial Officials Now Paid by Fees and the Extent of the Remuneration They Should Receive.
Report. Toronto: Warwick Bros. & Rutter, 1895. 95 p.

Chairman/Président: J.A. Boyd.

Commissioners/Commissaires: T. Brooks, J. Fleming, J.I. Hobson, J.J. Mason, J.B. Robinson.

Also known as/Également connue sous le nom de: Fees Commission.

Loc.: BVA, OKQ, OONL, OOP, OTAR, OTL, OTY, OTYL

130 **Commission on the Discipline in the University of Toronto.**
Report. Toronto: Warwick Bros. & Rutter, 1895. 34 p.

Chairman/Président: T.W. Taylor.

Commissioners/Commissaires: B.M. Britton, J. Campbell, J.J. Kingsmill, E.J. Senkler.

Loc.: OONL, OTAR, OTL, OTP, OTU

131 **1898-1900**

Royal Commission on Forestry Protection in Ontario.
Royal Commission on Forestry in Ontario: preliminary report. Toronto: Warwick Bro's & Rutter, 1898. 14 p.

Loc.: BVAU, OODF, OONL, OOP, OPAL, OTAR, OTL, OTP

———.

Report. Toronto: L.K. Cameron, Printer to the Queen's Most Excellent Majesty, 1900. 29 p.

Chairman/Président: E.W. Rathbun.

Commissioners/Commissaires: J. Bertram, A. Kirkwood, J.B. McWilliams, T. Southworth.

Loc.: BVAU, OONL, OPAL, OTAR, OTL, OTP

132 **1898**

Royal Commission on the Questions of Prices of School Books, Royalties, etc.
Report. Toronto: Warwick Bro's. & Rutter, 1898. 19 p.

Commissioners/Commissaires: J. Bain, Jr., E. Morgan, C.B. Robinson.

Loc.: OONL, OTAR, OTC, OTL, OTYL

133 **1899**

Commission of Enquiry Concerning the Operation of the San Jose Scale Act.
Report. Toronto: Warwick Bro's. & Rutter, 1899. 8 p.

Commissioners/Commissaires: W.H. Bunting, J. Dearness, J. Mills.

Loc.: OOAGE, OONL, OTAR, OTL

134 **1900**

Royal Commission on the Financial Position of the Province of Ontario.
Report. Toronto: Warwick Bro's. & Rutter, 1900. 26 p.

Chairman/Président: B.E. Walker.

Commissioners/Commissaires: J. Hoskin, A. Kirkland.

Loc.: OKQ, OLU, OOF, OONL, OTAR, OTL, OTP, OTU.

135 **1901-1902**

Ontario Assessment Commission.
Report of the Ontario Assessment Commission being the interim or first report and record of proceedings. Toronto: L.K. Cameron, Printer to the King's Most Excellent Majesty, 1901. xii, 605 p.

———.

Report. Toronto: L.K. Cameron, Printer to the King's Most Excellent Majesty, 1902. 75, 115 p.

Chairman/Président: J. Maclennan.

Commissioners/Commissaires: M.J. Butler, K.W. McKay, H. MacMahon, T.H. Macpherson, A. Pratt, D.R. Wilkie.

Loc.: OONL, OOP, OTAR, OTL, OTP

136 **1901**

West Elgin Election Investigation.
Report. Toronto: L.K. Cameron, Printer to the King's Most Excellent Majesty, 1901. 16p.

Chairman/Président: J.A. Barron.

Commissioners/Commissaires: D.B. MacTavish, E. Morgan.

Loc.: OONL, OTAR, OTL

137 **1903**

Royal Commission re Gamey Charges.
Report. Toronto: L.K. Cameron, Printer to the King's Most Excellent Majesty, 1903. 952, 98, 48 p.

Commissioners/Commissaires: J.A. Boyd, W.G. Falconbridge.

Also known as/Également connue sous le nom de: Bribery Charges Commission.

Loc.: OOA, OOL, OONL, OOP, OTAR, OTL, OTP, OTYL, SRL

138 **1905**

Commission Appointed to Inquire into and Report upon the Matters Referred to in a Resolution of the Senate of the University of Toronto on the 20th Day of January, 1905.
Report. Toronto: L.K. Cameron, Printer to the King's Most Excellent Majesty, 1905. 14 p.

Chairman/Président: W.R. Meredith.

Commissioners/Commissaires: A.B. Aylesworth, T.C.S. Macklem, C. Moss, W.P.R. Street.

Loc.: OONL, OTAR, OTL

139 **Ontario Commission on Railway Taxation.**
Report. Toronto: L.K. Cameron, Printer to the King's Most Excellent Majesty, 1905. 219 p.

Chairman/Président: H.J. Pettypiece.

Commissioners/Commissaires: A. Bell, A. Shortt.

Loc.: NSHPL, OKQ, OONL, OTAR, OTL, OTP

140 **1906**

Commission of Inquiry Concerning Certain Charges Against Charles Edward Whelihan, Esq., Registar of Deeds for the Registry Division of the South Riding of Perth.
Report. [Listowel, Ont., 1906] 12 *l.* (typescript)

Commissioner/Commissaire: H.B. Morphy.

Loc.: OTAR

141 **Royal Commission on the University of Toronto.**
Report. Toronto: L.K. Cameron, Printer to the King's Most Excellent Majesty, 1906. lx, 268 p.

Chairman/Président: J.W. Flavelle.

Commissioners/Commissaires: H.J. Cody, A.H.U. Colquhoun, D.B. Macdonald, W.R. Meredith, G. Smith, B.E. Walker.

Loc.: BVAU, MWU, NBSAM, OOC, OONL, OOP, OTAR, OTL, OTU, QQL, SRL

142 **1907**

Commission to Enquire into all such Matters and Things as Are Charged or May Be Charged against Thomas McDonald of the Village of Morrisburgh in the County of Dundas, Registrar of Deeds.
Report. [London, Ont., 1907] 11 *l.* (typescript)

Commissioner/Commissaire: J.C. Judd.

Loc.: OTAR

143 **Commission to Enquire into and Report upon the Workings of the Deaf and Dumb Institute at Belleville.**
Report. [Belleville, Ont., 1907] 25 *l.* (typescript)

Commissioner/Commissaire: A.J.R. Snow.

Loc.: OTAR

144 **Commission to Enquire into and Report upon the Workings of the Institute for the Blind at Brantford.**
Report. [Brantford, Ont.?, 1907] 50 *l.* (manuscript copy)

Commissioner/Commissaire: A.J.R. Snow.

Loc.: OTAR

145 **Text Book Commission.**
Report. Toronto: L.K. Cameron, Printer to the King's Most Excellent Majesty, 1907. 389 p.

Chairman/Président: T.W. Crothers.

Commissioner/Commissaire: A.C. Casselman, J.A. Cooper.

Loc.: AEU, OH, OONL, OTAR, OTC, OTL, OTP, OTYL, SSU

146 **1909**

Enquiry into the Conduct of W.R. Andrews, the License Inspector of East Elgin.
Return to an order of the House that the report of the Commissioner who held the recent enquiry into the conduct of W.R. Andrews the license inspector of East Elgin together with the evidence on which same is based, be laid on the table of the House. Toronto: L.K. Cameron, Printer to the King's Most Excellent Majesty, 1909. 80 p.

Commissioner/Commissaire: E. Saunders.

Loc.: OONL, OTAR, OTL

147 **1910**

Milk Commission Appointed to Enquire into the Production, Care and Distribution of Milk.
Report. Toronto: L.K. Cameron, Printer to the King's Most Excellent Majesty, 1910. 142 p.

Chairman/Président: A.R. Pyne.

Commissioners/Commissaires: J.R. Dargaval, F.G. Macdiarmid, W.F. Nickle.

Loc.: BVAU, OLU, OOAG, OONL, OTAR, OTL, OTP

148 **1911**

Commission of Inquiry in the Cause, or Causes, of the Destruction, or Partial Destruction, of Certain Dams on the Napanee River, Called the Dams at the Third, Fourth and Fifth Depot Lakes.
Report. [Napanee, Ont., 1911] 4 *l.* (typescript)

Commissioner/Commissaire: W. Rankin.

Loc.: OTAR

149 **1912**

Commission to Inquire into the Charges Made by one Michael Farr of the Town of Goderich, against William Patterson, Chairman of the Board of License Commissioners of the License District of Centre Huron.
Report. [Toronto, 1912] 5 *l.* (typescript)

Commissioner/Commissaire: E. Saunders.

Loc.: OTAR

150 **Ontario Game and Fisheries Commission.**
Final report. Toronto: L.K. Cameron, Printer to the King's Most Excellent Majesty, 1912. 304 p.

Commissioner/Commissaire: K. Evans.

Loc.: NSHPL, OOC, OODF, OOFI, OOG, OONL, OL, OSTCB, OTAR, OTL, OTP, OTY

151 **1912-1913**

Workmen's Compensation Commission.
Interim report on laws relating to the liability of employers to make compensation to their employees for injuries received in the course of their employment which are in force in other countries. Toronto: L.K. Cameron, Printer to the King's Most Excellent Majesty, 1912. 478 p.

————.

Second interim report on laws relating to the liability of employers with draft of an act to provide for compensation to workmen for injuries sustained and industrial diseases contracted in the course of their employment. Toronto: L.K. Cameron, Printer to the King's Most Excellent Majesty, 1913. 40 p.

————.

Final report. Toronto: L.K. Cameron, Printer to the King's Most Excellent Majesty, 1913. 18 p.

Commissioner/Commissaire: W.R. Meredith.

Loc.: OH, OONL, OTAR, OTL

152 **1913**

Commission to Enquire into Certain Irregularities in Connection with Voting on a Certain By-Law of the Town of Welland, on August 6, 1912.
Report. Toronto, 1913. 6 *l.* (typescript)

Commissioner/Commissaire: J.W. Bain.

Also known as/Également connue sous le nom de: Welland Investigation.

Loc.: OTAR

153 **1914**

Public Roads and Highways Commission of Ontario.
Report. Toronto: L.K. Cameron, Printer to the King's Most Excellent Majesty, 1914. 277 p.

Chairman/Président: C.A. Magrath.

Commissioners/Commissaires: W.A. McLean, A.M. Rankin.
Also known as/Également connue sous le nom de: Good Roads Commission.

Loc.: NSHPL, OQK, OLU, OOAG, OONL, OORD, OOU, OPAL, OTAR, OTL, OTMCL, OTP, OTY, OW

154 **1915-1916**

Ontario Commission on Unemployment.
Interim report. Toronto: L.K. Cameron, Printer to the King's Most Excellent Majesty, 1915. 11 p.

Loc.: OONL, OTAR

————.

Report. Toronto: A.T. Wilgress, Printer to the King's Most Excellent Majesty, 1916. viii, 334 p.

Chairman/Président: J.S. Willison.

Commissioners/Commissaires: G.F. Beer, W.L. Best, H.J. Cody, A.T. DeLury, J. Gibbons, W.P. Gundy, G.E. Jackson, W.K. McNaught, N. McNeil, D. Strachan.

Loc.: AEP, BVAU, BVIV, MWU, OH, OLU, OOAG, OOL, OONL, OTAR, OTL, OTP, OTV, OTY, SRU

155 **1917**

Royal Commission to Inquire into the Administration, Management and Welfare of the Ontario School for the Blind.
Report. Toronto: A.T. Wilgress, Printer to the King's Most Excellent Majesty, 1917. 35 p.

Commissioner/Commissaire: N.B. Gash.

Loc.: OH, OONL, OTAR, OTL, OTP

156 **Royal Ontario Nickel Commission.**
Report. Toronto: A.T. Wilgress, Printer to the King's Most Excellent Majesty, 1917. various pagings

Chairman/Président: G.T. Holloway.

Commissioners/Commissaires: T.W. Gibson, W.G. Miller, M. Young.

Loc.: BVA, BVAU, MWU, NBFU, NBS, OKQ, OOND, OONL, OOP, OOTC, OTAR, OTL, QMBM, QQL

157 **1918**

Commission of Inquiry re Waterworks Regulations and Electrical Development Company of Ontario.
Report. [Toronto, 1918] 8 *l.* (typescript)

Commissioners/Commissaires: H.T. Kelly, W.R. Meredith, R.F. Sutherland.

Loc.: OTAR

158 **Commission on Medical Education in Ontario.**
Report. Toronto: A.T. Wilgress, Printer to the King's Most Excellent Majesty, 1918. 177 p.

Commissioner/Commissaire: F.E. Hodgins.

Loc.: OONL, OTAR, OTL

159 **Commission to Inquire into and Report upon the Administration, Management, Conduct and Welfare of the Industrial Farm at Burwash, Ontario.**
Report. [Toronto, 1918] 42 *l.* (typescript)

Commissioner/Commissaire: E. Coatsworth.

Loc.: OTAR

160 **1918-1919**

Royal Commission on the Care and Control of the Mentally Defective and Feeble-minded in Ontario [and the Prevalence of Venereal Disease].
Interim report on venereal diseases and copy of an Act for the Prevention of Venereal Disease. Toronto: A.T. Wilgress, Printer to the King's Most Excellent Majesty, 1918. 21 p.

Loc.: OONL, OTAR, OTL, OTP

―――――――.
Report on venereal diseases. Toronto: A.T. Wilgress, Printer to the King's Most Excellent Majesty, 1919. 25 p.

Loc.: OOA, OONL, OTAR, OTL

―――――――.
Report. Toronto: A.T. Wilgress, Printer to the King's Most Excellent Majesty, 1919. 236 p.

Commissioner/Commissaire: F.E. Hodgins.

Loc.: OLUM, OOA, OOCC, OONH, OONL, OOP, OTAR, OTL, OTMCL, OTP, OTYL

161 **1919**

Commission Appointed to Enquire into and Report upon the Building Department of the Board of Education of the City of Toronto.
Report. [Toronto, 1919] 91 *l.* (typescript)

Commissioner/Commissaire: H.I.S. Lennox.

Loc.: OTAR

162 **Insurance Commission.**
Report. Toronto: A.T. Wilgress, Printer to the King's Most Excellent Majesty, 1919. 107 p.

Commissioner/Commissaire: C.A. Masten.

Loc.: BVA, BVAU, OOAG, OOCI, OONL, OTAR, OTL, OTP

163 **Royal Commission on Police Matters.**
Report. [Toronto, 1919] 58 *l.* (typescript)

Chairman/Président: W.R. Meredith.

Commissioners/Commissaires: J.T. Gunn, S.R. Parsons.

Loc.: OTAR

164 **1920**

Commission of Enquiry, Kapuskasing Colony.
Report. Toronto: A.T. Wilgress, Printer to the King's Most Excellent Majesty, 1920. 15 p.

Chairman/Président: W.F. Nickle.

Commissioners/Commissaires: J.I. McLaren, J. Sharp.

Loc.: OONL, OTAR, OTL

165 **Commission to Inquire in the Matter of Certain Charges as to the Administration of the Ontario Temperance Act.**
Report. In Ontario. Legislative Assembly. *Sessional papers.* v. 52, part 8. 15th Legislature, 6th Session. Toronto: C.W. James, Printer to the King's Most Excellent Majesty, 1920. p. 20-31. (Sessional paper no. 66).

Commissioner/Commissaire: W.R. Meredith.

Loc.: BVAU, BVIP, MWP, OH, OHM, OL, OLU, OOA, OONL, OOP, OTAR, OTDRE, OTL, OTMCL, OTU, OTY, OWTL, OWTU, QMHE, QMM, QQL

166 **Commission to Inquire into and Report upon the Rates of Wages Paid to Men Employed by the Hydro-Electric Power Commission in the Construction of the Queenston-Chippawa Development, as Compared with the Rates Paid for Similar Service by Other Employers: the Ability of the Queenston-Chippawa Project to Pay Increased Wages and the Living Conditions of the Men so Employed.**
Report. Toronto: C.W. James, Printer to the King's Most Excellent Majesty, 1920. 7 p.

Chairman/Président: E. Watson.

Commissioners/Commissaires: W.H. Casselman, M. MacBride, A.E. Ross, J.C. Tolmie.

Loc.: OONL, OOP, OTAR, OTL, OTP

167 **Inquiry Respecting the Ontario Hospital, Hamilton.**
Report. [Toronto, 1920] 20 *l.* (typescript)

Commissioner/Commissaire: C.G. Snider.

Loc.: OTAR

168 **1921**

Commission Appointed to Inquire into Certain Charges against F.B. Taber and C.R. Deacon.
Report. [Toronto, 1921] 5 *l.* (typescript)

Commissioner/Commissaire: J.K. Dowsley.

Loc.: OTAR

169 **Commission Appointed to Inquire into Hydro-Electric Railways.**
Reports. Toronto: C.W. James, Printer to the King's Most Excellent Majesty, 1921. 234 p.

Chairman/Président: R.F. Sutherland.

Commissioners/Commissaires: W.A. Amos, A.F. McCallum, C.H. Mitchell.

Also known as/Également connue sous le nom de: Radial Railway Commission.

Loc.: BVAU, OLU, OONL, OOP, OTAR, OTL, OTP

170 **Commission Appointed to Inquire into the Truth or Falsity of Certain Charges Made against David Hastings, Police Magistrate of Dunnville.**
Report. [Toronto? 1921] 19 *l.* (typescript)

Commissioner/Commissaire: J.A. Patterson.

Loc.: OTAR

171 **Commission Appointed to Investigate Certain Charges Made by George Laing against John Goodwin, Police Magistrate of the City of Welland, and Other Officers.**
Report. [St. Catharines, Ont., 1921] 11 *l.* (typescript)

Commissioner/Commissaire: J.S. Campbell.

Also known as/Également connue sous le nom de: Welland Enquiry.

Loc.: OTAR

172 **Commission to Conduct an Inquiry into the Truth or Falsity of the Charges Relating to the Toronto Police Court.**
Report. [Toronto, 1921] 48 *l.* (typescript)

Commissioner/Commissaire: H.A. Ward.

Loc.: OTAR

173 **Commission to Make Inquiries and Report upon all Matters and Things Connected with or Relative or Incidental to the Seizure on or about the 21st of April, 1920, of a Car of Whiskey at the City of Chatham.**
Report. [London, Ont., 1921] 16 *l.* (typescript)

Commissioner/Commissaire: T. Macbeth.

Loc.: OTAR

174 **Commission Upon the Victoria Industrial School for Boys.**
Report. [Toronto, 1921] 7 *l.* (typescript)

Chairman/Président: J. Waugh.

Commissioners/Commissaires: J.J. Kelso, H. MacMurchy.

Loc.: OTAR

175 **Royal Commission on University Finances.**
Report. Toronto, C.W. James, Printer to the King's Most Excellent Majesty, 1921. 2 v.

Chairman/Président: H.J. Cody.

Commissioners/Commissaires: A.P. Deroche, T.A. Russell, C.R. Somerville, J.A. Wallace, J.S. Willison.

Loc.: BVIV, NFSM, OKQ, OOC, OONL, OOP, OTAR, OTL, OTU, SSU

176 **1921-1922**

Royal Commission to Inquire into, Consider and Report upon the Best Mode of Selecting, Appointing, and Remunerating Sheriffs, etc., etc.
Interim report respecting sheriffs. Toronto: C.W. James, Printer to the King's Most Excellent Majesty, 1921. 37 p.

Loc.: AEU, OONL, OTAR, OTL, OTLS

─────────.

Interim report respecting police magistrates. Toronto: C.W. James, Printer to the King's Most Excellent Majesty, 1921. 21 p.

Loc.: OH, OONL, OTAR, OTL, OTLS, OTP

─────────.

Interim report respecting issuers of marriage licenses. Toronto: C.W. James, Printer to the King's Most Excellent Majesty, 1921. 7 p.

Loc.: OONL, OTAR, OTL, OTLS

─────────.

Interim report respecting Toronto Police Court. Toronto: C.W. James, Printer to the King's Most Excellent Majesty, 1921. 28 p.

Loc.: OTAR, OTL, OTLS, OTMCL

─────────.

Interim report respecting coroners. Toronto: C.W. James, 1921. 10 p.

Loc.: OONL, OTAR, OTL, OTLS, OTR, OTU

─────────.

Interim report respecting extension of land titles system in Northern Ontario. Toronto: C.W. James, Printer to the King's Most Excellent Majesty, 1922. 6 p.

Loc.: OH, OONL, OTAR, OTL, OTLS, OTP, OTYL.

———.
Interim report respecting Osgoode Hall. Toronto: C.W. James, Printer to the King's Most Excellent Majesty, 1922. 5-28 p.

Loc.: OH, OTAR, OTL, OTLS, OTP

———.
Interim report respecting Toronto and York registry offices. Toronto: C.W. James, Printer to the King's Most Excellent Majesty, 1922. 6 p.

Chairman/Président: W.D. Gregory.

Commissioners/Commissaires: H.L. Brittain, A. Hellyer, E.A. Pocock, N. Sommerville.

Also known as/Également connue sous le nom de: Public Service Commission.

Loc.: AEU, OONL, OTAR, OTL, OTLS, OTP

177 **1921-1922**

Timber Commission.
Interim reports (first, second and third) of the Commission to investigate and report upon the accuracy or otherwise of all returns made pursuant to the Crown Timber Act, Section 14, by any holder of a timber license, etc., etc., etc. Toronto: C.W. James, Printer to the King's Most Excellent Majesty, 1921. 8 p.

———.
Report. Toronto: C.W. James, Printer to the King's Most Excellent Majesty, 1922. 65 p.

Commissioners/Commissaires: F.R. Latchford, W.R. Riddell.

Loc.: OONL, OTAR, OTL, OTP

178 **1922**

Commission Appointed to Investigate the Financial Affairs of the Town of Oshawa.
Report. Toronto, 1922. 13 *l.* (typescript)

Commissioner/Commissaire: H. Pettit.

Loc.: OTAR

179 **Commission to Inquire into the Truth or Falsity of Certain Charges, etc., Contained in a Speech Delivered by A.C. Lewis, Esq., M.L.A. in the Legislative Assembly, Reflecting on the Administration of the Attorney General's Department in Respect of the Investigation into the Death of Captain Orville Huston, at Fort Frances.**
Report. Toronto: C.W. James, Printer to the King's Most Excellent Majesty, 1922. 54 p.

Commissioner/Commissaire: J.A. Macintosh.

Loc.: OLU, OOC, OOP, OTAR, OTL, OTP, OTYL

180 **Inquiry into the Financial Affairs of the Town of Cobourg and any Matter Connected Therewith.**
Interim report. Toronto, 1922. 2 *l.* (typescript)

———.
Report. Toronto, 1922. 42 *l.* (typescript)

Commissioner/Commissaire: G.A. Peters.

Loc.: OTAR

181 **1922**

Northern Ontario Fire Investigation.
Report of the Provincial Fire Marshall E.P. Heaton following investigation into the Northern Ontario conflagration of October 4th, 1922. [Toronto, 1922] 51 *l.* (typescript)

Commissioner/Commissaire: E.P. Heaton.

Loc.: OTAR, OTL

182 **1924**

Hydro-Electric Inquiry Commission.
General report. [Toronto, 1924] 2 v. (typescript)

Chairman/Président: W.D. Gregory.

Commissioners/Commissaires: M.J. Haney, L. Harris, J.A. Ross, R.A. Ross.

Also known as/Également connue sous le nom de: The Gregory Commission.

Loc.: OTAR, OTL, OTU

183 **Inquiry into Charges Made by One E.C. Settell with Regard to the Administration of the Affairs of the Hydro-Electric Power Commission of Ontario.**
Report. [Toronto] 1924. 94 *l.* (typescript)

Commissioner/Commissaire: C.G. Snider.

Loc.: MWP, MWU, OOP, OTAR, OTMCL, OW

184 **1925**

Commission Appointed to Inquire and Report upon Ownership of Lots Numbers Ninety-Four and Ninety-Five, in the Third Concession, Township of Glenelg, County of Grey.
Report. [Toronto, 1925] 10 *l.* (typescript)

Commissioner/Commissaire: F.E. Titus.

Loc.: OTAR

185 **Commission to Inquire into Financial Affairs of the Township of Markham.**
Report. [Toronto, 1925] unpaged (typescript)

Commissioner/Commissaire: W.J. McCoy.

Loc.: OTAR

186 **1926**

Commission on the Prices of Gasoline and Oils Sold to the People of Ontario.
Report. Toronto: C.W. James, Printer to the King's Most Excellent Majesty, 1926. 27 p.

Commissioner/Commissaire: G.T. Clarkson.

Loc.: OKQ, OONL, OOP, OTL

187 **Inquiry into the Industrial Farm at Langstaff and the Women's Farm at Concord.**
Report. [Toronto, 1926] 7 *l.* (typescript)

Commissioners/Commissaires: W.W. Denison, A.L. McPherson.

Loc.: OTAR

188 **1927**

> **Ottawa Collegiate Institute Inquiry.**
> *Report.* [Toronto, 1927] 20 *l.* (typescript)
>
> **Commissioner/Commissaire:** J.F. Orde.
>
> Also known as/Également connue sous le nom de: Royal Commission on Ottawa Collegiate Conditions, 1926.
>
> Loc.: OTAR

189 **1928**

> **Commission Appointed to Enquire into Certain Irregularities in Connection with the Ballots for the Electoral District of South Ottawa.**
> *Report.* [Toronto, 1928] 19 *l.* (typescript)
>
> **Commissioners/Commissaires:** F.E. Hodgins, J. Magee.
>
> Loc.: OTAR

190 **Commission to Inquire into, Investigate and Report upon the General Administration, Management, Conduct, and all Matters Pertaining to the Safe-Guarding of the Prisoners in the County Gaol of the County of Middlesex, at the City of London, Ontario.**
Report. [Simcoe, Ont., 1928] 21 *l.* (typescript)

> **Commissioner/Commissaire:** A.T. Boles.
>
> Also known as/Également connue sous le nom de: London Gaol Inquiry.
>
> Loc.: OTAR

191 **Hollinger Fire Inquiry.**
Report. [Toronto, 1928] 21, 13 *l.* (typescript)

> **Commissioner/Commissaire:** T.E. Godson.
>
> Also known as/Également connue sous le nom de: Hollinger Mine Inquiry.
>
> Loc.: OTAR.

192 **1930**

Royal Commission on Automobile Insurance Premium Rates.
Interim report on compulsory insurance and safety responsibility laws.
2d ed. Toronto: Printer to the King's Most Excellent Majesty, 1930. 85 p.

———.
Report. 2d ed. Toronto: H.H. Ball, Printer to the King's Most Excellent Majesty, 1930. 116 p.

Commissioner/Commissaire: F.E. Hodgins.

Loc.: MWP, NSHPL, OOCI, OONL, OOP, OTAR, OTL, OTUL, OTY, OTYL, QQL, SRL

193 **The Royal Commission on Public Welfare.**
Report. Toronto: Printer to the King's Most Excellent Majesty, 1930. ii, 111 p.

Chairman/Président: P.D. Ross.

Commissioners/Commissaires: J.M. McCutcheon, D.M. Wright.

Loc.: BVA, BVAU, MWHP, MWU, NSHDL, OHM, OKQ, OOAG, OONL, OOP, OTAR, OTL, OTY, OWTU, QMU, SRL, SSU

194 **1931**

Commission in the Matter of Application for Patent of North One-Half of Lot Number Seven, Ninth Concession, Township of Glenelg, County of Grey, Province of Ontario.
Report. [Toronto, 1931] 16 *l.* (typescript)

Commissioner/Commissaire: F.E. Titus.

Loc.: OTAR

195 **1932**

Commission in the Matter of the Workmen's Compensation Act.
Report. Toronto: H.H. Ball, Printer to the King's Most Excellent Majesty, 1932. 17 p.

Commissioner/Commissaire: W.E. Middleton.

Loc.: OOL, OONL, OOP, OTAR, OTL, OTP

196 **The Royal Commission Appointed to Inquire into Certain Matters Concerning the Hydro-Electric Power Commission of Ontario Namely: (a) The Mississippi and Madawaska Purchase. (b) The Possible Relationship of the Payment to John Aird, Jr., to the Purchase of Power from the Beauharnois Interests. (c) Purchase of the Assets of the Dominion Power and Transmission Company Limited.**
Report. Toronto: H.H. Ball, Printer to the King's Most Excellent Majesty, 1932. 11 p.

Commissioners/Commissaires: W.R. Riddell, G.H. Sedgewick.

Loc.: OH, OKQ, OONL, OOP, OPAL, OTAR, OTL, OWTU, SRL

197 **Royal Commission on the Use of Radium and X-Rays in the Treatment of the Sick, etc.**
Report. Toronto: H.H. Ball, Printer to the King's Most Excellent Majesty. 1932. 171 p.

Chairman/Président: H.J. Cody.

Commissioners/Commissaires: W.T. Connell, A.R. Ford, J.C. McLennan.

Loc.: MWM, OKQ, OLU, OOM, OON, OONL, OTAR, OTL, QMMM, SRL

198 **1933**

Commission Appointed to Inquire into the Events and Circumstances Relating to the Arrest of Albert Dorland and William Toohey.
Report. [Toronto, 1933] xliii *l*. (typescript)

Commissioner/Commissaire: A.C. Kingstone.

Also known as/Également connue sous le nom de: Dorland Commission.

Loc.: OTAR, OTL

199 **Royal Commission of Inquiry as to the Administration of Relief at York Township, Ontario.**
Report. [Toronto, 1933] 74 *l*. (typescript)

Commissioner/Commissaire: J.M. Hall.

Loc.: OTAR

200 **Royal Commission of Enquiry as to the Handling of Unemployment and Direct Relief at Sturgeon Falls, Ontario.**
Report. [Toronto? 1933] 79 *l.* (typescript)

Commissioner/Commissaire: J.M. Hall.

Loc.: OTAR

201 **1934**

Commission Appointed Respecting the Appointment and Resignation of Daniel McCaughrin, Police Magistrate.
Report. [Toronto, 1934] 8 *l.* (typescript)

Commissioner/Commissaire: R.G. Fisher.

Loc.: OTAR

202 **Inquiry into Ontario Provincial Air Service.**
Report. [Toronto, 1934] 15 *l.* (typescript).

Commissioner/Commissaire: D.W. Lang.

Loc.: OTAR, OTL

203 **Niagara Parks Commission Inquiry.**
Report. [Toronto, 1934] 17 *l.* (typescript)

Commissioners/Commissaires: A. Racine, H.J. Welch.

Loc.: OTAR, OTL

204 **Royal Commission Appointed to Inquire into the Purchase of the Bonds of the Ontario Power Service Corporation by the Hydro-Electric Power Commission of Ontario and the Government of Ontario, and the Payment Therefor in the Bonds of the Hydro-Electric Power Commission of Ontario, and all the Circumstances Connected Therewith.**
Report. [Toronto, 1934] 43 *l.* (typescript)

Commissioners/Commissaires: F.R. Latchford, R. Smith.

Also known as/Également connue sous le nom de: Inquiry into the Hydro-Electric Power Commission.

Loc.: OONL, OTAR, OTL

205 **1935**

Commission Appointed Respecting the General Election of the Legislative Assembly of the Province of Ontario Held on the 19th Day of June, 1934.
Report. [Toronto, 1935] 12 *l.* (typescript)

Commissioner/Commissaire: I.A. Humphries.

Also known as/Également connue sous le nom de: Elections Inquiry Commission.

Loc.: OTAR

206 **Commission to Inquire into and Report upon the Internal Management of the Ontario Hospital, Mimico.**
Ontario Hospital Mimico: report of a Royal Commission inquiring into the internal management. Toronto, 1935. 28 *l.* (typescript)

Commissioner/Commissaire: W.B. Common.

Loc.: OTAR

207 **Commission to Inquire into the Ontario Athletic Commission.**
Report. [Toronto, 1935] 16 *l.* (typescript)

Commissioner/Commissaire: C.S. Walters.

Loc.: OTAR

208 **Liquor Control Board Inquiry.**
Report. [St. Thomas, Ont., 1935] 48 *l.* (typescript)

Commissioner/Commissaire: D.C. Ross.

Loc.: OTAR

209 **Royal Commission on Border Cities Amalgamation.**
Report. Toronto: T.E. Bowman, Printer to the King's Most Excellent Majesty, 1935. 59 p.

Chairman/Président: J.J. Couglin.

Commissioners/Commissaires: H.L. Brittain, H.L. Cummings, J.C. Keith, S.E. McGorman.

Loc.: OLU, OTAR, OTL

210 **Temiskaming and Northern Ontario Railway Inquiry.**
Report. Toronto: T.E. Bowman, Printer to the King's Most Excellent Majesty, 1935. 25 p.

Commissioner/Commissaire: A. Racine.

Loc.: OOP, OTAR, OTL

211 **1936**
Commission to Inquire into and Report upon all Matters Arising out of the Evidence Given by One, W.J. Watt, before the Board of Commissioners of Police for the City of Toronto, and Generally with Respect to the Conduct of the Toronto Police Force, or Any of its Members.
Report. [Toronto, 1936] 50 *l.* (typescript)

Commissioners/Commissaires: J.J. Coughlin, D.C. Ross.

Also known as/Également connue sous le nom de: Toronto Police Inquiry.

Loc.: OONL, OTL

212 **Royal Commission Appointed to Inquire into and Report upon certain Charges of Mismanagement and Impropriety in Connection with the Administration of the Affairs of the Department of Northern Development in the District of South Cochrane.**
Report. [Toronto, 1936] 32 *l.* (typescript)

Commissioner/Commissaire: W.B. Common.

Loc.: OTAR

213 **1937**

Commission to Inquire into the Financial Affairs of the Corporation of the Town of Collingwood.
Report. [Toronto, 1937] 39 *l.* (typescript).

Commissioner/Commissaire: W.D. Roach.

Loc.: OTAR

214 **Commission to Inquire into the Recent Disturbances of and among the Prisoners at the Ontario Reformatory at Guelph.**
Inquiry into recent disturbances at the Ontario Reformatory, Guelph. [Toronto, 1937] 36 *l.* (typescript)

Commissioner/Commissaire: J.E. Madden.

Loc.: OONL, OTAR, OTL

215 **1938**

Royal Commission on the Operation of the Mental Hospitals Act.
Report. [Toronto, 1938] 84 *l.* (typescript)

Chairman/Président: C.R. Magone.

Commissioners/Commissaires: W.H. Avery, L.P. Conacher.

Loc.: OTAR, OTL

216 **1939**

Royal Commission on Transportation.
Report. Toronto: T.E. Bowman, Printer to the King's Most Excellent Majesty, 1939. xv, 293 p.

Chairman/Président: E.R.E. Chevrier.

Commissioners/Commissaires: E.R. Sayles, C.R. Young.

Loc.: BVAU, OH, OKQ, OOB, OOF, OONL, OTAR, OTL, OTP, SRL

217 **1941**

Royal Commission Inquiring into the Affairs of the Abitibi Power & Paper Company, Limited.
Report. [Toronto, 1941] 20 p.

Chairman/Président: C.P. McTague.

Commissioners/Commissaires: J. Dunn, A.E. Dyment.

Loc.: OHM, OLU, OPET, OTAR, OTL

218 **1942**

Commission to Investigate, Inquire into and Report upon all Matters Pertaining to a Statement Appearing in the Issue of March 31, 1942, of the *Globe and Mail*, as follows: "Controller Duncan Said He Had Evidence to the Effect that Many Toronto Reliefees Had Died from Malnutrition Due to the "Inadequacy" of the Past Relief Schedules."
Report. [Toronto, 1942] 3 *l.* (typescript)

Commissioner/Commissaire: S. Lawson.

Loc.: OTAR

219 **1944**

Royal Commission Appointed to Examine into and Report upon the Safety of Premises in the Province of Ontario Hired for Use by the Public as Places of Public Assembly or in Respect of which an Admission is Charged to the Public for Entrance or a Fee is Charged for Entertainment.
Report. [Toronto, 1944] 51 *l.* (typescript)

Commissioner/Commissaire: I.M. Macdonnell.

Also known as/Également connue sous le nom de: Royal Commission on the Safety of Public Buildings.

Loc.: OTAR

220 **Royal Ontario Mining Commission.**
Report. [Toronto] 1944. 8 pts. in 1 v.

Chairman/Président: N.C. Urquhart.

Commissioners/Commissaires: J.R. Gordon, K.C. Gray, J.H. Jessup, R.J. Jowsey, H.C. McCloskey, H.W. Sutcliffe, C.G. Williams.

Loc.: BVAU, MWU, NFSM, OHM, OKQ, OLU, OOC, OOF, OOG, OOM, OON, OOP, OPET, OTAR, OTL, OTP, OTRM, OTY, SRL, SSU

221 **1945**

Ontario Agricultural Commission of Inquiry.
Report. [Toronto] 1945. various pagings (typescript)

Chairman/Président: A. Leitch.

Commissioners/Commissaires: C. Boynton, W. Breckon, S. Brown, M.B. Cochran, H. Craise, W.A. Dryden, N.A. Fletcher, R.W. Graham, F. Griesbach, J. Henderson, C. Holmes, H. Huffman, R. Lick, A. McKinney, G. Mitchell, W. Montgomery, M.M. Robinson, H. Scott, R.J. Scott, H. Wilson.

Loc.: OKQ, OOAG, OONL, OOP, OTAR, OTL, OTP

222 **Royal Commission Appointed May 28th, 1945 to Investigate Charges Made by Mr. Edward B. Joliffe, K.C., in a Radio Address on May 24th, 1945.**
Report. Toronto: T.E. Bowman, Printer to the King's Most Excellent Majesty, 1945. 62 p.

Commissioner/Commissaire: A.M. LeBel.

Loc.: OOCC, OTAR, OTL, OTY

223 **1947-1948**

Ontario Research Commission.
Interim report. Toronto: H.E. Brown, Acting Printer to the King's Most Excellent Majesty, 1947. 152 p.

———.

Final report. Toronto: B. Johnston, Printer to the King's Most Excellent Majesty, 1948. 66 p.

Chairman/Président: R.C. Wallace.

Commissioners/Commissaires: C.E. Burke, G.I. Christie, W.S. Fox, E.H. Gurney, T.H. Hogg, W.E. Phillips, S. Smith, E.T. Sterne, R.K. Stratford, H.M. Turner, C.R. Young.

Loc.: BVAU, BVIV, MWU, OKQ, OLU, OON, OONH, OONL, OOP, OTAR, OTL, OTP, OTRF, OTU, OTY, OWTU, SRL, SSU

224 **1947**

Ontario Royal Commission on Forestry.
Report. Toronto: B. Johnston, Printer to the King's Most Excellent Majesty, 1947. 196 p.

Commissioner/Commissaire: H. Kennedy.

Loc.: NFBU, OOAG, OOC, OOF, OOND, OONL, OOP, OOT, OTAR, OTL, OTP, QMU

225 **Ontario Royal Commission on Milk.**
Report. Toronto: B. Johnston, Printer to the King's Most Excellent Majesty, 1947. xv, 157, 205 p.

Commissioner/Commissaire: D.C. Wells.

Loc.: AEU, BVAU, MWU, OOAG, OOF, OOL, OONL, OTAR, OTL, OTP, OTU, QQL, SSU

226 **1949**

Royal Commission to Inquire into and Report upon any Charge or Complaint Made Against any Police Officer or Public Official in a Report Made by Provincial Constable J.E. Keays.
Report. [Toronto, 1949] 35 *l.* (typescript)

Commissioner/Commissaire: J.K. MacKay.

Loc.: OTAR

227 **1950**

Commission Appointed to Inquire into and Report upon, and to Make Recommendations Regarding the Workmen's Compensation Act upon Subjects Other than Detail Administration.
Report. Toronto: B. Johnston, Printer to the King's Most Excellent Majesty, 1950. 125 p.

Commissioner/Commissaire: W.D. Roach.

Loc.: BVIV, NSHPL, OKQL, OOL, OTAR, OTL, OTLS, OTP, SRL

228 **Royal Commission on Education in Ontario.**
Report. Toronto: B. Johnston, Printer to the King's Most Excellent Majesty, 1950. xxiii, 933 p.

Chairman/Président: J.A. Hope.

Commissioners/Commissaires: M.A. Campbell, A.V. Chapman, W.H. Clarke, C.R. Conquergood, E.F. Henderson, R.S. Houck, A. Kelly,
N. McLeod, B. Marshall, R.J. Neelands, H.I. New, J.M. Pigott, L.H. Reid, H. Saint-Jacques, C.R. Sanderson, H.M. Sheppard, S.E. Smith,
W.A. Townshend, W.L. Whitelock.

Loc.: NFSM, NSHPL, OOCC, OONH, OONL, OORD, OTAR, OTER, OTL, OTMCL, OTP, OTREC, OTY

229 **1952**

Commission to Inquire into and Report upon the Financial Affairs of the East Windsor Health Association..
Report. [Toronto, 1952] 183 *l.* (typescript)

Commissioner/Commissaire: G.L. Fraser.

Also known as/Également connue sous le nom de: Royal Commission re East Windsor Health Association.

Loc.: OTAR

230 **Royal Commission Appointed to Enquire into Conditions at the Don Jail, Toronto.**
Report. [Toronto, 1952] 65*l.* (typescript)

Commissioner/Commissaire: I.M. Macdonnell.

Loc.: OTAR

231 **1954**

Inquiry into the Arrest and Detention of Robert Wright and Michael Griffin.
Report. [Toronto, 1954] 35 *l.* (typescript)

Commissioner/Commissaire: W.D. Roach.

Loc.: OTAR

232 **1958**

Royal Commission re: Individual Dump Truck Owners Assn. and International Brotherhood of Teamsters, Chauffeurs, Warehousemen and Helpers.
Report. [Toronto, 1958] 105, xx *l.* (typescript)

Commissioner/Commissaire: W.D. Roach.

Loc.: OOL, OONL, OOP, OTAR, OTL

233 **1959**

Royal Commission to Inquire into the Financial Affairs of the Corporation of the City of Belleville.
Report. [Toronto, 1959] 47 *l.* (typescript)

Commissioner/Commissaire: A.R. Wilmott.

Loc.: OOCC, OTAR

234 **1960**

Inquiry into Certain Financial Affairs of the Corporation of the Township of York Related to Sub-divisions of Land, Zoning By-laws and the Sales of Municipal Lands Owned by the Said Corporation of the Said Township of York and Matters Connected Therewith.
Report. [Toronto] 1960. 266, 17 *l.* (typescript)

Commissioner/Commissaire: J.A. Sweet.

Loc.: OONL, OOP, OTAR, OTL, OTP, OTU

235 **Royal Commission Appointed to Investigate Charges Relating to the Purchase of Lands in the City of Sarnia by the Hydro-Electric Power Commission of Ontario from Dimensional Investments Limited.**
Report. [Toronto, 1960] 133 *l.* (typescript)

Commissioner/Commissaire: G.A. McGillivray.

Also known as/Également connue sous le nom de: Royal Commission on Sarnia Indian Lands.

Loc.: OONL, OOP, OTAR, OTL, OTU, OW

236 **1961**

The Committee Appointed to Inquire into and Report upon the Fluoridation of Municipal Water Supplies.
Report. [Toronto] 1961. iii, 177 p. (typescript)

Chairman/Président: K.G. Morden.

Commissioners/Commissaires: E.L. Frankel, G.E. Hall, C. McKenzie.

Loc.: AEU, BVAU, MWUD, NFSM, OOC, OOHN, OONL, OOP, OTAR, OTL, OTMEN, OTP, OTY, OW, QMU

237 **The Royal Commission on Industrial Safety.**
Report. [Toronto, 1961] 87 p.

Chairman/Président: P.J. McAndrew.

Commissioners/Commissaires: J.D. Bateman, G.R. Harvey.

Loc.: MWP, OKQL, OONL, OORD, OTAR, OTL, OTU, OW, OWA

238 **1962**

Royal Commission of Inquiry Respecting the Arrest and Detention of Rabbi Norbert Leiner by the Metropolitan Toronto Police Force.
Report. [Toronto, 1962] 99 p.

Commissioner/Commissaire: D.C. Wells.

Loc.: BVAU, NSHPL, OONL, OOP, OTAR, OTL, OTU, QMML

239 **The Royal Commission on Labour-Management Relations in the Construction Industry.**
Report. [Toronto] 1962. 79 p.

Commissioner/Commissaire: H.C. Goldenberg.

Loc.: OONL, OTAR, OTL, OTYL

240 **1963**

Commission Appointed under the Public Inquiries Act by Letters Patent Dated December 11, 1961.
Report. [Toronto, 1963] 383 *l.* (typescript)

Commissioner/Commissaire: W.D. Roach.

Also known as/Également connue sous le nom de: Royal Commission on Crime in Ontario.

Loc.: BVA, OKQL, OONL, OOP, OTAR, OTL, OTP, OTU, OTY, OWA

241 **1964**

Medical Services Insurance Committee.
Report. [Toronto: Queen's Printer] 1964. ii, 71 p.

Chairman/Président: J.G. Hagey.

Commissioners/Commissaires: J.O. Aylen, W. Butt, D.J. Caswell, A.R. Coulter, R. Galloway, J. Hamilton, H. McArthur, W.S. Major, P.J. Mulrooney, C.A. Naylor, A. Reid, H. Simon, J.L. Whitney.

Loc.: BVAM, MWP, OHM, OKQL, OONH, OOP, OTAR, OTL, OTLS, OTP, OTU, OTY, OWTU

242 **Royal Commission on Compulsory Arbitration in Disputes Affecting Hospitals and their Employees.**
Report. [Toronto] 1964. 62 p.

Chairman/Président: C.E. Bennett.

Commissioners/Commissaire: R.V. Hicks, H. Simon.

Loc.: BVAU, OKQL, OONL, OTAR, OTL, OTY, QMML

243 **1965**

Commission under the Designation Fame Inquiry in Respect of the Affairs of Farmers' Allied Meat Enterprises Co-Operatives Limited.
Report. [Toronto, 1965] 114 p.

Commissioner/Commissaire: C. Grant.

Loc.: OONL, OOP, OTAR, OTL, OTLS, OTP, OTY, OTYL, OWA, OWAL, QMHE, QMU, QSHERU

244 **The Royal Commission on Metropolitan Toronto.**
Report. [Toronto] 1965. xv, 213 p.

Commissioner/Commissaire: H.C. Goldenberg.

Loc.: ACU, AEU, BVAU, BVIV, MW, MWU, NBFU, NFSM, NSHPL, OH, OKQL, OOC, OOCC, OONL, OOU, OTAR, OTL, OTU, OTY, OWAL, QMML, QMU, SRL, SSU

245 **The Royal Commission to Investigate Trading in the Shares of Windfall Oils and Mines Limited.**
Report. [Toronto] 1965. xviii, 177 p.

Commissioner/Commissaire: A. Kelly.

Loc.: ACU, AEU, BVA, BVAU, MWU, NFSM, NSHPL, OH, OKQL, OLU, OOB, OOCI, OOF, OONL, OOP, OTAR, OTB, OTL, OTLS, OTP, OTU, OTY, OWA, OWTU, QMML, SSU

246 **1967**

The Ontario Committee on Taxation.
Approach, background and conclusions. [Toronto] F. Fogg, Queen's Printer, [1967] xxiv, 343 p. (Report of The Ontario Committee on Taxation; v. 1)

———.

The local revenue system. [Toronto: F. Fogg, Queen's Printer, 1967] xv, 550 p. (Report of The Ontario Committee on Taxation; v. 2)

———.

The provincial revenue system. [Toronto: F. Fogg, Queen's Printer, 1967] xv, 473 p. (Report of The Ontario Committee on Taxation; v. 3)

Chairman/Président: L.J. Smith.

Commissioners/Commissaires: E. Hardy, R.C. McIvor, C. Pollock, R.B. Stapells.

Loc.: AE, AEU, BVA, BVAU, MW, MWU, NFSM, NSHPL, OKQL, OKR, OONL, OTAR, OTL, OTP, OTU, OTV, OW, QMML, QMU, QQL, SSU

247 **The Royal Commission in the Matter of the Workmen's Compensation Act.**
Report. [Toronto] 1967. xx, 217 p.

Commissioner/Commissaire: G.A. McGillivray.

Loc.: AEU, BVA, BVAS, MWU, NSHPL, OKQL, OLU, OOCW, OONH, OONL, OOP, OOU, OOUD, OTAR, OTL, OTP, OTU, OTY, QMML, SSU

248 **1968**

Committee Appointed to Inquire into and Report upon the Pollution of Air, Soil, and Water in the Townships of Dunn, Moulton, and Sherbrooke Haldimand County.
Report. [Toronto: F. Fogg, Queen's Printer, 1968] xx, 355 p.

Chairman/Président: G.E. Hall.

Commissioners/Commissaires: A. McKinney, W.C. Winegard.

Loc.: NFSG, OH, OLU, OOCC, OOED, OONL, OTAR, OTL, OTP, OTU, OTYL, SSU

249 **Inquiry re Magistrate Frederick J. Bannon and Magistrate George W. Gardhouse.**
Report. [Toronto] 1968. xi, 69 p.

Commissioner/Commissaire: C. Grant.

Loc.: AEU, MWU, NSHPL, OKQL, OPET, OTAR, OTL, OTP, OTY, OTYL

250 **1968-1971**

Royal Commission Inquiry into Civil Rights.
Report. [Toronto: F. Fogg, Queen's Printer] 1968-1971. 5 v.

Commissioner/Commissaire: J.C. McRuer.

Loc.: AEU, BVAS, MW, MWU, NBSAM, NFSM, NSHPL, OKQL, OLU, OOCS, OONL, OOSC, OOSS, OOU, OOUD, OTAR, OTC, OTL, OTY, OTYL, OW, QMML, QMU, QQLA, SRL

251 **Royal Commission Inquiry into Labour Disputes.**
Report. [Toronto: F. Fogg, Queen's Printer] 1968. xxv, 263 p.

Commissioner/Commissaire: I.C. Rand.

Loc.: AEU, BVAS, NBSAM, NSHPL, OKQL, OLU, OOCI, OONL, OOUD, OTAR, OTL, OTYL, QMMSC, QQLA

252 **The Royal Commission to Investigate Allegations Relating to Coroners' Inquests.**
Report. [Toronto] 1968. xiii, 132 p.

Commissioner/Commissaire: W.D. Parker.

Loc.: AEU, BVAM, MWU, NSHPL, OKQL, OONH, OONL, OTAR, OTL, OTYL

253 **1969**

Inquiry re Provincial Judge Lucien Coe Kurata.
Report. [Toronto] 1969. xiv, 140 p.

Commissioner/Commissaire: D.A. Keith.

Loc.: AE, AEU, OLU, OPA, OPET, OTAR, OTB, OTL, OTMCL, OW

254 **The Royal Commission Appointed to Inquire into the Failure of Atlantic Acceptance Corporation, Limited.**
Report. [Toronto: The Commission] 1969. 4 v.

Commissioner/Commissaire: S.H.S. Hughes.

Loc.: AEU, BVA, BVAU, MWU, NSHPL, OLU, OOB, OOCC, OOF, OONL, OOP, OOSC, OTAR, OTL, OTU, OTY, OW, QMM, QSHERU, SSU

255 **1970**

Commission of Inquiry re Alleged Improper Relationships between Personnel of the Ontario Provincial Police Force and Persons of Known Criminal Activity under the Public Inquiries Act by Letters Patent Dated 28th July, 1970.
Report. [Toronto: W. Kinmond, Queen's Printer, 1970] x, 118 p.

Commissioner/Commissaire: C. Grant.

Loc.: AEU, BVAS, BVAU, MWU, OLU, OONL, OOP, OOSC, OTAR, OTL, OTMCL, OTU, OTY, OTYL

256 **Committee on the Healing Arts.**
Report. [Toronto: Queen's Printer, 1970] 3 v.

Chairman/Président: I.R. Dowie.

Commissioners/Commissaires: H. Krever, M.C. Urquhart.

Loc.: AEU, BVAU, BVIV, MWM, MWUD, OKQH, OLU, OOC, OOF, OONH, OOL, OTAR, OTL, OTMCL, OTU, OTY, QMMM, QMU, QQL

257 **The Royal Commission Appointed to Inquire into the Use of Pesticides and the Death of Waterfowl on Toronto Island.**
Report. [Toronto: W. Kinmond, Queen's Printer] 1970. unpaged

Commissioner/Commissaire: M.H. Edwards.

Loc.: BVAS, BVAU, NSHPL, OLT, OOAG, OONL, OTAR, OTL, OTY, OWAL

258 **1971**

Commission of Inquiry into Certain Matters Relating to and Arising from the Report of Professor Leonard Gertler Dated June, 1968, Entitled "Niagara Escarpment Study – Conservation and Recreation Report."
Report. [Toronto] 1971. 101 *l.* (typescript)

Commissioner/Commissaire: C.E. Bennett.

Also known as/Également connue sous le nom de: Royal Commission Inquiry into Niagara Escarpment Land Transactions.

Loc.: OLU, OTAR, OTL, OTMCL, OTY, OTYL

259 **1972**

The Royal Commission Appointed to Inquire into the Egg Industry in Ontario.
Report. [Thunder Bay, Ont.] 1972. x, 105 *l.* (typescript)

Commissioner/Commissaire: J.F.W. Ross.

Loc.: BVAU, OLU, OOAG, OOB, OOCI, OOP, OTAR, OTB, OTL, OTMCL, OTY, OTYL, OWAL, QSHERU, SRL

260 **The Royal Commission of Inquiry in Relation to the Conduct of the Public and the Metropolitan Toronto Police Force.**
Report. [Toronto, 1972] 181 *l.* (typescript)

Commissioner/Commissaire: I.A. Vannini.

Loc.: BVAU, NSHPL, OKQL, OONL, OTAR, OTL, OTU, OTY, OS

261 **1972-1975**

Solandt Commission.
Interim report. [Toronto] 1972. various pagings (typescript)

Loc.: BVAS, BVAU, MWP, OKQL, OLU, OOC, OONL, OOP, OPAL, OS, OTAR, OTL, OTLS, OTMCL, OTU, OTY, OTYL, QMML

———.
Report: a public inquiry into the transmission of power between Nanticoke and Pickering. [Toronto] 1974. various pagings

Loc.: AEU, BVAS, BVAU, MWP, NFSM, OKQL, OOC, OONL, OOP, OOSH, OPET, OTAR, OTL, OTLS, OTU, OTUL, OTY, OWAL

———.

Report: a public inquiry into the transmission of power between Lennox and Oshawa. [Toronto] 1975. xii, 213 p.

Commissioner/Commissaire: O.M. Solandt.

Loc.: AEU, BVA, BVAU, MWP, NFSM, OKQL, OLU, OOC, OON, OONL, OOP, OOS, OS, OTAR, OTL, OTU, OTY, OTYL, OWAL.

262 **1973**

Royal Commission on Book Publishing.
Canadian publishers & Canadian publishing: final report. [Toronto: Ministry of the Attorney General, 1973] 371 p.

Chairman/Président: R.H. Rohmer.

Commissioners/Commissaires: D.K. Camp, M. Jeanneret.

Loc.: AC, AEU, BVAS, MWP, MWU, NBSU, NFSM, NHSPL, OKQ, OLUS, OOA, OOCI, OONL, OOP, OOU, OTAR, OTL, OTLS, OTU, OTY, OWA, QLB, QMML, QQLA, SRL, SSU

263 **1974**

Inquiry in respect to the Affairs of the Township of Kingston.
Report. [Toronto?] 1974. 90 *l.* (typescript)

Commissioner/Commissaire: E.M. Shortt.

Loc.: OKQL, OTL, OTLS, OTY

264 **Royal Commission on Certain Sectors of the Building Industry.**
Report. [Toronto] J.C. Thatcher, Queen's Printer, [1974] 2 v.

Commissioner/Commissaire: H.Waisberg.

Loc.: OOC, OONL, OTAR, OTL, OTUL, OTYL, OW, QMMSC, SSU

265 **1975**

> **Royal Commission Inquiry into the Grand River Flood, 1974.**
> *Report.* [Toronto: Ministry of the Attorney General, 1975] 93 p.
>
> **Commissioner/Commissaire:** W.W. Leach.
>
> Loc. AEU, BVAS, BVAU, MWP, NFSM, OOFF, OONL, OOP, OPAL, OS, OTAR, OTL, OTLS, OTMCL, OTY, OW

266 **The Royal Commission on the Conduct of Police Forces at Fort Erie on the 11th of May, 1974.**
Report. [Toronto, 1975] 91 *l.* (typescript)

> **Commissioner/Commissaire:** J.A. Pringle.
>
> Loc.: AEU, BVAS, BVAU, NFSM, OKQL, OLU, OOC, OOSC, OOSG, OOUD, OTAR, OTL, OTUL, OTY, OW, QMML, QMU, QSHERU, SSU

267 **1976**

> **The Royal Commission into Metropolitan Toronto Police Practices.**
> *Report.* [Toronto, 1976] xix, 272 p.
>
> **Commissioner/Commissaire:** D.R. Morand.
>
> Loc.: AEU, BVA, BVAU, MWP, NFSM, OONL, OS, OTAR, OTB, OTL, OTU, OTUL, OTY, OW, OWAL, QMML, QMU, SSU

268 **1976-1980**

> **Royal Commission on Electric Power Planning.**
> *Shaping the future: the first report.* [Toronto: The Commission] 1976. 51 p.
>
> Loc.: AEU, BVAU, BVIV, MWU, NFSM, NSHPL, OCKA, OKQL, OON, OONE, OONL, OOP, OOTC, OTB, OTCSA, OTY, OTYL, OW
>
> ———.
>
> *Interim report on nuclear power in Ontario.* [Toronto: The Commission, 1978] xviii, 227 p.
>
> Loc.: AEU, MWP, MWU, OCKA, OOAECB, OOCI, OOEC, OOF, OOFF, OOMI, OON, OONE, OONL, OOP, OS, OTB, OTCSA, OTMCL, OTV, OW, OWAL, SRL

―――――.
Concepts, conclusions, and recommendations. [Toronto: The Commission, 1980] xxiii, 225 p. (Report of the Royal Commission on Electric Power Planning; v. 1)

―――――.
The electric power system in Ontario. [Toronto: The Commission, 1980] xiv, 128 p. (Report of the Royal Commission on Electric Power Planning; v. 2)

―――――.
Factors affecting the demand for electricity in Ontario. [Toronto: The Commission, 1980] xi, 74 p. (Report of the Royal Commission on Electric Power Planning; v. 3)

―――――.
Energy supply and technology for Ontario. [Toronto: The Commission, 1980] xvi, 105 p. (Report of the Royal Commission on Electric Power Planning; v. 4)

―――――.
Economic considerations in the planning of electric power in Ontario. [Toronto: The Commission, 1980] xiv, 135 p. (Report of the Royal Commission on Electric Power Planning; v. 5)

―――――.
Environmental and health implications of electric energy in Ontario. [Toronto: The Commission, 1980] xvi, 124 p. (Report of the Royal Commission on Electric Power Planning; v. 6)

―――――.
The socio-economic and land-use impacts of electric power in Ontario. [Toronto: The Commission, 1980] xiv, 96 p. (Report of the Royal Commission on Electric Power Planning; v. 7)

―――――.
Decision-making, regulation, and public participation: a framework for electric power planning in Ontario for the 1980s. [Toronto: The Commission, 1980] xv, 83 p. (Report of the Royal Commission on Electric Power Planning; v. 8)

―――――.
A bibliography to the report. [Toronto: The Commission, 1980] xi, 90 p. (Report of the Royal Commission on Electric Power Planning; v. 9)

Chairman/Président: A. Porter.

Commissioners/Commissaires: G.A. McCague, S. Plourde-Gagnon, W.W. Stevenson.

Loc.: BVA, MPW, MWU, OCKA, OKF, OOAECB, OOF, OONE, OONL, OOP, OOPW, OOSH, OS, OTAR, OTL, OTU, OW, QMHE, QQERE, SRL

269 **The Royal Commission on Petroleum Products Pricing.**
Report. [Toronto] The Commission, 1976. iv, 192 p.

Commissioner/Commissaire: C.M. Isbister.

Loc.: AC, AEU, BVAS, BVAU, MWP, OKQL, OLU, OOCI, OOEC, OONE, OOP, OOTC, OPET, OTAR, OTL, OTMCL, OTUL, OTY, QMMSC

270 **Royal Commission on the Health and Safety of Workers in Mines.**
Report. [Toronto: Ministry of the Attorney General, 1976] xi, 329 p.

Commissioner/Commissaire: J.M. Ham.

Loc.: AC, AEU, BVA, BVAU, BVIP, MWU, NFSM, OKQ, OLU, OOC, OOL, OON, OONH, OONL, OOS, OOSH, OPET, OTLS, OTMCL, OTU, OTY, QMM, SRL, SRU

271 **1976-1977**

The Royal Commission on Violence in the Communications Industry.
Interim report. [Toronto: The Commission] 1976. various pagings (issued also in French)

Loc.: AEU, BVA, BVAS, BVIV, MWP, MWU, NFSM, OLU, OOC, OOL, OON, OONL, OOP, OOTC, OOU, OTAR, OTB, OTC, OTL, OTLS, OTMCL, OTU, OTY, OTYL, OWAL, QMM, QMML, SSU

─────────.

Approaches, conclusions and recommendations. [Toronto: The Commission, 1977] 497 p. (Report of The Royal Commission on Violence in the Communications Industry; v. 1) (issued also in French)

─────────.

Violence and the media: a bibliography. [Toronto: The Commission, 1977] 171 p. (Report of The Royal Commission on Violence in the Communications Industry; v. 2)

─────────.

Violence in television films and news. [Toronto: The Commission, 1977] 703 p. (Report of The Royal Commission on Violence in the Communications Industry; v. 3)

———.

Violence in print and music. [Toronto: The Commission, 1977] 239 p. (Report of The Royal Commission on Violence in the Communications Industry; v. 4)

———.

Learning from the media. [Toronto: The Commission, 1977] 313 p. (Report of The Royal Commission on Violence in the Communications Industry; v. 5)

———.

Vulnerability to media effects. [Toronto: The Commission, 1977] 401 p. (Report of The Royal Commission on Violence in the Communications Industry; v. 6)

———.

The media industries: from here to where? [Toronto: The Commission, 1977] 325 p. (Report of The Royal Commission on Violence in the Communications Industry; v. 7)

Chairman/Présidente: J.V. LaMarsh.

Commissioners/Commissaires: L.A. Beaulieu, S.A. Young.

Loc.: AC, ACU, AEU, BVA, BVAU, MWP, MWU, NBFU, NFSM, NSHPL, OKF, OKQL, OOC, OOEC, OOF, OOL, OONL, OOP, OORT, OOS, OOSH, OTAR, OTB, OTC, OTE, OTL, OTMCL, OTU, OTV, OTY, QMML, QMU, SRL, SSM, SSU

1976-1977

La Commission royale d'enquête sur la violence dans le secteur des communications.
Rapport intérimaire. [Toronto: La Commission, 1976] pagination multiple (publié aussi en anglais)

Loc.: OOC, OOF, OOMI, OONL, OOP, OORT, OOS, OOSS, OOTC, OTMCL, OTY, OTYL, OW, QMU, QQLA

La Commission royale sur la violence dans l'industrie des communications.
Exposé du problème, conclusions et recommandations. [Toronto: La Commission, 1977] 544 p. (publié aussi en anglais)

Présidente/Chairman: J.V. LaMarsh.

Commissaires/Commissioners: L.A. Beaulieu, S.A. Young.

Loc.: OOC, OOMI, OONL, OOP, OOSC, OORT, OTMCL, OW, QMHE

1977

272 **Commission of Inquiry into the Acquisition by the Ministry of Housing of Certain Lands in the Community of North Pickering.**
Report. [Toronto: The Commission, 1977] xiv, 163 p.

Chairman/Président: J.F. Donnelly.

Commissioners/Commissaires: R.M. Grant, G.P. Marriott.

Loc.: AEU, MWP, MWU, OONL, OTAR, OTL, OTMCL, OTYL

273 **Inquiry in Respect to the Affairs of the Township of Malden.**
Report. [Toronto, 1977] 97 *l.* (typescript)

Commissioner/Commissaire: B.J.S. Macdonald.

Also known as/Également connue sous le nom de: Malden Inquiry.

Loc.: OTAR, OTL

274 **Public Inquiry into Ronto Development Company.**
Report. [Toronto, 1977] 58 p.

Commissioner/Commissaire: J.D. Cromarty.

Loc.: AEU, MWP, OKQL, OONL, OOP, OOUD, OTAR, OTL, OTUL, OTY

275 **The Royal Commission of Inquiry on Algoma University College.**
Reports. [Toronto: The Commission, 1977] various pagings

Commissioner/Commissaire: J.W. Whiteside.

Loc.: AEU, MWP, OLU, OOC, OOCU, OONL, OOP, OTER, OTL, OTMCL, OTY

276 **The Royal Commission on Metropolitan Toronto.**
Metropolitan Toronto: a framework for the future. [Toronto: The Commission] 1977. xxxii, 62 p. (Report of The Royal Commission on Metropolitan Toronto; v. 1)

———.
Detailed findings and recommendations. [Toronto: The Commission] 1977. xxxii, 64-395 p. (Report of The Royal Commission on Metropolitan Toronto; v. 2)

Commissioner/Commissaire: J.P. Robarts.

Loc.: AEU, BVA, BVAU, MWP, MWU, NBSU, NSHPL, OKQL, OLU, OOC, OONL, OOSG, OTV, OTYL, OW, OWAL, QMBM, QMM

277 **1978-1979**

Commission of Inquiry on Aluminium Wiring.
Report. [Toronto] J.C. Thatcher, Queen's Printer, 1978-1979. 3 v.

Commissioner/Commissaire: J.T. Wilson.

Loc.: BVA, OCKA, OON, OONL, OOP, OTAR, OTCSA, OTL, OTMCL, OW

278 **1978**

Commission of Inquiry re: Provincial Judge Harry J. Williams.
Report. [Toronto: The Commission] 1978. ix, 29 p.

Commissioner/Commissaire: S.L. Robins.

Loc.: AEU, MWP, MWU, OKQL, OONL, OOP, OOUD, OTAR, OTL, OTMCL, OTYL, OW, OWAL, QMML

279 **Hamilton-Wentworth Review Commission.**
Report. [Toronto: The Commission] 1978. 227 p.

Chairman/Président: H.E. Stewart.

Members/Membres: H. Dixon, J.A. Johnson.

Loc.: MWP, MWU, OONL, OOP, OTAR, OTL, OTMCL, OTU, OTYL, OW, OWAL

280 **The Royal Commission Appointed to Inquire into Waste Management Inc., et cetera.**
Report. [Toronto: The Commission, 1978] 133 p.

Commissioner/Commissaire: S.H.S. Hughes.

Loc.: AEU, MWP, MWU, OONL, OOP, OTAR, OTL, OTMCL, OW, OWAL

281 **The Royal Commission on the Northern Environment.**
Interim report. [Toronto: The Commission] 1978. 41 p. (issued also in French)

Commissioner/Commissaire: E.P. Hartt (1977-1978), J.E.J. Fahlgren (1978-).

N.B.: The Royal Commission is still sitting.

Loc.: AEU, MWP, OLU, OOFF, OONL, OOP, OORD, OTAR, OTB, OTL, OTU, OTYL, OW

Commission royale sur l'environnement du Nord.
Rapport intérimaire. [Toronto: La Commission, 1978] 47, 4 p. (publié aussi en anglais)

Commissaire/Commissioner: E.P. Hartt (1977-1978), J.E.J. Fahlgren (1978-).

N.B.: La Commission royale siège encore.

Loc.: OONL, OORD

282 **Royal Commission on the Toronto Jail and Custodial Services.**
Report. [Toronto] Queen's Printer, [1978] 4 v.

Commissioner/Commissaire: B.B. Shapiro.

Loc.: BVA, MWD, MWU, OLU, OONL, OOSE, OOUD, OS, OTAR, OTL, OTMCL, OTUL, OTYL, OW, QMML, SRP, SSU

283 **1979**

Waterloo Region Review Commission.
Report. [Waterloo, Ont.] 1979. xiv, 348 p.

Commissioner/Commissaire: W.H. Palmer.

Loc.: MWU, OONL, OOP, OTAR, OTMCL

284 **1980**

Commission of Inquiry into the Confidentiality of Health Information.
Report. [Toronto: J.C. Thatcher, Queen's Printer, 1980] 3 v.

Commissioner/Commissaire: H. Krever.

Loc.: BVA, BVAM, MWM, MWU, NBS, OKQL, OLU, OOCN, OOF, OOMI, OONL, OOP, OOS, OTLS, OTU, QMML, SRL

285 **The Commission on Freedom of Information and Individual Privacy.**
Public government for private people. [Toronto: The Commission] 1980. xxi, 51 p. (Report of The Commission on Freedom of Information and Individual Privacy; v. 1)

―――――.
Public government for private people: freedom of information. [Toronto: The Commission] 1980. xi, 53 - 493 p. (Report of The Commission on Freedom of Information and Individual Privacy; v. 2)

―――――.
Public government for private people: protection of privacy. [Toronto: The Commission] 1980. x, 495 - 812 p. (Report of The Commission on Freedom of Information and Individual Privacy; v. 3)

Chairman/Président: D.C. Williams.

Commissioners/Commissaires: G.H.U. Bayly, D.J. Burgoyne.

Loc.: BVA, BVAWC, MWU, OKQL, OLU, OOB, OOCI, OOCS, OOEC, OOF, OOMI, OON, OONL, OOAG, OOP, OOS, OOSC, OOSH, OOSS, OS, OTAR, OTL, OTLS, OTU, OW, OWAL, QMML, QMNF, QQL, SRL, SSU

286 **Royal Commission of Inquiry into Discounting and Allowances in the Food Industry in Ontario.**
Report. [Toronto] The Commission, 1980. xviii, 593 p.

Commissioner/Commissaire: W.W. Leach.

Loc.: BVA, MWU, OOCI, OOF, OONL, OOP, OOSC, OS, OTAR, OTL, OTLS, OW, SRL

287 **Royal Commission on the Status of Pensions in Ontario.**
Design for retirement. [Toronto: Government of Ontario, 1980] xxi, 248 p. (Report of the Royal Commission on the Status of Pensions in Ontario; v. 1)

―――――.
Design for retirement. [Toronto: Government of Ontario, 1980] 323 p. (Report of the Royal Commission on the Status of Pensions in Ontario; v. 2)

———.

Design for retirement. [Toronto: Government of Ontario, 1980] 253 p. (Report of the Royal Commission on the Status of Pensions in Ontario; v. 3)

———.

Your income in retirement. [Toronto: Government of Ontario, 1980] 86 p. (Report of the Royal Commission on the Status of Pensions in Ontario; v. 4)

———.

Ontario and the Canada Pension Plan. [Toronto: Government of Ontario, 1981] xiv, 327 p. (Report of the Royal Commission on the Status of Pensions in Ontario; v. 5)

———.

Pensions for Ontario public sector employees. [Toronto: Government of Ontario, 1981] xiii, 226 p. (Report of the Royal Commission on the Status of Pensions in Ontario; v. 6)

Loc.: BVA, MWU, OKF, OLU, OOF, OOL, OONL, OOP, OOS, OOSC, OOSH, OTAR, OTL, OTLS, OW, OWAL

———.

Summary report: a plan for the future. [Toronto: Government of Ontario, 1981] x, 107 p.

Chairman/Président: D.J. Haley.

Commissioners/Commissaires: A.H. Cordell, D.G.M. Coxe, C. McDonald, W.G. Upshall.

Loc: BVA, MWU, OLU, OOP, OOCU, OOCW, OOL, OOMI, OONL, OONLB, OOSH, OTAR, OTL, QMHE, SRL

288 **1981**

Commission of Inquiry into the Toronto Islands.
Pressure island: report. [Toronto, 1981] xii, 598 p.

Commissioner/Commissaire: B.B. Swadron.

Loc.: OONL, OTAR, OTL

QUÉBEC

289 **1874**

Commission d'enquête sur la conduite de C.E. Belle, écuyer, agent d'immigration, à Montréal.
Réponse à une adresse de l'Assemblée législative, demandant copie des documents concernant l'enquête sur la conduite de C.E. Belle, écuyer, agent d'immigration, a Montréal. Québec, 1874. 341 p.

Commissaire/Commissioner: C.A. Leblanc.

Loc.: OONL, OTYL, QQL

290 **1876**

Commissaires nommés pour s'enquérir des affaires des chemins à barrières de la Rive nord et de la Rive sud à Québec.
Rapport. Québec: L. Brousseau, 1876. 37 p. (publié aussi en anglais)

Commissaires/Commissioners: E.J. Deblois, J.A. Defoy, P. Mackay.

Commissioners Appointed to Enquire into the Affairs of the Quebec North and South Shore Turnpike Trusts.
Return. Quebec: "Le Canadien", 1876. 37 p. (issued also in French)

Commissioners/Commissaires: E.J. Deblois, J.A. Defoy, P. Mackay.

Loc.: OONL, QQL

291 **1879**

Commission d'enquête sur les bureaux du protonotaire de la Cour supérieure, du greffier de la Cour de Circuit, du greffier de la Couronne et de la Paix et sur le Bureau de police.
A l'honorable Luc Letellier de St. Just, Lieutenant-gouverneur de la province de Québec: rapport de J.E. Robidoux, ecr. [Montréal] 1879. 24 p.

Commissaire/Commissioner: J.E. Robidoux.

Loc.: OONL, QQL

Président/Chairman: L.A. Jetté.

Commissaires/Commissioners: G. Baby, C.P. Davidson.

Loc.: BVAU, OOA, OONL, OOP, QQL

Royal Commission. Inquiry into the Baie des Chaleurs Railway Matter.
Reports, proceedings of the Commission and deposition of witnesses, appendices and indices. Quebec, 1892. 1071 p. (issued also in French)

Chairman/Président: L.A. Jetté.

Commissioners/Commissaires: G. Baby, C.P. Davidson.

Loc.: BVAU, OOA, OOP, OWA, QMBM, QQL

298 **Commission royale émise sous le Grand Sceau de la Province de Québec, le onzième jour de janvier, l'an mil huit cent quatre-vingt-douze pour faire enquête sur divers sujets et matières, se rattachant au bon gouvernement de cette Province, sous l'autorité des articles 596 et suivants des statuts refondus de la dite Province, au sujet des enquêtes sur les affaires publiques.**
Procès-verbaux des séances et dépositions des témoins. Québec: L. Brousseau, 1892. 271 p. (publié aussi en anglais)

———.

Procès-verbaux des séances et dépositions des témoins. [Rapport des commissaires] Montréal: "L'Etendard", 1892. 270 p. (publié aussi en anglais)

Président/Chairman: M. Mathieu (janvier 1892), S. Pagnuelo (février 1892).

Commissaires/Commissioners: D. MacMaster, D. Masson.

Loc.: OONL, OOP

Royal Commission Issued under the Great Seal of this Province of Quebec, the Eleventh Day of January, in the Year One Thousand Eight Hundred and Ninety-Two, to Make Enquiry into Different Matters and Things, Concerning the Good Government of this Province, under the Authority of Article 596 and Following the Revised Statutes of this Province, on the Subject of Enquiries Concerning Public Matters.
Notes and proceedings and evidence of witnesses. Levis, Quebec: Mercier & Co., 1892. 272, 268 p. (issued also in French)

Chairman/Président: M. Mathieu (January 1892),
S. Pagnuelo (February 1892).

Commissioners/Commissaires: D. MacMaster, D. Masson.

Loc.: OOP, QQLA

299 **1904**

Commission de colonisation de la Province de Québec.
Rapport. Québec: C. Pageau, Imprimeur de Sa Très Excellente Majesté le Roi, 1904. 125 p. (publié aussi en anglais)

Président/Chairman: J.H. Legris.

Commissaires/Commissioners: J.L. Brodie, P.N. Thivierge.

Loc.: OOA, OONL, OOP, QQL

Colonization Commission of the Province of Quebec.
Report. Quebec: C. Pageau, Printer to the King's Most Excellent Majesty. 1904. 119 p. (issued also in French)

Chairman/Président: J.H. Legris.

Commissioners/Commissaires: J.L. Brodie, P.N. Thivierge.

Loc.: OOA, OONL, OOP, QQL

300 **1907-1908**

Commission royale chargée de faire enquête et rapport sur bien-fondé des accusations portées contre le gouvernement de cette province relativement aux négociations pour la vente d'un bloc de terrain dans la région du lac Abittibi (sic).
Procès-verbaux des séances. [Québec, 1907] pagination multiple (manuscrit)

Pièces du dossier. [Québec, 1908] pagination multiple (manuscrit)

Commissaires/Commissioners: M. Charbonneau, F. Langelier.

Loc.: QQL, QQLA

301 **1908**

Commission sur les accidents du travail.
Rapport. [Montréal, 1908] 60 p. (publié aussi en anglais)

Président/Chairman: A. Globensky.

Commissaires/Commissioners: C.B. Gordon, G. Marois.

Loc.: QQL

Commission on Labour Accidents.
Report. [Montreal, 1908] 61 p. (issued also in French)

Chairman/Président: A. Globensky.

Commissioners/Commissaires: C.B. Gordon, G. Marois.

Loc.: QQL

302 **1909-1910**

Commission royale de la tuberculose.
Rapport. Québec, 1909-1910. 161 p. (publié aussi en anglais)

Président/Chairman: E.P. Lachapelle.

Commissaires/Commissioners: J.G. Adami, M.J. Ahern, G. Bourgeois, J. Burland, J.E. Dubé, J.J. Guérin, C.M. Holt, J. Lespérance, C.R. Paquin, E. Pelletier, T.G. Roddick, A. Rousseau, A. Simard.

Loc.: OOA, OOSJ, OTY, QMBN, QMM, QMML, QMU, QQL, QSHERU

Royal Commission on Tuberculosis.
Report. Quebec, 1909-1910. 156 p. (issued also in French)

Chairman/Président: E.P. Lachapelle.

Commissioners/Commissaires: J.G. Adami, M.J. Ahern, G. Bourgeois, J. Burland, J.E. Dubé, J.J. Guérin, C.M. Holt, J. Lespérance, C.R. Paquin, E. Pelletier, T.G. Roddick, A. Rousseau, A. Simard.

Loc.: NSHDM, OOP, OOSJ, OTY, QMBM, QMM, QMU, QQL

303 **1909**

Commission royale pour faire enquête générale et complète sur l'administration des affaires de la Cité de Montréal.
Rapport. [Québec ?] 1909. 149 p. (manuscrit dactylographié)

Commissaire/Commissioner: L.J. Cannon.

Loc.: QQA

304 **1911**

Commission royale concernant les écoles catholiques de Montréal.
Rapport de la Commission royale scolaire. In Québec (Province) Assemblée législative. *Documents de la session.* v. 44, no 4. [Québec, 1911] 16 p. (Réponses aux adresses no 68) (publié aussi en anglais)

Président/Chairman: R. Dandurand.

Commissaires/Commissioners: E.-J.-C. Kennedy, P. Perrier.

Loc.: NFSM, OHM, OOCC, OONL, OOP, OOU, QMHE, QQL, QQLA, QSHERU

Royal Commission with Respect to the Catholic Schools of Montreal.
Report of the Royal Commission on schools. In Quebec (Province) Legislative Assembly. *Sessional papers.* v. 44, 4. [Quebec, 1911] 14 p. (Returns to addresses no. 68) (issued also in French)

Chairman/Président: R. Dandurand.

Commissioners/Commissaires: E.-J.-C. Kennedy, P. Perrier.

Loc.: AEP, BVAU, BVIP, MWP, OLU, OOA, OONL, OOP, OTL, OTMCL, OTU, OTY, OWTU, QMBM, QMBN, QMF, QMHE, QMM, QQL

305 **1913**

Commission des licences.
Rapport. Québec, 1913. 60 p. (publié aussi en anglais)

President/Chairman: H.G. Carroll.

Commissaires/Commissioners: A.G. Cross, A. Tessier.

Loc.: OONL, OOP, QQL, QQLA

License Commission.
Report. Montreal, 1913. 54 p. (issued also in French)

Chairman/Président: H.G. Carroll.

Commissioners/Commissaires: A.G. Cross, A. Tessier.

Loc.: OONL, OOP, QQL, QQLA

306 **1925**

Commission d'étude sur la réparation des accidents du travail.
Rapport. Québec: L.-A. Proulx, Imprimeur du Roi, 1925. 74 p. (publié aussi en anglais)

Président/Chairman: E. Roy.

Commissaires/Commissioners: P. Beaulé, J.-A. Bothwell, E.-G. Brousseau, G. Francq.

Loc.: OTY, QQL

Investigation Commission on the Compensation in Labor Accidents.
Report. Quebec: LS.A. Proulx, Printer to His Majesty the King, 1925. 73 p. (issued also in French)

Chairman/Président: E. Roy.

Commissioners/Commissaires: P. Beaule, J.-A. Bothwell, E.-G. Brousseau, G. Francq.

Loc.: QQL

307 **Enquête royale sur tous les faits qui seraient de nature à faire croire à l'existence d'irrégularités, au cours des dernières années, dans les examens des Mesureurs de Bois, ou propres à faire planer des soupçons sur quelques-unes des personnes chargées de faire passer ces examens.**
Rapport. [Québec ?] 1925. 25 f. (lettre dactylographiée)

Commissaire/Commissioner: W. Amyot.

Loc.: QQA

308 **1927**

Commission royale chargée de faire enquête sur l'incendie du "Laurier Palace" et sur certaines autres matières d'intérêt général.
Rapport. [Québec, 1927] 31 p.

Commissaire/Commisioner: L. Boyer.

Loc.: OONL, QQL

309 **1932-1933**

Commission des assurances sociales de Québec.
Rapports. Québec, 1932-1933. 350 p. (publié aussi en anglais)

Président/Chairman: E. Montpetit.

Membres/Members: G. Courchesne, J.T. Foster, A. Lessard, G. Savoy, F.G. Scott, G. Tremblay.

Loc.: OONL, OOP, OOU, QMML, QMU, QQL, QQLA, QSHERU

Quebec Social Insurance Commission.
Reports. Quebec, 1932-1933. 332 p. (issued also in French)

Chairman/Président: E. Montpetit.

Members/Membres: G. Courchesne, J.T. Foster, A. Lessard, G. Savoy, F.G. Scott, G. Tremblay.

Loc.: BVAU, NSHD, OONH, OONL, OOP, OOU, OTP, OTY, QMML, QQL, SRL

310 **1935**

Commission de l'électricité de la Province de Québec.
Rapport. [Montréal] 1935. 65 p. (publié aussi en anglais)

Président/Chairman: E. Lapointe.

Membres/Members: A. Frigon, G.C. McDonald.

Loc.: OONL, OOP, QMU, QQL

Electricity Commission of the Province of Quebec.
Report. [Montreal] 1935. 48 p. (issued also in French)

Chairman/Président: E. Lapointe.

Members/Membres: A. Frigon, G.C. McDonald.
Loc.: OONL, QMU, QQL

311 **1943**

Commission chargée de faire enquête sur certaines difficultés survenues aux usines de Price Brothers & Company Limited, et de Lake St. John Power & Paper Company, Limited.
Rapport. [Québec, 1943] 25 f. (manuscrit dactylographié) (publié aussi en anglais)

Commissaires/Commissioners: S. McDougall, G. Pratte, J.A. Prévost.

Loc.: QQL, QQLA

Commission Appointed to Inquire into Certain Disputes in the Mills of Price Brothers & Company, Limited and Lake St. John Power & Paper Company, Limited.
Report. [Quebec, 1943] 18 p. (typescript) (issued also in French)

Commissioners/Commissaires: S. McDougall, G. Pratte, J.A. Prévost.

Loc.: OOL, QQL, QQLA

312 **1944**

Commission royale nommée pour s'enquérir des activités de la Sûreté provinciale et de la police des liqueurs dans le district de Montréal, depuis le 26 août 1936 jusqu'au 15 mars 1944.
Rapport. Montréal, 1944. 52 f. (manuscrit dactylographié)

Commissaire/Commissioner: L. Cannon.

Loc.: QQL

313 **1946**

Commission d'enquête sur la répartition des impôts municipaux et scolaires.
Rapport sur les aspects financiers du problème scolaire. [Québec, 1946] 15 f. (manuscrit dactylographié)

N.B.: Les noms des commissaires n'apparaissent pas/The names of the Commissioners are not mentioned.

Loc.: QQL

314 **1952**

Commission d'enquête sur le problème du logement.
Rapport. Montréal, 1952. ii, 178 *f.* (manuscrit dactylographié)

Président/Chairman: J. Gingras.

Commissaires/Commissioners: O. Filion, J.-A. Fortin, J.R. Latter.

Loc.: QQL

315 **1955**

Comité d'enquête pour la protection des agriculteurs et des consommateurs.
Rapport. [Montréal, 1955] 455 p.

Président/Chairman: G.-H. Héon.

Membres/Members: A. Larue, J.-A. Marion.

Loc.: NBFU, OOAG, OOP, OOU, QMM, QMU, QQL, QQLA, QSHERU

316 **1956**

Commission royale d'enquête sur les problèmes constitutionnels.
Aperçu historique. Finances publiques. [Québec] 1956. xv, 398 p.
(Rapport de la Commission royale d'enquête sur les problèmes constitutionnels; v. 1) (publié aussi en anglais)

———.

La province de Québec et le cas canadien-français. Le fédéralisme.
[Québec] 1956. 336 p. (Rapport de la Commission royale d'enquête sur les problèmes constitutionnels; v. 2) (publié aussi en anglais)

———.

Analyse des besoins et recommandations: la juridiction provinciale.
[Québec] 1956. 377 p.
(Rapport de la Commission royale d'enquête sur les problèmes constitutionnels; v. 3.1) (publié aussi en anglais)

———.

Analyse des besoins et recommandations: les problèmes municipaux et scolaires; les relations fiscales et financières. [Québec] 1956. 346 p.
(Rapport de la Commission royale d'enquête sur les problèmes constitutionnels; v. 3.2) (publié aussi en anglais)

Documentation. [Québec] 1956. 424 p. (Rapport de la Commission royale d'enquête sur les problèmes constitutionnels; v. 4) (publié aussi en anglais)

Président/Chairman: T. Tremblay.

Commissaires/Commissioners: R. Arès, P.-H. Guimont, E. Minville, H. Parent, J.P. Rowat.

Loc.: OOC, OONL, OOP, OOPW, OOSC, OOSS, OOU, OOUD, OTMCL, OTY, QMBM, QMHE, QMU, QQL, QQLA, QRCN, QRUQR, QSHERU, QSTJ, SSU

Royal Commission of Inquiry on Constitutional Problems.
Historical outline. Public finances. [Quebec] 1956. xv, 390 p. (Report of the Royal Commission of Inquiry on Constitutional Problems; v. 1) (issued also in French)

The Province of Quebec and the French-Canadian case. Federalism. [Quebec] 1956. 332 p. (Report of the Royal Commission of Inquiry on Constitutional Problems; v. 2) (issued also in French)

Analysis of needs and recommendations: provincial jurisdiction. [Quebec] 1956. 368 p. (Report of the Royal Commission of Inquiry on Constitutional Problems; v. 3.1) (issued also in French)

Analysis of needs and recommendations: municipal and school problems; fiscal and financial relations. [Quebec] 1956. 338 p. (Report of the Royal Commission of Inquiry on Constitutional Problems; v. 3.2) (issued also in French)

Documentation. [Quebec] 1956. 424 p. (Report of the Royal Commission of Inquiry on Constitutional Problems; v. 4) (issued also in French)

Chairman/Président: T. Tremblay.

Commissioners/Commissaires: R. Arès, P.-H. Guimont, E. Minville, H. Parent, J.P. Rowat.

Loc.: ACU, BVA, BVAU, MWP, MWU, NBSAM, NFSM, NSHPL, OH, OHM, OKQ, OKQL, OLU, OOA, OOC, OONL, OOP, OOSC, OOU, OPAL, OPET, OSTCB, OTER, OTP, OTU, OTY, OWA, OWTU, QLB, QMBM, QMM, QMU, QQL, QQLA, SRL, SSM, SSUL

317 **1960**

Commission d'enquête sur Taxi Owners Reciprocal Insurance Association.
Rapport. [Québec, 1960 ?] 42 *f.* (manuscrit dactylographié)

Commissaire/Commissioner: V. Chabot.

Loc.: QQL

318 **1960-1961**

Commission d'étude du système administratif de Montréal.
Rapport. [Montréal, 1960-1961] 2 v. (publié aussi en anglais)

Président/Chairman: P. Champagne.

Commissaires/Commissioners: C.F. Carsley, L.-A. Lapointe, H. Parent, G. Picard.

Loc.: OONL, OOU, OOUD, QQL

Commission to Inquire into the Administrative System of Montreal.
Report. [Montreal, 1960-1961] 2 v. (issued also in French)

Chairman/Président: P. Champagne.

Commissioners/Commissaires: C.F. Carsley, L.-A. Lapointe, H. Parent, G. Picard.

Loc.: BVA, OOF, OONL, OOU, OOUD, OTU, QMML, QQL

319 **1961**

Commission d'enquête sur l'organisation et l'administration de l'Hôpital Jean-Talon de Montréal.
Rapport. [Québec, 1961] 220 *f.* (manuscrit dactylographié)

Commissaires/Commissioners: G. Auger, V. Chabot, J.H. Charbonneau.

Loc.: OONL, OOP, QMU, QQL, QSHERU

320 **1962**

Comité d'étude sur l'enseignement technique et professionnel.
Rapport. [Québec, 1962] 2 v.

Loc.: AEU, NFSM, OOC, OONL, OOP, OOSS, OOU, OTER, OTMCL, OTYL, OWTU, QCU, QMBM, QMG, QMM, QMU, QQER, QQL, QQLA, QRUQR, QSHERU, QTU

———.
Rapport: résumé des principales constatations et recommandations. Québec, 1962. 147 p. (publié aussi en anglais)

Président/Chairman: A. Tremblay.

Membres/Members: R.L. Campbell, L.-P. Fortin, D. Gauthier, R. Lair, A. Landry, L. Thibeault, P. Vaillancourt.

Loc.: AEU, OOF, OOP, OOSS, OOU, OTYL, OWTU, QMBN, QMG, QMU, QQL, QQLA, QSHERU, QTU

Study Committee on Technical and Vocational Education.
Report: summary of the principal findings and recommendations. Quebec, 1962. 148 p. (issued also in French)

Chairman/Président: A. Tremblay.

Members/Membres: R.L. Campbell, L.-P. Fortin, D. Gauthier, R. Lair, A. Landry, L. Thibeault, P. Vaillancourt.

Loc.: OONL, QMM, QQLA

321 **Commission d'enquête à l'Ecole normale Jacques-Cartier de Montréal.**
Rapport. [Montréal] 1962. 32 p. (manuscrit dactylographié)

Président/Chairman: A. Montpetit.

Commissaires/Commissioners: V. Décarie, P. Garigue, J.-M. Mathieu, E. Minville.

Loc.: OONL, QQL

322 **Commission d'enquête sur l'organisation et l'administration de l'Hôpital Général Fleury Inc., la corporation de l'Hôpital Général Fleury et du Docteur J.-A. Dionne.** [Montréal] 1962. 91 f. (manuscrit dactylographié)

Commissaire/Commissioner: J. Tellier.

Loc.: QQL

323 Commission d'enquête sur l'organisation et l'administration de l'Hôpital St. Michel.
Rapport. [Montréal, 1962] 83 f. (manuscrit dactylographié)

Commissaire/Commissioner: J. Tellier.

Loc.: QQL

324 Commission d'enquête sur la vente du réseau de gaz de l'Hydro-Québec à la Corporation de gaz naturel du Québec.
Rapport. [Montréal, 1962] 2, 102, 5 f. (manuscrit dactylographié) (publié aussi en anglais)

Président/Chairman: E. Salvas.

Commissaires/Commissioners: J.-M. Guérard, H.I. Ross.

Loc.: OONL, OOP, QQL

Commission of Inquiry Concerning the Sale of the Gas Network of Hydro-Quebec to the Quebec Natural Gas Corporation.
Report. [Montreal, 1962] 2, 102, 5 l. (typescript) (issued also in French)

Chairman/Président: E. Salvas.

Commissioners/Commissaires: J.-M. Guérard, H.I. Ross.

Loc.: OONL, OTLS, OTU

325 **1963**

Commission d'enquête de l'Hôpital Général Fleury Inc.
Rapport. Montréal, 1963. 150 f. (manuscrit dactylographié)

Commissaire/Commissioner: J. Tellier.

Loc.: OONL, MWP, QMU, QQL, QQLA, QSHERU

326 Commission d'enquête sur le commerce du livre dans la Province de Québec.
Rapport. Montréal, 1963. 250 f. (manuscrit dactylographié)

Commissaire/Commissioner: M. Bouchard.

Loc.: BVAU, NFSM, OOC, OONL, OOP, OOU, OOS, OTMCL, OTY, OTYL, QMCB, QMU, QQL, QQLA, QRCN, QSHERU

327 **Commission d'enquête sur le Sanatorium Bégin de Sainte-Germaine de Dorchester.**
Rapport. [Québec ? 1963] 51 *f.* (manuscrit dactylographié)

Commissaire/Commissioner: V. Chabot.

Loc.: QQL

328 **Commission d'enquête sur le Sanatorium Ross de Gaspé.**
Rapport. [Québec ? 1963] 78 *f.* (manuscrit dactylographié)

Commissaire/Commissioner: V. Chabot.

Loc.: QQL

329 **Commission d'enquête sur les méthodes d'achat utilisées au Département de la colonisation et au Service des achats du gouvernement du 1er juillet 1955 au 30 juin 1960.**
Rapport. [Montréal] 1963. 4, 216 *f.* (manuscrit dactylographié) (publié aussi en anglais)

Président/Chairman: E. Salvas.

Commissaires/Commissioners: J.-M. Guérard, H.I. Ross.

Loc.: OONL, OOP, OOU, OOUD, QMU, QMBM, QQL, QQLA, QSHERU, SSU

Commission of Inquiry Concerning the Purchasing Methods Used in the Department of Colonization and the Government Purchasing Service from July 1st, 1955 to June 30th, 1960.
Report. [Montreal] 1963. 4, 216 *l.* (typescript) (issued also in French)

Chairman/Président: E. Salvas.

Commissioners/Commissaires: J.-M. Guérard, H.I. Ross.

Loc.: MWP, OOCC, OONL, OTU, OTYL, OWAL, OWTU, QQL

330 **1963-1966**

Commission royale d'enquête sur l'enseignement.
Les structures supérieures du système scolaire. [Québec] 1963. xiii, 121 p. (Rapport de la Commission royale d'enquête sur l'enseignement; v. 1) (publié aussi en anglais)

———.
Les structures pédagogiques du système scolaire: les structures et les niveaux de l'enseignement. [Québec] 1964. ix, 404 p. (Rapport de la Commission royale d'enquête sur l'enseignement; v. 2) (publié aussi en anglais)

———.
Les structures pédagogiques du système scolaire: les programmes d'étude et les services éducatifs. [Québec] 1964. 391 p. (Rapport de la Commission royale d'enquête sur l'enseignement; v. 3) (publié aussi en anglais)

———.
L'administration de l'enseignement: diversité religieuse, culturelle, et unité de l'administration. [Québec] 1966. ix, 244 p. (Rapport de la Commission royale d'enquête sur l'enseignement; v. 4) (publié aussi en anglais)

———.
L'administration de l'enseignement: le financement, les agents de l'éducation. [Québec] 1966. v, 287 p. (Rapport de la Commission royale d'enquête sur l'enseignement; v. 5) (publié aussi en anglais)

———.
Index analytique du rapport de la Commission royale d'enquête sur l'enseignement. [Québec, 1966] 120 p. (publié aussi en anglais)

Président/Chairman: A.-M. Parent.

Commissaires/Commissioners: G. Filion, J. Lapointe, P. Larocque, J. McIlhone, D. Munroe, G. Rocher, Sr. Marie-Laurent de Rome.

Loc.: AE, BVAS, MWP, NBFL, NFSM, OOA, OOC, OONL, OOP, OOSS, OOU, OPET, OSTCB, OTC, OTER, OTMCL, OTY, OWA, QMBM, QMG, QMHE, QMJ, QMM, QMU, QQER, QQL, QQLA, QRCN, QSHERU

Royal Commission of Inquiry on Education.
The structure of the educational system at the provincial level. [Quebec] 1963. xix, 121 p. (*Report of the Royal Commission of Inquiry on Education; v. 1*) *(issued also in French)*

———.
The pedagogical structures of the educational system: the structures and the levels of education. [Quebec] 1964. xix, 402 p. (Report of the Royal Commission of Inquiry on Education; v. 2) (issued also in French)

———.
The pedagogical structures of the educational system: the programmes of study and the educational services. [Quebec] 1965. xiii, 363 p. (Report of the Royal Commission of Inquiry on Education; v. 3) (issued also in French)

———.
Educational administration: religious and cultural diversity within a unified administration. [Quebec] 1966. xvii, 229 p. (Report of the Royal Commission of Inquiry on Education; v. 4) (issued also in French)

———.
Educational administration: finances, participants in education. [Quebec] 1966. xv, 272 p. (Report of the Royal Commission of Inquiry on Education; v. 5) (issued also in French)

———.
Index to the report of the Royal Commission of Inquiry on Education. [Quebec, 1967] 123 p. (issued also in French)

Chairman/Président: A.-M. Parent.

Commissioners/Commissaires: G. Filion, J. Lapointe, P. Larocque, J. McIlhone, D. Munroe, G. Rocher, Sr. Marie-Laurent de Rome.

Loc.: AEU, BVAU, BNND, MWP, MWU, NFSG, NFSM, OH, OKQ, OLU, OOA, OONH, OOS, OOU, OPET, OTER, OTL, OTP, OTU, OTY, OWA, QMBM, QMG, QMJ, QMM, QMU, QQLA, QSHERU, SSU

331 **1964**

Comité d'étude sur l'enseignement dans les écoles d'architecture de Montréal et de Québec.
Rapport. [Québec, 1964] 181 p.

Président/Chairman: L. Lamontagne.

Commissaires/Commissioners: J.-P. Carlhian, P.-M. Côté, J.-M. Martin, J. Michaud.

Loc.: BVAU, BVIV, MWP, OOC, OOF, OON, OONL, OOP, OOSS, OOU, OTY, QMCB, QMML, QMU, QQL, QQLA, QSHERU, SRL

332 **Commission d'enquête Brossard sur l'affaire Coffin.**
Rapport. Québec, 1964. 3 v. (manuscrit dactylographié) (comprend du texte en anglais)

Commissaire/Commissioner: R. Brossard.

Loc.: AEU, MWP, NFSM, OONL, OOP, OOU, OTU, OTY, OWAL, OWTU, QMCB, QMHE, QMU, QQL, QQLA, QSHERU

333 **Commission d'enquête sur l'administration de l'Institut Albert Prévost quant à son personnel médical et hospitalier.**
Rapport. [Montréal, 1964] 2, 126 *f.* (manuscrit dactylographié)

Commissaires/Commissioners: A. Cousineau, R. Parenteau, A. Régnier.

Loc.: OONL, OTY, QMML, QMU, QQL, QQLA, QSHERU

334 **Commission d'enquête sur la Commission des écoles catholiques de la Cité de Jacques-Cartier, la Commission des écoles catholiques de Verdun et les commissaires d'écoles pour la municipalité d'Alma.**
La Commission des écoles catholiques de la Cité de Jacques-Cartier. [Montréal, 1964] 199, 21 *f.* (Rapport de la Commission d'enquête sur la Commission des écoles catholiques de la Cité de Jacques-Cartier, la Commission des écoles catholiques de Verdun et les commissaires d'écoles pour la municipalité d'Alma; v. 1) (manuscrit dactylographié)

———.
La Commission des écoles catholiques de Verdun. [Montréal, 1964] 118 *f.* (Rapport de la Commission d'enquête sur la Commission des écoles catholiques de la Cité de Jacques-Cartier, la Commission des écoles catholiques de Verdun et les commissaires d'écoles pour la municipalité d'Alma; v. 2) (manuscrit dactylographié)

———.
Les commissaires d'écoles pour la municipalité d'Alma. [Montréal, 1965] 122 *f.* (Rapport de la Commission d'enquête sur la Commission des écoles catholiques de la Cité de Jacques-Cartier, la Commission des écoles catholiques de Verdun et les commissaires d'écoles pour la municipalité d'Alma; v. 3) (manuscrit dactylographié)

Président/Chairman: R. Morcel.

Commissaires/Commissioners: J.-Y. Drolet, J. St-Laurent.

Loc.: OOP, QMML, QQL, QQLA

335 **Commission d'étude du système administratif de la Cité de Québec.**
Rapport. [Québec, 1964] iv, 120 *f.*

Président/Chairman: C.A. Sylvestre.

Commissaires/Commissioners; G. Fortier, P. Letarte.

Loc.: OONL, OOP, OOU, OOUD, OTCT, QMU, QQL, QQLA

336 **Commission of Inquiry Appointed to Investigate the Real Estate Transactions of the Protestant School Board of Greater Montreal and the School Boards Under its Control During the Ten Year Period 1953 to 1963.**
Report. [Montreal, 1964 ?] 162 *l.* (typescript)

Commissioner/Commissaire: A.I. Smith.

Loc.: OTLS, QQL

337 **1965**

Commission d'enquête sur l'administration de la justice à la Cour municipale de Québec.
Rapport. [Québec, 1965] pagination variée (manuscrit dactylographié)

Président/Chairman: C.A. Sylvestre.

Commissaires/Commissioners: G. Fortier, P. Letarte.

Loc.: AE, AEU, MWP, OONL, OOP, OTU, OTY, OTYL, QMU, QMML, QQL, QQLA, QSHERU

338 **Commission d'enquête sur l'extension de la distribution du gaz naturel dans la province de Québec.**
Rapport. Montréal, 1965. 113 *f.* (manuscrit dactylographié)

Président/Chairman: J. Vadboncoeur.

Commissaires/Commissioners: A. Cossette-Trudel, M. Messier.

Loc.: QMU, QQL, QSHERU

339 **Commission d'enquête sur les faillites, liquidations, concordats et cessions de biens.**
Rapport/Report. [Québec] 1965. 22, 22 p. (texte tête-bêche en français et en anglais)

Commissaire/Commissioner: L. Mercier.

Commission of Inquiry Concerning Bankruptcies, Liquidations, Proposals and Voluntary Assignments.
Report/Rapport. [Québec] 1965. 22, 22 p. (text in English and French on inverted pages)

Commissioner/Commissaire: L. Mercier.

Loc.: BVAU, MWP, NBFU, OOCI, OONL, OOUD, OTY, OTYL, QMML, QMU, QQL, QSHERU, SRL

340 **Commission royale d'enquête sur la chiropraxie et l'ostéopathie.**
La chiropraxie. [Québec, 1965] 359 f. (Rapport de la Commission royale d'enquête sur la chiropraxie et l'ostéopathie; v. 1) (manuscrit dactylographié) (publié aussi en anglais)

———.
La chiropraxie: annexes. [Québec, 1965] pagination variée (Rapport de la Commission royale d'enquête sur la chiropraxie et l'ostéopathie; v. 2) (manuscrit dactylographié) (publié aussi en anglais)

———.
L'ostéopathie. **[Québec, 1965] pagination variée (Rapport de la Commission royale d'enquête sur la chiropraxie et l'ostéo pathie; v. 3) (manuscrit dactylographié) (publié aussi en anglais)**

Commissaire/Commissioner: G. Lacroix.

Loc.: MWP, OOC, OONL, OOD, OOU, QMHE, QMML, QMU, QQL, QQLA, QRCN, QRUQR, QSHERU

Royal Commission of Inquiry on Chiropraxy & Osteopathy.
Chiropraxy. [Quebec, 1965] 166 p. (Report of the Royal Commission of Inquiry on Chiropraxy & Osteopathy; v. [1]) (issued also in French)

———.
Chiropraxy: annexes. [Quebec, 1965] various pagings (Report of the Royal Commission of Inquiry on Chiropraxy & Osteopathy; v. [2]) (issued also in French)

———.
Osteopathy. [Quebec, 1965] various pagings (Report of the Royal Commission of Inquiry on Chiropraxy & Osteopathy; v. [3]) (issued also in French)

Commissioner/Commissaire: G. Lacroix.

Loc.: ACU, BVAS, OONL, OTU, QMHE

341 **Commission royale d'enquête sur la fiscalité.**
Rapport. Québec: [R. Lefebvre, Imprimeur de la Reine] 1965. 552 p. (publié aussi en anglais)

Président/Chairman: M. Bélanger.

Commissaires/Commissioners: H.C. Goldenberg, C.-H. Perrault.

Loc.: BVAU, MWP, OOA, OOB, OOCC, OOCI, OOEC, OOF, OONL, OOP, OOSS, OOU, OPET, OTU, OTYL, QMCB, QMML, QMU, QQL, QQLA, QRCN, QSHERU

Royal Commission on Taxation.
Report. Quebec: [R. Lefebvre, Queen's Printer] 1965. 512 p. (issued also in French)

Chairman/Président: M. Bélanger.

Commissioners/Commissaires: H.C. Goldenberg, C.-H. Perrault.

Loc.: ACU, AEU, BVA, BVAU, MWP, MWU, NFSM, NSHPL, OHM, OKQL, OOB, OOCC, OOEC, OOF, OONL, OOP, OOTC, OPAL, OPET, OTER, OTLS, OTP, OTU, OTYL, OWAL, QMG, QMMSC, QMU, QQL, QQLA, SRL, SSU

342 **1966**

Comité d'étude de la cédule des justes salaires au sujet des taux de transport.
Rapport. [Québec, 1966] 104 f. (manuscrit dactylographié)

Président/Chairman: R. Lippé.

Membres/Members: G.-E. Legault, J. Parizeau.

Loc.: QQL

343 **Commission d'enquête sur l'observance du dimanche dans les usines de pâtes et papiers du Québec.**
Rapport/Report. [Québec] 1966. 145 p. (texte en français et en anglais)

Commissaires/Commissioners: R. Alleyn, R.M. Fowler, J.-P. Geoffroy.

Public Inquiry Commission Concerning Sunday Observance in Quebec Pulp & Paper Mills.
Report/Rapport. [Quebec] 1966. 145 p. (text in English and French)

Commissioners/Commissaires: R. Alleyn, R.M. Fowler, J.-P. Geoffroy.

Loc.: AEU, BVAS, MWP, OKQL, OOC, OOFF, OOL, OONL, OOP, OOU, OTMCL, OTYL, OWTU, QMML, QMU, QQL, QQLA, QSHERU, SRL

344 **1967**

Commission d'enquête sur l'acquisition d'immeubles par la Régie des alcools du Québec.
Rapport. [Montréal, 1967] 79, 2 p. (publié aussi en anglais)

Commissaire/Commissioner: A.I. Smith.

Loc.: OOP, QQL.

Commission Appointed to Investigate Land Purchases by Quebec Liquor Board.
Report. [Montreal, 1967] 83, 4 p. (issued also in French)

Commissioner/Commissaire: A.I. Smith.

Loc.: QQL

345 **1967-1972**

Commission d'enquête sur la santé et le bien-être social.
L'assurance-maladie. [Québec: R. Lefebvre, Imprimeur de la Reine] 1967. xii, 338 p. (Rapport de la Commission d'enquête sur la santé et le bien-être social; v. 1) (publié aussi en anglais)

──────── .

Les médecins internes et les résidents. [Québec: R. Lefebvre, Imprimeur de la Reine] 1967. 79 p. (Rapport de la Commission d'enquête sur la santé et le bien-être social; v. 2) (publié aussi en anglais)

──────── .

Le développement. [Québec: R. Lefebvre, Éditeur officiel du Québec] 1971. 251 p. (Rapport de la Commission d'enquête sur la santé et le bien-être social; v. 3.1) (publié aussi en anglais)

──────── .

Le développement. [Québec: R. Lefebvre, Éditeur officiel du Québec] 1971. 279 p. (Rapport de la Commission d'enquête sur la santé et le bien-être social; v. 3.2) (publié aussi en anglais)

———.

La santé: la situation actuelle. [Québec: R. Lefebvre, Éditeur officiel du Québec] 1970. 212 p. (Rapport de la Commission d'enquête sur la santé et le bien-être social; v. 4.1) (publié aussi en anglais)

———.

La santé: le régime de la santé. [Québec: R. Lefebvre, Éditeur officiel du Québec] 1970. 209 p. (Rapport de la Commission d'enquête sur la santé et le bien-être social; v. 4.2) (publié aussi en anglais)

———.

La santé: le régime de la santé. [Québec: R. Lefebvre, Éditeur officiel du Québec] 1970. 198 p. (Rapport de la Commission d'enquête sur la santé et le bien-être social; v. 4.3) (publié aussi en anglais)

———.

La santé: les ressources: l'instauration du régime de la santé. [Québec: R. Lefebvre, Éditeur officiel du Québec] 1970. 331 p. (Rapport de la Commission d'enquête sur la santé et le bien-être social; v. 4.4) (publié aussi en anglais)

———.

La sécurité du revenu: la situation actuelle: les fondements d'une politique de sécurité du revenu. [Québec: R. Lefebvre, Éditeur officiel du Québec] 1971. 343 p. (Rapport de la Commission d'enquête sur la santé et le bien-être social; v. 5.1)

———.

La sécurité du revenu: les nouveaux régimes. [Québec: R. Lefebvre, Éditeur officiel du Québec] 1971. 276 p. (Rapport de la Commission d'enquête sur la santé et le bien-être social; v. 5.2)

———.

La sécurité du revenu: l'instauration des nouveaux régimes. [Québec: R. Lefebvre, Éditeur officiel du Québec] 1971. 171 p. (Rapport de la Commission d'enquête sur la santé et le bien-être social; v. 5.3)

———.

Les services sociaux. [Québec: R. Lefebvre, Éditeur officiel du Québec] 1972. 381 p. (Rapport de la Commission d'enquête sur la santé et le bien-être social; v. 6.1) (publié aussi en anglais)

———.

Les services sociaux. [Québec: R. Lefebvre, Éditeur officiel du Québec] 1972. 492 p. (Rapport de la Commission d'enquête sur la santé et le bien-être social; v. 6.2) (publié aussi en anglais)

———.

Les professions et la société. [Québec: R. Lefebvre, Éditeur officiel du Québec] 1970. 101 p. (Rapport de la Commission d'enquête sur la santé et le bien-être social; v. 7.1) (publié aussi en anglais)

Les établissements à buts lucratifs. [Québec: R. Lefebvre, Éditeur officiel du Québec] 1970. 68 p. (Rapport de la Commission d'enquête sur la santé et bien-être social; v. 7.2) (publié aussi en anglais)

Président/Chairman: C. Castonguay (1966-1970), G. Nepveu (1970-1972).

Membres/Members: J. de la Chevrotière, J. Dinelle, W.A. Dyson, A.-M. Guillemette, G.A. Lachaîne, E. Laurent, J.D. LeMay Warren.

Loc.: OOCW, OOL, OON, OONL, OOSS, OOU, OTMCL, QMCB, QMML, QMMM, QMU, QQL, QQLA, QRUQR, QSHERU

Commission of Inquiry on Health and Social Welfare.
Health insurance. [Québec: R. Lefebvre, Québec Official Publisher] 1967. xii, 318 p. (Report of the Commission of Inquiry on Health and Social Welfare; v. 1) (issued also in French)

———.

Interns and residents. [Québec: R. Lefebvre, Québec Official Publisher] 1967. 79 p. (Report of the Commission of Inquiry on Health and Social Welfare; v. 2) (issued also in French)

———.

Development. [Québec: R. Lefebvre, Québec Official Publisher] 1971. 245 p. (Report of the Commission of Inquiry on Health and Social Welfare; v. 3.1) (issued also in French)

———.

Development. [Québec: R. Lefebvre, Québec Officiel Publisher] 1971. 253 p. (Report of the Commission of Inquiry on Health and Social Welfare; v. 3.2) (issued also in French)

———.

Health: the present situation. [Québec: R. Lefebvre, Québec Official Publisher] 1970. 194 p. (Report of the Commission of Inquiry on Health and Social Welfare; v. 4.1) (issued also in French)

———.

Health: the health plan. [Québec: R. Lefebvre, Québec Official Publisher] 1970. 191 p. (Report of the Commission of Inquiry on Health and Social Welfare; v. 4.2) (issued also in French)

———.

Health: the health plan. [Québec: R. Lefebvre, Québec Official Publisher] 1970. 180 p. (Report of the Commission of Inquiry on Health and Social Welfare; v. 4.3) (issued also in French)

———.

Health: resources: establishment of the health plan. [Québec: R. Lefebvre, Québec Official Publisher] 1970. 293 p. (Report of the Commission of Inquiry on Health and Social Welfare; v. 4.4) (issued also in French)

———.

Income security: the present situation: foundations of an income security policy. [Québec: R. Lefebvre, Québec Official Publisher] 1971. 340 p. (Report of the Commission of Inquiry on Health and Social Welfare; v. 5.1) (issued also in French)

———.

Income security: the new plans. [Québec: R. Lefebvre, Québec Official Publisher] 1971. 271 p. (Report of the Commission of Inquiry on Health and Social Welfare; v. 5.2) (issued also in French)

———.

Income security: establishment of the new plans. [Québec: R. Lefebvre, Québec Official Publisher] 1971. 166 p. (Report of the Commission of Inquiry on Health and Social Welfare; v. 5.3) (issued also in French)

———.

Social services. [Québec: R. Lefebvre, Québec Official Publisher] 1972. 368 p. (Report of the Commission of Inquiry on Health and Social Welfare; v. 6.1) (issued also in French)

———.

Social services. [Québec: R. Lefebvre, Québec Official Publisher] 1972. 447 p. (Report of the Commission of Inquiry on Health and Social Welfare; v. 6.2) (issued also in French)

———.

The professions and society. [Québec: R. Lefebvre, Québec Official Publisher] 1970. 88 p. (Report of the Commission of Inquiry on Health and Social Welfare; v. 7.1) (issued also in French)

———.

Profit-making institutions. [Québec: R. Lefebvre, Québec Official Publisher] 1970. 68 p. (Report of the Commission of Inquiry on Health and Social Welfare; v. 7.2) (issued also in French)

Chairman/Président: C. Castonguay (1966-1970), G. Nepveu (1970-1972).

Members/Membres: J. de la Chevrotière, J. Dinelle, W.A. Dyson, A.-M. Guillemette, G.A. Lachaîne, E. Laurent, J.D. LeMay Warren.

Loc.: BVAS, BVIP, NFSM, OOC, OOCW, OONL, OOP, OTMCL, OWAL, QMML, QMMM, QQL, QQLA

346 1967-1969

Commission royale d'enquête sur l'agriculture au Québec.
L'assainissement des sols au Québec. [Québec: R. Lefebvre, Imprimeur de la Reine, 1967] 143 p. (Rapport de la Commission d'enquête sur l'agriculture au Québec; v. [1])

―――――.
Le crédit agricole au québec. [Québec: R. Lefebvre, Imprimeur de la Reine, 1967] 57 p. (Rapport de la Commission royale d'enquête sur l'agriculture au Québec; v. [2])

―――――.
L'industrie et le commerce des engrais chimiques au Québec. [Québec: R. Lefebvre, Imprimeur de la Reine, 1967] 61 p. (Rapport de la Commission royale d'enquête sur l'agriculture au Québec; v. [3])

―――――.
La médecine vétérinaire et les produits de médecine vétérinaire au Québec. [Québec: R. Lefebvre, Imprimeur de la Reine, 1967] 75 p. (Rapport de la Commission Royale d'enquête sur l'agriculture au Québec; v. [4])

―――――.
L'évolution de l'agriculture et le développement économique du Québec, 1946 à 1976. [Québec: R. Lefebvre, Imprimeur de la Reine, 1967] 156 p. (Rapport de la Commission royale d'enquête sur l'agriculture au Québec; v. [5])

―――――.
La mise en marché de la viande et de la volaille au Québec. [Québec: R. Lefebvre, Imprimeur de la Reine, 1967] 129 p. (Rapport de la Commission royale d'enquête sur l'agriculture au Québec; v. [6])

―――――.
L'industrie laitière au Québec. [Québec: R. Lefebvre, Imprimeur de la Reine, 1967] 164 p. (Rapport de la Commission royale d'enquête sur l'agriculture au Québec; v. [7])

―――――.
Les coopératives agricoles et les plans conjoints au Québec. [Québec: R. Lefebvre, Imprimeur de la Reine, 1968] 96 p. (Rapport de la Commission royale d'enquête sur l'agriculture au Québec; v. [8])

―――――.
La culture et la mise en marché du tabac au Québec. [Québec: R. Lefebvre, Imprimeur de la Reine, 1968] 22 p. (Rapport de la Commission royale d'enquête sur l'agriculture au Québec; v. [9])

———.

Les grains de provende au Québec. [Québec: R. Lefebvre, Imprimeur de la Reine, 1968] 31 p. (Rapport de la Commission royale d'enquête sur l'agriculture au Québec; v. [10])

———.

La mise en marché des fruits et légumes au Québec. [Québec: R. Lefebvre, Imprimeur de la Reine, 1968] 94 p. (Rapport de la Commission royale d'enquête sur l'agriculture au Québec; v. [11])

———.

La mise en marché des fruits et légumes au Québec: annexes. [Québec: R. Lefebvre, Imprimeur de la Reine, 1968?] non paginé (Rapport de la Commission royale d'enquête sur l'agriculture au Québec; v. [12])

———.

La consolidation des fermes au Québec, par Nolasque April. [Québec: R. Lefebvre, Éditeur officiel du Québec, 1969] 78 p. (Rapport de la Commission royale d'enquête sur l'agriculture au Québec; v. [13])

———.

L'intégration en agriculture au Québec, par Nolasque April. [Québec: R. Lefebvre, Éditeur officiel du Québec, 1969] 96 p. (Rapport de la Commission royale d'enquête sur l'agriculture au Québec; v. [14])

Président/Chairman: N. April.

Membres/Members: R. Cousineau, E. Dugas, C. Neapole, R.P. Poirier, G. Thompson, M. Tremblay.

Loc.: AEU, BVIV, MWP, OOF, OONL, OOP, OTY, OTYL, QMAC, QMML, QMU, QQL, SRL

347 **1968-1970**

Commission d'enquête sur l'administration de la justice en matière criminelle et pénale au Québec.
La société face au crime: principes fondamentaux d'une nouvelle action sociale. [Québec: R. Lefebvre, Éditeur officiel du Québec, 1968] 99 p. (Rapport de la Commission d'enquête sur l'administration de la justice en matière criminelle et pénale au Québec: v. 1) (publié aussi en anglais)

———.

La société face au crime: la sécurité judiciaire. [Québec: R. Lefebvre, Éditeur officiel du Québec, 1969] 723 p. (Rapport de la Commission d'enquête sur l'administration de la justice en matière criminelle et pénale au Québec; v. 2.1) (publié partiellement en anglais)

_____.
La société face au crime: la sécurité judiciaire. [Québec: R. Lefebvre, Éditeur officiel du Québec, 1969?] 364 p. (Rapport de la Commission d'enquête sur l'administration de la justice en matière criminelle et pénale au Québec; v. 2.2)

_____.
La société face au crime: le crime au Québec: les tendances de la criminalité québécoise. [Québec: R. Lefebvre, Éditeur officiel du Québec, 1969] 416 p. (Rapport de la Commission d'enquête sur l'administration de la justice en matière criminelle et pénale au Québec; v. 3.1) (publié partiellement en anglais)

_____.
La société face au crime: le crime au Québec: les sommets de la criminalité québécoise. [Québec: R. Lefebvre, Éditeur officiel du Québec, 1969] 980 p. (Rapport de la Commission d'enquête sur l'administration de la justice en matière criminelle et pénale au Québec; v. 3.2) (publié partiellement en anglais)

_____.
La société face au crime: le crime au Québec: le crime organisé. [Québec: R. Lefebvre, Éditeur officiel du Québec, 1969] 623 p. (Rapport de la Commission d'enquête sur l'administration de la justice en matière criminelle et pénale au Québec; v. 3.3)

_____.
La société face au crime: la cour de bien-être social. [Québec: R. Lefebvre, Éditeur officiel du Québec, 1970] 1057 p. (Rapport de la Commission d'enquête sur l'administration de la justice en matière criminelle et pénale au Québec; v. 4.1)

_____.
La société face au crime: étude comparative sur les tribunaux pour mineurs: Grande-Bretagne, France, Suède. [Québec: R. Lefebvre, Éditeur officiel du Québec, s.d.] 381 p. (Rapport de la Commission d'enquête sur l'administration de la justice en matière criminelle et pénale au Québec; v. 4.2)

_____.
La société face au crime: étude comparative sur les tribunaux pour mineurs: Québec. [Québec: R. Lefebvre, Éditeur officiel du Québec, s.d.] 378 p. (Rapport de la Commission d'enquête sur l'administration de la justice en matière criminelle et pénale au Québec; v. 4.3)

_____.
La société face au crime: omnibus. [Québec: R. Lefebvre, Éditeur officiel du Québec, 1970] 1123 p. (Rapport de la Commission d'enquête sur l'administration de la justice en matière crimi nelle et pénale au Québec; v. 5)

Président/Chairman: Y. Prévost.

Commissaires/Commissioners: H. Gould, L. Laplante.

Loc.: AEU, BVAU, MWU, OKQL, OOC, OOND, OONH, OONL, OOSC, OOU, OTMCL, OTU, OTYL, QMU, QQL, QRCN, QSHERU

Commission of Enquiry into the Administration of Justice on Criminal and Penal Matters in Quebec.
Crime, justice and society: fundamental principles of a new social action programme. [Québec: R. Lefebvre, Québec Official Publisher, 1968] 93 p. (Report of the Commission of Enquiry into the Administration of Justice on Criminal and Penal Matters in Quebec; v. 1) (issued also in French)

———.

Crime, justice and society: legal security. [Québec: R. Lefebvre, Québec Official Publisher, 1969] 215 p. (Report of the Commission of Enquiry into the Administration of Justice on Criminal and Penal Matters in Quebec; v. 2) (issued also in French)

———.

Crime, justice and society: crime in Quebec: trends in Quebec criminality. [Québec: R. Lefebvre, Québec Official Publisher, 1969] 269 p. (Report of the Commission of Enquiry into the Administration of Justice on Criminal and Penal Matters in Quebec; v. 3.1) (issued also in French)

———.

Crime, justice and society: crime in Quebec: the peaks of Quebec criminality. [Québec: R. Lefebvre, Québec Official Publisher, 1969] 273 p. (Report of the Commission of Enquiry into the Administration of Justice on Criminal and Penal Matters in Quebec; v. 3.2) (issued also in French)

———.

Crime, justice and society: crime in Quebec: organized crime. [Québec: R. Lefebvre, Québec Official Publisher, 1969] 207 p. (Report of the Commission of Enquiry into the Administration of Justice on Criminal and Penal Matters in Quebec; v. 3.3) (issued also in French)

Chairman/Président: Y. Prévost.

Commissioners/Commissaires: H. Gould, L. Laplante.

Loc.: AEU, BVAS, BVAU, BVIV, MWU, NFSM, NSHPL, OKQL, OOC, OOEC, OOND, OONL, OOSG, OOTC, OOU, OTLS, OTP, OTU, OTY, OWAL, QMCB, QMML, QMU, QQL, QQLA, SRL, SSU

348 **Commission d'enquête sur l'Hôpital Saint-Louis de Windsor Inc.**
Rapport. [Québec? 1968] 162 *f.* (manuscrit dactylographié)

Président/Chairman: J. Trahan.

Commissaires/Commissioners: P. Bourgeois, E. Gagnon, Y. Leboeuf.

Loc.: QQL

349 **Commission d'enquête sur le transport scolaire.**
Rapport. [Québec: R. Lefebvre, Éditeur officiel du Québec] 1968. 342 p.

Président/Chairman: L. Lachapelle.

Commissaires/Commissioners: A. Barré, R. Martin, J.-A. Pelletier, J.E. Perry, C. Pomerleau, O. Tremblay.

Loc.: MWP, NFSM, OONL, OOP, OOU, OTY, QMML, QMU, QQL, QRCN, QSHERU, SRL

350 **1969**

Commission d'enquête sur l'enseignement des arts au Québec.
Rapport. [Québec] Éditeur officiel du Québec [1969] 4 v.

Président/Chairman: M. Rioux.

Commissaires/Commissioners: J. Deslauriers, R. Gauthier, J. Ouellet, F. Ouellet, A. Paradis.

Loc.: BVA, BVAS, BVAU, MWP, NFSM, OOC, OOF, OONL, OOP, OOSS, OOTC, OOU, OTER, OTMCL, QLB, QMBM, QMM, QMML, QMU, QQL, QQLA, QRCN, QSHERU, SRL

351 **1971**

Commission d'enquête sur le commerce des boissons alcooliques.
Rapport. Québec: [R. Lefebvre, Éditeur officiel du Québec] 1971. 359 p.

Président/Chairman: L. Thinel.

Commissaires/Commissioners: M. Bélanger, O. Thur.

Loc.: AEU, MWP, NFSM, OOC, OOEC, OOF, OONL, OOP, OOU, OOUD, OTMCL, OTY, OTYL, QJH, QMML, QMU, QQL, QSHERU, SRL

352 **1972**

Commission d'enquête sur l'Hôpital Charles Lemoyne.
Rapport. [Montréal: Fédération nationale des services, 1972] 158 p.

Président/Chairman: J. Trahan.

Commissaires/Commissioners: P. Bourgeois, J.-C. Deschênes, R. Dubord, E.D. Gagnon.

Loc.: OONL, QMBN, QMU, QQL

353 **Commission d'enquête sur la situation de la langue française et sur les droits linguistiques au Québec.**
La langue de travail: la situation du français dans les activités de travail et de consommation des Québécois. Québec: [Éditeur officiel du Québec] 1972. viii, 379 p. (Rapport de la Commission d'enquête sur la situation de la langue française et sur les droits linguistiques au Québec; v. 1) (publié aussi en anglais)

———.
Les droits linguistiques. Québec: [Éditeur officiel du Québec] 1972. viii, 474 p. (Rapport de la Commission d'enquête sur la situation de la langue française et sur les droits linguistiques au Québec; v. 2) (publié aussi en anglais)

———.
Les groupes ethniques: les autres groupes ethniques et l'épanouissement du français au Québec. Québec: [Éditeur officiel du Québec] 1972. viii, 570 p. (Rapport de la Commission d'enquête sur la situation de la langue française et sur les droits linguistiques au Québec; v. 3) (publié aussi en anglais)

Président/Chairman: J.-D. Gendron.

Commissaires/Commissioners: M. Doyon-Ferland, A. Gagné, E. McWhinney, N.M. Matte.

Loc.: AEU, NSCS, OKF, OOCI, OOMI, OOND, OONL, OOP, OOSC, OOPW, OOU, OOUD, OTLS, OTMCL, OTY, OW, QMBM, QMCB, QMG, QMHE, QMM, QMMN, QMU, QQLA, QTU, SRL

Commission of Inquiry on the Position of the French Language and on Language Rights in Québec.
The language of work: the position of French in work and consumer activities of Québecers. Québec: [Éditeur officiel du Québec] 1972. viii, 362 p. (Report of the Commission of Inquiry on the Position of the French Language and on Language Rights in Québec; v. 1) (issued also in French)

———.
Language rights. [Québec: Éditeur officiel du Québec] 1972. xii, 484 p. (Report of the Commission of Inquiry on the Position of the French Language and on Language Rights in Québec; v. 2) (issued also in French)

———.
The ethnic groups: other ethnic groups and the enhancement and development of French in Québec. Québec: [Éditeur officiel du Québec] 1972. viii, 557 p. (Report of the Commission of Inquiry on the Position of the French Language and on Language Rights in Québec; v. 3) (issued also in French)

Chairman/Président: J.-D. Gendron.

Commissioners/Commissaires: M. Doyon-Ferland, A. Gagné, E. McWhinney, N.M. Matte.

Loc.: AE, BVA, BVAS, BVAU, MW, MWP, NFSM, OKQL, OOC, OOF, OOMI, OOND, OONL, OOP, OOPW, OOS, OOU, OSUL, OTB, OTC, OTMCL, OTUL, OW, OWA, QLB, QMU, QQL, QQLA, SSM

354 **1973**

Commission d'enquête sur la formation des jeunes avocats.
Rapport. [Montréal] 1973. 1 v. (manuscrit dactylographié)

Commissaire/Commissioner: G. Guérin.

Loc.: OOU, OOUD, QMML, QQL

355 **1974**

Comité d'étude sur l'assurance automobile.
Rapport. [Québec: Éditeur officiel du Québec] 1974. 412 p. (publié aussi en anglais)

Président/Chairman: J.-L. Gauvin.

Membres/Members: C. Belleau, J.-M. Bouchard, E. Rankin.

Loc.: BVIV, MWP, NFSM, OONL, OOP, OOUD, QLB, QMCB, QMMSC, QMU, QQL

Committee of Inquiry on Automobile Insurance.
Report. [Québec: Éditeur officiel du Québec] 1974. 415 p. (issued also in French)

Chairman/Président: J.-L. Gauvin.

Members/Membres: C. Belleau, J.-M. Bouchard, E. Rankin.

Loc.: BVAS, OONL, OOP, QMG, QMU, SRL

356 **1975**

Commission d'enquête sur l'exercice de la liberté syndicale dans l'industrie de la construction.
Rapport. [Québec: Éditeur officiel du Québec, 1975] 355 p. (publié aussi en anglais)

Président/Chairman: R. Cliche.

Commissaires/Members: G. Chevrette, B. Mulroney.

Loc.: AEU, BVA, BVAU, MWP, NBSAM, NFSM, NSHDL, OKQL, OOC, OOE, OOL, OONL, OOP, OOPS, OOSG, OOU, OPET, OTMCL, OTU, OWAL, QLB, QMBM, QMG, QMML, QMU, QQL, QQLA, QRCN, QSHERU, SRL

Commission of Inquiry on the Exercise of Union Freedom in the Construction Industry.
Report. [Québec: Éditeur officiel du Québec, 1976] 603 p. (issued also in French)

Chairman/Président: R. Cliche.

Members/Commissaires: G. Chevrette, B. Mulroney.

Loc.: MWP, NFSM, NSHPL, OOL, OOMI, OONL, OOP, OTMCL, OTUL, OTY, OTYL, OWAL, QLB, QMG, QMML, QMMSC, QQL, SRL

357 **Commission d'enquête sur les incendies.**
Rapports d'enquêtes au Procureur général de la Province de Québec au sujet des incendies survenus dans la ville de Montréal entre le 31 octobre 1974 et le 3 novembre inclusivement. Montréal, 1975. 126 f. (manuscrit dactylographié)

Commissaire/Commissioner: G.A. Allison.

Loc.: QQL

358 **1976**

Comité d'étude sur la salubrité dans l'industrie de l'amiante.
Rapport préliminaire. [Québec: Éditeur officiel du Québec] 1976. vii, 404 p. (Annexe)

———.
Rapport final. [Québec: Éditeur officiel du Québec] 1976. 3 v.

Président/Chairman: R. Beaudry.

Membres/Members: L. Juteau, G. Lagacé.

Loc.: MWP, OOCI, OOL, OOMI, OON, OONL, OOP, OOUD, OTY, QMCB, QMU, QQER, QQL, QQLA

359 **1980**

Commission d'enquête sur le coût de la 21e olympiade.
Rapport. [Québec: Éditeur officiel du Québec, 1980] 4 v. (publié aussi en anglais)

Président/President: A.H. Malouf.

Commissaires/Commissioners: J.-G. Laliberté, G. Poirier.

Loc.: OODP, OOF, OONL, OOP, OOUD, QQL

Commission of Inquiry into the Cost of the 21st Olympiad.
Report. [Québec: Éditeur officiel du Québec, 1980] 4 v. (issued also in French)

Chairman/Président: A.H. Malouf.

Commissioners/Commissaires: J.-G. Laliberté, G. Poirier.

Loc.: OONL, NBS, QMBN, QQL

360 **1981**

Commission d'enquête sur des opérations policières en territoire québécois.
Rapport. [Québec: Direction générale des publications gouvernementales, Ministère des communications, 1981] xv, 451 p.

Commissaire/Commissioner: J.F. Keable.

Loc.: BVA, NSHDL, OOF, OONF, OONL, OOP, OOSC, OOUD, OTLS, OWAL, QMBM, QMML, QQL

361 **1981-1982**

Commission d'enquête sur la tragédie de la mine Belmoral et les conditions de sécurité dans les mines souterraines.
Rapport final sur les circonstances, les conditions préalables et les causes de la tragédie du 20 mai 1980. [Québec: La Commission] 1981. xviii, 284 p. (Rapport de la Commission d'enquête sur la tragédie de la mine Belmoral et les conditions de sécurité dans les mines souterraines; v. 1)

———.
Le sauvetage. [Québec: La Commission] 1981. xiv, 243 p. (Rapport de la Commission d'enquête sur la tragédie de la mine Belmoral et les conditions de sécurité dans les mines souterraines; v. 2)

———.
La sécurité dans les mines souterraines. [Québec: La Commission] 1982. xix, 342 p. (Rapport de la Commission d'enquête sur la tragédie de la mine Belmoral et les conditions de sécurité dans les mines souterraines; v. 3)

Président/Chairman: R. Beaudry.

Commissaire/Commissioner: L. Juteau.

Loc.: OONL, OOP, QQL

362 **1982**

Commission d'étude sur la formation des adultes.
Apprendre: une action volontaire et responsable: énoncé d'une politique globale de l'éducation des adultes dans une perspective d'éducation permanente. [Québec: Direction de l'édition du Ministère des communications, 1982] xxxii, 869 p.

Présidente/President: M. Jean.

Commissaires/Commissioners: M. Blondin, C. Desmarais, M. Lemay, F.C. McKenzie, C. Perreault, L. Rayson, R. Routhier.

Loc.: OLU, OOCS, OOMI, OONL, OOP, OOSS, QMBM, QMFA, QMHE, QRUQR

MANITOBA

363 **1875**

Commission pour instituer une enquête sur certains faits se rattachant (sic) à la dernière élection d'un membre de l'Assemblée Législative, pour la division électorale de Kildonan.
Rapport. In Manitoba. Assemblée législative. *Journal.* 2ième Parlement, 1re session. St. Boniface, Man.: Imprimerie du Journal "Le Metis", 1875. p. xlvii-lxxxvii. (Appendice H) (publié aussi en anglais)

Commissaire/Commissioner: L. Betournay.

Loc.: BVA, BVAU, BVIP, MWA, MWU, NBFU, NSHL, OHM, OOA, OONL, OOP, OPET, OSUL, OTMCL

Commission to Enquire into Certain Matters Respecting the Late Election of a Member to Serve in the Legislative Assembly for the Electoral Division of Kildonan.
Report. In Manitoba. Legislative Assembly. *Journals.* 2nd Parliament, 1st Session. Winnipeg: J.A. Kenny, Queen's Printer, 1875. p. xlvii-lxxxiv. (Appendix [H]) (issued also in French)

Commissioner/Commissaire: L. Betournay.

Loc.: BVAU, BVIP, BVIV, MWP, NBFU, NFSM, OHM, OOA, OONL, OPET, OSUL, OTL, OTMCL, OTU, QMM, QQL

364 **1886**

Commission Appointed by his Honour the Lieutenant-Governor-in-Council on the 19th August, 1885, upon the Subject of the Municipal Laws of the Province of Manitoba.
Report. In Manitoba. Legislative Assembly. *Journals.* v. 17. 5th Legislature, 4th Session. Winnipeg: G. Bourdeau, Queen's Printer, 1886. p. 77-82.

Chairman/Président: T.W. Taylor.

Commissioners/Commissaires: T.A. Bernier, J.H.D. Munson.

Loc.: BVAU, BVIP, MWP, NBFU, NFSM, OHM, OOA, OONL, OPET, OSUL, OTL, OTU, OTY, QMM, QQL

365 Royal Commission to Examine into and Report upon the Charges Made Against the First Minister.
Report. In Manitoba. Legislative Assembly. *Journals.* v. 18. 5th Legislature, 4th Session. Winnipeg: G. Bourdeau, Queen's Printer, 1886. p. 189-195.

Commissioner/Commissaire: L. Wallbridge.

Loc.: BVAU, BVIP, MWP, NBFU, OHM, OOA, OONL, OPET, OSUL, OTL, OTU, OTY, QMM, QQL

366 **1888**

Royal Commission to Make Examination and Inquiry into Certain Charges made by the "Call" and "Free Press" Newspapers Against the Government of Manitoba, and Particularly the First Minister and the Attorney General.
Report. Winnipeg, 1888. 12 *l.* (manuscript)

Commissioner/Commissaire: A.C. Killam.

Loc.: MWP

367 **1896**

Commissioners Appointed to Represent the Province of Manitoba at the Conference Held with the Representatives of the Dominion Government on the School Question.
Report. [Winnipeg] D. Philip, Queen's Printer [1896] 24 p.

Commissioners/Commissaires: J.D. Cameron, C. Sifton.

Loc.: ACG, BVIPA, MWP, MWU, OOA, OONL, OTER, OTP, OTYL, OWAL, SSU

368 **1900**

Royal Commission Appointed by the Lieutenant-Governor-in-Council, on the 31st day of January, A.D. 1900, to Inquire into the Financial Affairs of the Province.
Report. In Manitoba. Legislative Assembly. *Sessional papers.* v. 33. 10th Legislature, 1st Session. [Winnipeg, 1900] p. 389-538. (Sessional paper no. 21)

Chairman/Président: C.A. Kennedy.

Members/Membres: C. Bartlett, G.H. Halse.

Loc.: AEP, BVAU, BVIP, MWP, MWU, NBFL, NBFU, OOA, OONL, OSUL, OTL, OTMCL, QMBN, QQL, SSU

369 **1903**

Agricultural College Commission.
Report. In Manitoba. Legislative Assembly. *Journals.* v. 35. 10th Legislature, 4th Session. Winnipeg: J. Hooper, Printer to the King's Most Excellent Majesty, 1903. p. 491-502. (Sessional paper no. 17)

Chairman/Président: W. Patrick.

Commissioners/Commissaires: J.A.M. Aikins, G.H. Halse, H. Irwin, J.S. Miller, H.C. Simpson.

Loc.: BVAS, BVAU, BVIP, MWP, MWUC, OOA, OONL, OTU, OTY, QMM, QQL

370 **1907**

Beef Commission Appointed to Inquire into, Investigate and Report to the Lieutenant-Governor-in-Council upon and with Regard to all Matters Having to do with the Purchase and Sale of Cattle, Hogs, Sheep and Meat in the Provinces of Manitoba and Alberta.
Report. [Winnipeg: J. Hooper, King's Printer for the Province of Manitoba, 1907] 36 p.

Chairman/Président: A.M. Campbell.

Commissioner/Commissaire: A. Middleton.

Loc.: AEP, MWP, OOAG, OONL, SRL

371 **1910**

Royal Commission Appointed to Report on the Compensation to be Allowed to Workmen for Accidental Injuries.
Report. In Manitoba. Legislative Assembly. *Journals.* v. 42. 12th Legislature, 3rd Session. Winnipeg: J. Hooper, Printer to the King's Most Excellent Majesty, 1910. p. 634-655. (Sessional paper no. 24)

Chairman/Président: C. Locke.

Commissioners/Commissaires: T.R. Deacon, A.W. Puttee.

Loc.: BVAS, BVAU, BVIP, MWP, OOA, OONL, OTL, OTU, OTY, QMM, QQL

372 **Royal Commission on the University of Manitoba.**
Report. Winnipeg: J.A. Hooper, Printer to the King's Most Excellent Majesty, 1910. 92 p.

Chairman/Président: J.A.M. Aikins.

Commissioners/Commissaires: J.D. Cameron, A.A. Cherrier, J.L. Gordon, J.A. Machray, W.A. McIntyre, G.B. Wilson.

Loc.: MWP, MWU, OOCU, OONL, OTP, SSU

373 **1911**

Commission to Investigate into and Report upon all and any the Charges Referred to in a Resolution of the Council of the City of Winnipeg, Passed on the Twenty-first Day of November, A.D. 1910, Which Recites as Follows: "Whereas, According to Reports Contained in the Press Allegations of Graft Have Been Made Against the Police Authorities in the City of Winnipeg, and It Is Stated that Houses of Prostitution Pay for Police Protection..."
Report. Winnipeg, 1911. 21 *l.* (typescript)

Commissioner/Commissaire: H.A. Robson.

Loc.: MWP

374 **1912**

Royal Commission on Technical Education and Industrial Training.
Report. Winnipeg: Telegram Job Printers, for J. Hooper, King's Printer for the Province of Manitoba, 1912. 78 p.

Chairman/Président: G.R. Coldwell.

Commissioners/Commissaires: W.J. Bartlett, W.J. Black, R.J. Buchanan, F.C. Chambers, M. Christie, R. Fletcher, E. Fulcher, I.F. Hafenbrak, W.H. Head, H. Irwin, A.B. Juniper, G.A. Lister, D. McIntyre, W.W. Miller, A.W. Puttee, R.A. Rigg, H. Sampson, G. Seal, R.S. Ward, J.S. Woodsworth, J. Yuill.

Also known as/Également connue sous le nom de: Technical School Commission.

Loc.: MWP, MWU, OOAG

375 **Royal Commission to Investigate and Report upon the Conduct and Methods of the Administration of the Manitoba Government Telephones.**
Interim report. In Manitoba. Legislative Assembly. *Journals.* v. 44. 13th Legislature, 2nd Session. Winnipeg: J. Hooper, Printer to the King's Most Excellent Majesty, 1912. p. 508-509. (Sessional paper no. 19)

Commissioners/Commissaires: R.L. Barry, G.R. Crowe, C. Locke.

Loc.: BVAS, BVAU, BVIP, MWP, OOA, OONL, OTL, OTMCL, OTU, OTY, QMM, QQL

376 **1915**

Royal Commission Appointed to Inquire into Certain Matters Relating to the New Parliament Buildings.
Report. Winnipeg: J. Hooper, Printer to the King's Most Excellent Majesty, 1915. 82 p.

Chairman/Président: T.G. Mathers.

Commissioners/Commissaires: D.A. Macdonald, H.J. Macdonald.

Loc.: BVAU, MPW, MWP, OONL, OOP, SSU

377 **1916**

Royal Commission Appointed to Investigate the Charges Made in the Statement of C.P. Fullerton, K.C.
Report. In Manitoba. Legislative Assembly. *Sessional papers.* v. 48. 15th Legislature, 1st Session. [Winnipeg] 1916. p. 953-969. (Sessional paper no. 18)

Chairman/Président: W.E. Perdue.

Commissioners/Commissaires: A.C. Galt, H.A. Robson.

Loc.: BVAU, BVIP, MWP, MWU, MWUC, OLU, OOA, OONL, OTL, OTMCL, OTU, QMM, QQL, SRL, SSU

378 **Special Commissioner Appointed to Investigate into the Management and Supervision of the Gaol and Prison Farm of the Eastern Judicial District of Manitoba.**
Report. In Manitoba. Legislative Assembly. *Sessional papers.* v. 48. 15th Legislature, 1st Session. [Winnipeg] 1916. p. 1125-1157. (Sessional paper no. 21)

Commissioner/Commissaire: J.P. Curran.

Loc.: BVAU, BVIP, MWP, MWU, MWUC, OLU, OOA, OONL, OTL, OTMCL, OTU, QMM, QQL, SRL, SSU

379 **1917**

Royal Commission Constituted to Inquire into all Matters Pertaining to the Manitoba Agricultural College.
First and second interim reports. [Winnipeg? 1917] 46, 48 p.

Commissioner/Commissaire: A.C. Galt.

Loc.: MWP, OONL, OOP

380 **Royal Commission Constituted to Inquire into and Report on all Expenditures for Road Work during the Year 1914.**
Report. In Manitoba. Legislative Assembly. *Sessional papers.* v. 49. 15th Legislature, 2nd Session. [Winnipeg] 1917. p. 1363-1424. (Sessional paper no. 42)

Commissioner/Commissaire: G. Paterson.

Loc.: AEP, BVAU, BVIP, MWP, MWU, NBFU, OOA, OONL, OTL, OTMCL, OTU, OWA, QMM, SRL

381 **1918-1920**

Public Welfare Commission of Manitoba.
First interim report. [Winnipeg] 1918. 7 *l.* (typescript)

———.

Second interim report. Winnipeg: P. Purcell, Printer to the King's Most Excellent Majesty, 1919. 154 p.

———.

Third and final report. Winnipeg: P. Purcell, King's Printer for the Province of Manitoba, 1920. 50 p.

Chairman/Président: T.H. Johnson.

Commissioners/Commissaires: S.E. Clement, R. Forke, W.J. Fulton, J. Halpenny, D.B. Harkness, E. Johns, A.T. Mathers, H.J. Symington, J.M. Thompson.

Loc.: MWP

382 **Royal Commission on "The Workmen's Compensation Board".**
Report. In Manitoba. Legislative Assembly. *Sessional papers.* n.p.: n.p., 1918. 11 p. (Sessional paper no. 20)

Chairman/Président: W.S. Fallis.

Commissioners/Commissaires: A.R.D. Paterson, A.W. Puttee.

Loc.: AEP, BVAU, BVIP, MWP, MWU, OOA, OONL, OTL, OTMCL, QMM, QQL, SRL

383 **Royal Commission on Winnipeg Police Appointed to Enquire into Certain Declarations of Fannie Cooper et al. with Respect to Vice Protection in the City of Winnipeg.**
Report. [Winnipeg, 1918] 49 *l.* (typescript)

Commissioner/Commissaire: J.E.P. Prendergast.

Loc.: MWP

384 **1919**

Royal Commission to Enquire into and Report upon the Causes and Effects of the General Strike which Recently Existed in the City of Winnipeg for a Period of Six Weeks, Including the Methods of Calling and Carrying on Such Strike.
Report. [Winnipeg, 1919] 31 p.

Commissioner/Commissaire: H.A. Robson.

Loc.: BVAS, BVAU, MWP, NFSM, OKQ, OOL, OONL, OOP, OTMCL, OTY, SSU

385 **1920**

Commission to Inquire into Loans for Erecting and Modernizing Houses in the Municipality of Assiniboia.
Report. [Winnipeg, 1920] 10 *l.* (typescript)

Commissioner/Commissaire: G. Paterson.

Loc.: MWP

386 **1921**

Manitoba Drainage Commission.
Report. Winnipeg: P. Purcell, King's Printer, 1921. 24 p.

Chairman/Président: J.G. Sullivan.

Commissioners/Commissaires: H. Grills, J.A. Thomson.

Loc.: MWP

387 **1923**

Commission Appointed to Inquire into the Operation of "The Rural Credits Act".
Report. [Winnipeg] 1923. 22 p.

Commissioners/Commissaires: F.J. Collyer, W.T. Jackman.

Loc.: BVAU, MWP, OONL, SRU

388 **1924**

Educational Commission.
Report. Winnipeg: P. Purcell, King's Printer for the Province of Manitoba, 1924. 149 p.

———.

Reports on the College of Agriculture and the University of Manitoba submitted by the Royal Commission on Education and the Carnegie Foundation for the Advancement of Teaching. [Winnipeg] 1924. 62 p.

Chairman/Président: W.C. Murray.

Commissioners/Commissaires: W.J. Bulman, G.F. Chipman, D. McIntyre, F.W. Ransom.

Also known as/Également connue sous le nom de: Royal Commission on Education.

Loc.: BVAU, MWP, MWU, OOCU

389 **1928**

Commission Appointed to Enquire into the Conditions Existing at the Brandon Hospital for Mental Diseases.
Report. [Winnipeg, 1928] 6 *l.* (typescript)

Chairman/Président: G. Barrett.

Commissioners/Commissaires: A.W. Puttee, T. Sharpe.

Loc.: MWP

390 **Royal Commission Appointed by Order-in-Council Number 747-28 to Inquire into the Administration of the Child Welfare Division of the Department of Health and Public Welfare.**
Report. [Winnipeg?] 1928. various pagings (typescript)

Commissioner/Commissaire: C. Whitton.

Also known as/Également connue sous le nom de: The Manitoba Child Welfare Inquiry, 1928.

Loc.: MWHP, MWP, OKQ, OOCC, OONH, OONL

391 **1929**

Royal Commission re Seven Sisters Falls Agreement.
Report. In Manitoba Free Press, May 1, 1929. p. 1+

―――――.
Report of Commissioner A.K. Dysart. In Manitoba Free Press, May 7, 1929. p. 1+

Chairman/Président: D.A. Macdonald.

Commissioners/Commissaires: A.K. Dysart, J.F. Kilgour.

Loc.: AEU, BVAU, BVIV, MW, MWP, OKQ, OLU, OOCC, OONL, QMG, SRU

Royal Grain Inquiry Commission.

see/voir

Saskatchewan. Royal Grain Inquiry Commission.
(no. 693)

392 **1931**

Royal Commission to Inquire into all Matters Appertaining to the Welfare of Blind Persons within the Provinces of Manitoba and Saskatchewan.
Report. [Winnipeg] 1931. 45 p.

Commissioner/Commissaire: O.H. Burritt.

Loc.: MWHP, MWP

393 **Royal Commission to Inquire Into Charges Against Manitoba Pool Elevators Limited.**
Report; with which is printed the report of the auditor (omitting the schedules). Winnipeg: P. Purcell, King's Printer for the Province of Manitoba, 1931. 75 p.

Commissioner/Commissaire: E.K. Williams.

Loc.: MWP, MWU, OOAG, OOF, OONL, OOP, OTMCL, SRL, SSU

394 **1933-1934**

Commission Appointed to Investigate the Fishing Industry of Manitoba.
Report. Winnipeg, 1933-1934. 2 pts. (typescript)

Chairman/Président: H.C. Grant.

Commissioners/Commissaires: T.W. Laidlaw, J. McLenaghen, S. Sigfusson, R.A. Wardle.

Loc.: MWP, OOAG, OONL

395 **Royal Commission on Impairment of University of Manitoba Trust Funds 1932-1933.**
Report. [Winnipeg, 1933] 120 p. (typescript)

Chairman/Président: W.F.A. Turgeon.

Commissioners/Commissaires: W.C. Murray, C.G.K. Nourse.

Loc.: MWP

396 **1936**

The Land Drainage Arrangement Commission.
Report of The Land Drainage Arrangement Commission respecting municipalities containing land subject to levies under "The Land Drainage Act". Winnipeg, 1936. 67 p.

Chairman/Président: J.N. Finlayson.

Commissioners/Commissaires: J. Holland, J. Spalding.

Loc.: BVAU, MWP, OWU, OKQ, OOB, OOP

397 **1939**

Royal Commission on the Municipal Finances and Administration of the City of Winnipeg.
Report. Winnipeg: J.L. Cowie, King's Printer for Manitoba, 1939. xxiv, 567 p.

Chairman/Président: H.C. Goldenberg.

Commissioners/Commissaires: A.L. Crossin, J.T. Thorson.

Loc.: BVAU, MW, MWHP, MWP, MWU, OH, OKQ, OOA, OOB, OOCC, OOF, OONL, OOP, OTER, OTP, QMHE

398 **1940**

Commission Appointed to Enquire into the Matters Specified in Order-in-Council Dated the 15th Day of March, 1940, in Respect of the Police Force of the City of Winnipeg in Manitoba.
Report. [Winnipeg, 1940] 92 *l.* (typescript)

Chairman/Président: W.J. Donovan.

Commissioners/Commissaires: N.J. Black, A.S. McKechnie.

Loc.: MWP

399 **1945**

Manitoba Cancer Enquiry Commission.
Report. [Winnipeg] 1945. 18 p.

Chairman/Président: A. Savage.

Commissioners/Commissaires: W.L. Mann, A.F. Menzies, O.C. Trainor.

Loc.: BVA, MWHP, MWP, OKQ, OONL, OOP, QQL, SRL, SSUM

400 **1946**

The Commission on Investigation of Venereal Disease.
Report. [Winnipeg] 1946. 58 p.

Chairman/Président: I. Schultz.

Commissioners/Commissaires: J.C. Dryden, S.J. Farmer, S.W. Fox, C.E. Greenlay, W.A. Kardash, J.S. Poole, E. Prefontaine, E.J. Rutledge, J.R. Solomon, L. Stinson, D. Swailes, S.O. Thompson, G.S. Thorvaldson, E.F. Willis.

Also known as/Également connue sous le nom de: Venereal Disease Commission.

Loc.: MWHP, OONH, OOP, OTP, QQL, SRL

401 **1947**

Manitoba Royal Commission on Adult Education.
Report. Winnipeg: R.M. Fisher, Acting King's Printer for the Province of Manitoba, 1947. 170 p.

Chairman/Président: A.W. Trueman.

Members/Membres: J.J. Deutsch, J. Grierson, H.A. Innis, F. McKay.

Loc.: AEU, BVAU, MW, MWU, MWP, NSHPL, OH, OKQ, OLU, OOAG, OOCU, OOL, OONL, OOP, OOS, OPET, OTP, OTY, OWA, QMU, QQL, QQLA, SRL, SSU

402 **1948**

Manitoba Water Power Commission.
Report. Winnipeg: C.E. Leech, Printer to the King's Most Excellent Majesty, 1948. xi, 69 p.

Commissioner/Commissaire: T.H. Hogg.

Loc.: BVAU, BVIP, MWP, MWU, OKQ, OLU, OONL, OOP, OOS, QQL, SRL

403 **1949**

Royal Commission in Reference to Costs of Hospitalization.
Report. [Winnipeg, 1949] 6 *l.* (typescript)

Chairman/Président: E.A. McPherson.

Commissioners/Commissaires: A.L. Crossin, J. Spalding.

Loc.: MWP, OONL

404 **1955**

The Manitoba Crop Insurance Commission.
Interim report. [Winnipeg] 1955. 14 *l*. (typescript)

Loc.: MWP, OOAG, OONL, OOP

———.
Report. [Winnipeg] 1955. 87 p.

Chairman/Président: W.G. Malaher.

Commissioners/Commissaires: F.W. Crawford, R. Hedlin.

Loc.: BVA, MWA, MWP, OOAG, OOF, OONL, OOP, OTU, QQL, SRL

405 **Manitoba Liquor Enquiry Commission.**
Report. Winnipeg, 1955. 751 p.

Chairman/Président: J. Bracken.

Members/Membres: P. L'Heureux, C.A. McCrae, H.J. Riley, J.L. Whiteford.

Loc.: ACU, AE, BVA, BVAS, BVAU, MW, MWM, MWP, MWU, NFSM, NSHPL, OOAG, OOCI, OONL, OOP, OTCT, OTU, OTY, OWA, QMHE, QQL

406 **1958**

Commission to Inquire and Investigate Every Aspect of The Workmen's Compensation Act.
Report. [Winnipeg] R.S. Evans, Queen's Printer for Manitoba, 1958. iv, 107 p.

Commissioner/Commissaire: W.F.A. Turgeon.

Loc.: BVAS, BVAU, MWP, OKQL, OLU, OONL, OTYL

407 **1958-1959**

Manitoba Royal Commission on Education.
Interim report. [Winnipeg] 1958. 158 p. (typescript)

———.
Report. [Winnipeg] 1959. xxi, 284 p.

Chairman: R.O. MacFarlane.

Members/Membres: J.H. Bruns, J.A. Cuddy, S. Hansen, H. Wood.

Loc.: AEU, BVA, BVAU, MW, MWP, MWU, NSHPL, OKQ, OONL, OOP, OTER, OTLS, OTMCL, OTU, QQL, SRL, SSU

408 **The Natural Gas Distribution Enquiry Commission of Greater Winnipeg.**
Report. [Winnipeg, 1958] 75, 109 p. (typescript)

Chairman/Président: J.J. Deutsch.

Commissioners/Commissaires: E.F. Bole, S. Juba.

Loc.: AEU, BVA, BVAS, BVAU, BVIV, MWP, OKQ, OOAG, OOCC, OONL, OOP, OTP, OTU, OTY, QQL, SSU

409 **Royal Commission on Flood Cost Benefit.**
Report. Winnipeg, 1958. xii, 129 p.

Chairman/Président: H.W. Manning.

Commissioners/Commissaires: A.S. Beaubien, W.J. Macdonald, J. McDowell, W.C. Riley.

Loc.: AEU, BVA, BVAU, BVIV, MWA, MWP, MWU, OKQ, OOAG, OOF, OONL, OOP, OTYL, OWA

410 **1959**

The Greater Winnipeg Investigating Commission.
Report. Winnipeg: R.S. Evans, Queen's Printer for the Province of Manitoba, 1959. v. 1

Chairman/Président: J.L. Bodie.

Commissioners/Commissaires: J.G. Van Belleghem, T.B. Findlay, C.N. Kushner, G.E. Sharpe.

Loc.: ACU, BVAS, BVAU, BVIP, MW, MWP, MWU, OOP, OTYL, QQL

411 **The Mineral Transactions Inquiry Commission.**
Report. [Winnipeg] 1959. ix, 18 p.

Commissioner/Commissaire: W.E. Norton.

Loc.: BVAU, BVIV, MWP, NSHPL, OKQ, OOCC, OONL, OTY, OWA, QMML

412 **1960**

Margarine Enquiry Commission.
Report. [Winnipeg, 1960] 16 p.

Commissioner/Commissaire: W.J. Waines.

Loc.: BVAS, MWA, MWP, OONL, OTU, OTY, SRL

413 **1961**

The Brandon Packers Strike Commission.
Report. [Winnipeg] 1961. 95, vii p.

Commissioner/Commissaire: G.E. Tritschler.

Loc.: BVAS, BVAU, MW, MWU, OKQL, OOL, OONL, OTP, OTYL

414 **The Commission on Judicial Boundaries.**
Report. [Winnipeg] 1961. 27 p.

Chairman/Président: C.C. Miller.

Commissioners/Commissaires: J.C. Doak, H.G.H. Smith.

Loc.: BVAS, BVIV, MWP, OKQL, QMML, OONL

415 **1963**

Firearms Safety Inquiry.
Report. Winnipeg, 1963. 30 p.

Commissioner/Commissaire: J.W. Kimball.

Loc.: MWP

416 **1964**

Manitoba Royal Commission on Local Government Organization and Finance.
Report. Winnipeg: R.S. Evans, Queen's Printer for Manitoba, 1964. xlvii, 306 p.

Loc.: ACU, AEU, BVAS, BVAU, MW, MWA, MWHP, MWP, MWU, NFSM, NSHPL, OKQ, OOB, OOC, OOF, OONL, OOP, OOU, OPAL, OTCT, OTER, OTLS, OTU, OTYL, OWA, QMU, QQL, QQLA, SSU

―――――.
Final report. Winnipeg, 1964. 8 p.

Chairman/Président: R. Michener.

Members/Membres: D.L. Campbell, M.S. Donnelly, J.R. McInnes, J. Thompson.

Loc.: BVAS, MWP, OONL, OTU, OWA, QMU, QQL, QQLA, SSU

417 **The Metropolitan Corporation of Greater Winnipeg Review Commission.**
Report and recommendations. [Winnipeg] 1964. 33 *l.* (typescript)

Chairman/Président: L.R. Cumming.

Commissioners/Commissaires: G.S. Halter, R.H. Robbins.

Loc.: MWP, OKQ, OOCC, OONL, OOP, OTCT, OTYL, QSHERU, SRL

418 **1965**

The Tallin Commission on Real Property Mortgage Loan Transactions.
Report. [Winnipeg, 1965] 63 p.

Commissioner/Commissaire: G.P.R. Tallin.

Loc.: AEU, MWP, MWU, OOCI, OONL, OOP, OTLS, OTYL, SRL

419 **1966**

The Grand Rapids Water Haulage Inquiry Commission.
Report. [Winnipeg, 1966] 108 p.

Commissioner/Commissaire: G.E. Tritschler.

Loc.: AEU, BVA, BVAS, BVIV, MWP, OKQ, OLU, OONL, OTY, OWAL

420 **1966**

The Totogan Farms Limited Commission.
Report. [Winnipeg] 1966. 33 p.

Commissioner/Commissaire: R.G.B. Dickson.

Loc.: MWP

421 **1967**

Manitoba Vegetable Marketing Inquiry Commission.
Report. [Winnipeg] 1967. 114 p.

Commissioner/Commissaire: D.R. Baron.

Loc.: AEU, BVAS, MBC, MWA, MWP, MWU, OOAG, OONL, OOP, OWA, QSHERU

1968

Prairie Provinces Cost Study Commission.

see/voir

Alberta. Prairie Provinces Cost Study Commission.
(no. 666)

422 **1969**

Royal Commission Inquiry into Northern Transportation.
Report. [Winnipeg: R.S. Evans, Queen's Printer for the Province of Manitoba] 1969. 601 p.

Commissioner/Commissaire: A.V. Mauro.

Loc.: ACU, AEU, BVA, BVAS, BVAU, MW, MWP, MWU, NFSM, OKQ, OLU, OOB, OOCI, OOF, OON, OONL, OOP, OPAL, OSUL, OTCT, OTMCL, OTYL, OWAL, SRL, SSU

423 **1971**

    The Commission of Inquiry into Hospital Admissions.
Report. [Winnipeg] 1971. 86 p.

    Chairman/Président: J.M. Hunt.

    Commissioners/Commissaires: F.A. Ball, D.H. Crofford, J.C. Haworth, R.A. James, L.F. Kocsis.

    Loc.: AEU, BVAS, MWHP, MWP, NSHPL, OKQ, OLU, OONH, OONL, OOP, OTY, OWA, SRL, SSUM

424 **Manitoba Royal Commission on Brandon Boundaries.**
Report. Brandon, Man., 1971. xii, 106 p.

    Commissioner/Commissaire: A.L. Dulmage.

    Also known as/Également connue sous le nom de: Brandon Boundaries Commission.

    Loc.: AEU, BVA, BVAS, MWP, OONL, OOP, OTY

425 **1972**

    Commission of Inquiry Appointed to Inquire into and Report upon all Matters in any Way Contributing to or Connected with "Problem Metis Families, City of Brandon".
Report. Brandon, Man. [1972?] 160 *l*. (typescript)

    Commissioner/Commissaire: J. Toal.

    Loc.: MW, OWAL

426 **Taxicab Inquiry Commission.**
Report. [Winnipeg, 1972] 59 *l*. (typescript)

    Chairman/Président: H.L. Stevens.

    Members/Membres: F. Boothroyd, K. Chadwell.

    Loc.: BVAS, MWP, OGU, OKQ, OONL, OOP, OTY, OWA, OWAL, OWTU

427 **Commission of Inquiry into a Professional Boxing Card Held at the Winnipeg, Arena, in the City of Winnipeg, in Manitoba, on Monday, the 21st of February, 1972.**
Report. [Winnipeg, 1972] 133 p. (typescript)

Commissioner/Commissaire: B. Hewak.

Loc.: MWP, OONL, OWTU

428 **1973**

Commission of Inquiry into the Manufacture, Distribution and Pricing of Chemical Fertilizers in Manitoba.
Fertilizer marketing in Manitoba: report. [Winnipeg: R.S. Evans, Queen's Printer for the Province of Manitoba] 1973. various pagings

Commissioners/Commissaires: S.E. Brooks, J.H. Weijs.

Also known as/Également connue sous le nom de: Manitoba Fertilizer Marketing Inquiry.

Loc.: BVA, BVIV, NFSM, OOCI, OONL, OOP

429 **1974**

The Commission of Inquiry into The Pas Forestry and Industrial Complex at The Pas, Manitoba.
Report. [Winnipeg] 1974. 6 v.

Chairman/Président: C.R. Smith.

Commissioners/Commissaires: M.S. Donnelly, L. Mitchell.

Also known as/Également connue sous le nom de: The Pas Inquiry.

Loc.: BVA, BVAS, BVAU, MW, MWP, MWU, OKQL, OOC, OOCC, OOFF, OONL, OOP, OPAL, OTMCL, OTU, OTYL, OWTL, QMMSC, SSU

430 **1976**

Committee of Review, City of Winnipeg Act.
Report and recommendations. [Winnipeg] 1976. x, 162 p.

Chairman/Président: P. Taraska.

Members/Membres: E.A. Levin, A. O'Brien.

Loc.: ACU, AEU, BVAU, BVIV, MW, MWP, MWU, OONL, OOP, OTMCL, OTY

431 **1976**

Manitoba Livestock and Meat Commission.
Report of the enquiry into livestock marketing in Manitoba. [Winnipeg: Queen's Printer for the Province of Manitoba] 1976. 57 p.

Chairman/Président: A.W. Wood.

Commissioners/Commissaires: D.F. Pruden, R. Usick.

Loc.: ACU, AEU, BVAS, MWP, OOAG, OONL, OOP

432 **1977**

The Winnipeg Land Prices Inquiry Commission.
Report and recommendations. [Winnipeg] P.N. Crosbie, Queen's Printer for the Province of Manitoba, 1977. ix, 103 p.

Commissioner/Commissaire: R.C. Bellan.

Also known as/Également connue sous le nom de: Bellan Report.

Loc.: BVA, MW, MWP, OLU, OOCC, OONL, OOP, OTMCL, OWTU

433 **1979**

Commission of Inquiry into Manitoba Hydro.
Nelson-Churchill River Systems Hydro Inquiry: report. Winnipeg, 1979. 10 *l.* (typescript)

Loc.: OONL, OOP

———.
Final report. [Winnipeg] 1979. viii, 483 p.

Commissioner/Commissaire: G.E. Tritschler.

Loc.: MWU, OGU, OKQ, OON, OONL, OOP, OWA, OWTL, OWTU

434 **Manitoba Lotteries Review Committee.**
Final report. [Winnipeg] 1979. v, 256 p.

Commissioner/Commissaire: G.T. Haig.

Loc.: AEU, MW, MWP, NSHDL, OONL, OOP, OTU, SRL

435 **1982**

Commission of Inquiry into Surface Rights in Manitoba.
Report. [Winnipeg] 1982. ii, 93 p. (typescript)

Commissioner/Commissaire: R.A.L. Nugent.

Loc.: NSHDL, OONL, OOP, SRL

436 **1982**

Commission on Compulsory Retirement.
Report. [Winnipeg] 1982. vii, 322 *l.*

Commissioner/Commissaire: M.E. Rothstein.

Loc.: MWU, NSHDOL, OONL, OOP, SSU

BRITISH COLUMBIA/COLOMBIE-BRITANNIQUE

437 **1872**

Commission Appointed to Inquire into and Report upon a Deficiency Appearing in the Accounts of Warner Reeve Spalding-Manager of the Savings Bank Nanaimo.
Report. 1872. 2 p. (manuscript)

Commissioners/Commissaires: R. Ker, A.R. Robertson, F.J. Roscoe.

Loc.: BVIPA

438 **1875**

Royal Commission for Instituting Enquiries into the Acquisition of Texada Island.
Report. In British Columbia. Legislative Assembly. *Journals.* v. 4. 1st Parliament, 4th Session. Victoria: R. Wolfenden, Government Printer, 1875. p. 183-186. (Sessional papers)

Commissioners/Commissaires: M.B. Begbie, H.P.P. Crease, J.H. Gray.

Loc.: BVA, BVIP, OOA, OONL, OOP, OTMCL, OTU, SRL

439 **1878**

Royal Commission Appointed to Enquire into the Allegations Made by the Members for Kootenay Against the Hon. A.C. Elliott.
Report. In *The British Columbia Gazette*, v. 18, no. 46, November 16th, 1878. p. 306.

Commissioners/Commissaires: M.B. Begbie, H.P.P. Crease, J.H. Gray.

Also known as/Également connue sous le nom de: Kootenay Enquiry.

Loc.: ACU, BVIP, BVIV, NFSM, OONL, OOP

440 **1885**

Metlakatlah Inquiry, 1884.
Report. In British Columbia. Legislative Assembly. *Sessional papers.* 4th Parliament, 3rd Session. Victoria: R. Wolfenden, Government Printer, at the Government Printing Office, James Bay, 1885. p. 131 [i.e. 137]-136.

Commissioners/Commissaires: H.M. Ball, A.E.B. Davie, A.C. Elliott.

Also known as/Également connue sous le nom de: Metlakatlah Commission.

Loc.: BVA, BVAU, BVIP, BVIV, OLU, OOA, OONL, OOP, OTMCL, OTU, QMM, QQL, SRL

441 **1886**

Commission Appointed to Investigate the Claims of Dry Dock Creditors, with Names of Said Creditors, and the Amounts Paid to Each; also the Names of Those Whose Claims Were Rejected, and the Reason Assigned for Such Rejection.
Report. In British Columbia. Legislative Assembly. *Sessional papers.* 4th Parliament, 4th Session. Victoria: R. Wolfenden, Printer to Queen's Most Excellent Majesty, 1886. p. 445-448.

Commissioner/Commissaire: E. Johnson.

Loc.: BVA, BVAU, BVIP, BVIV, OLU, OOA, OONL, OOP, OPET, OTMCL, OTU, QMM, QQL, SRL

442 **Commission of Enquiry Concerning the Genuineness of an Alleged Transfer, Dated the 23rd of June, 1884, from Certain Indians to One J.M.M. Spinks.**
Report. In British Columbia. Legislative Assembly. *Sessional papers.* 4th Parliament, 4th Session. Victoria: R. Wolfenden, Printer to the Queen's Most Excellent Majesty, 1886. p. 217-223.

Commissioner/Commissaire: M.B. Begbie.

Also known as/Également connue sous le nom de: Coal Harbour Lands Commission.

Loc.: BVA, BVAU, BVIP, BVIV, OLU, OOA, OONL, OOP, OPET, OTMCL, OTU, QMM, QQL, SRL

443 **1888**

Commission on Conditions of Indians of the North-West Coast.
Report. In British Columbia. Legislative Assembly. *Sessional papers.* 5th Parliament, 2nd Session. Victoria: R. Wolfenden, Government Printer, at the Government Printing Office, James Bay, 1888. p. 415-425.

Commissioners/Commissaires: C.F. Cornwall, J.P. Planta.

Loc.: BVA, BVAU, BVIP, BVIV, NBFL, OLU, OOA, OONL, OOP, OPET, OTMCL, OTU, QMM, QQL, SRL

444 **1890**

Victoria Gaol Investigation.
Report. In British Columbia. Legislative Assembly. *Sessional papers*. 5th Parliament, 4th Session. Victoria: R. Wolfenden, Printer to the Queen's Most Excellent Majesty, 1890. p. 463.

Commissioner/Commissaire: M.W.T. Drake.

Loc.: BVA, BVAU, BVIP, BVIV, OLU, OOA, OONL, OOP, OPET, OTMCL, OTU, OWTU, QMM, QQL, SRL, SSU

445 **1892**

Commission Appointed to Enquire into Certain Charges Against Isaac H. Hallett, Esq., a Stipendiary Magistrate for the County of Westminster.
Report. In British Columbia. Legislative Assembly. *Sessional papers*. 6th Parliament, 2nd Session. Victoria: R. Wolfenden, Printer to the Queen's Most Excellent Majesty, 1892. p. 691-694.

Commissioner/Commissaire: H.P.P. Crease.

Loc.: BVA, BVAU, BVIP, BVIV, OOA, OONL, OOP, OTMCL, OTU, QMM, QQL, SRL, SSU

446 **Commission to Enquire into the Conduct of the Police Magistrate at Victoria.**
Report. In British Columbia. Legislative Assembly. *Sessional papers*. 6th Parliament, 2nd Session. Victoria: R. Wolfenden, Printer to the Queen's Most Excellent Majesty, 1892. p. 265-272.

Commissioner/Commissaire: H.P.P. Crease.

Loc.: BVA, BVAU, BVIP, BVIV, OOA, OONL, OOP, OTMCL, OTU, QMM, QQL, SRL, SSU

447 **Royal Commission in the Matter of an Inquiry in the Conduct of the Affairs of the Municipal Council of Victoria.**
Report. In British Columbia. Legislative Assembly. *Sessional papers*. 6th Parliament, 2nd Session. Victoria: R. Wolfenden, Printer to the Queen's Most Excellent Majesty, 1892. p. 481-512.

Commissioners/Commissaires: M.B. Begbie, M.W.T. Drake.

Loc.: BVA, BVAU, BVIP, BVIV, OOA, OONL, OOP, OTMCL, OTU, QMM, QQL, SRL, SSU

448 **1893**

Commission Appointed to Inquire into the Late Epidemic Outbreak of Small-Pox in the Province of British Columbia.
Report. In British Columbia. Legislative Assembly. *Sessional papers.* 6th Parliament, 3rd Session. Victoria: R. Wolfenden, Printer to the King's Most Excellent Majesty, 1893. p. 507-518.

Commissioners/Commissaires: M.B. Begbie, E.A. Praeger.

Loc.: BVA, BVAU, BVIP, BVIV, OOA, OONL, OOP, OTU, QMM, QQL, SRL, SSU

449 **1894**

Royal Commission Appointed to Inquire into Certain Matters Concerning the Nakusp and Slocan Railway.
Report. In *The British Columbia Gazette*, v. 34, no. 20, May 17th, 1894. p. 430-431.

Commissioners/Commissaires: M.B. Begbie, G.W. Burbidge.

Loc.: ACU, BNND, BVAU, BVIP, BVIV, MWP, NFSM, OONL, OOP, OOSC

450 **1895**

Commission Appointed to Enquire into Certain Charges Against Mr. J.P. Planta, Police Magistrate of the City of Nanaimo and into His General Conduct as a Police Magistrate.
Report. 1895. 20 p. (typescript)

Commissioner/Commissaire: E. Harrison.

Loc.: BVIPA

451 **Commission Appointed to Enquire into Certain Matters Connected with the Provincial Lunatic Asylum at New Westminster.**
Report. In British Columbia. Legislative Assembly. *Sessional papers.* 7th Parliament, 1st Session. Victoria: R. Wolfenden, Printer to the Queen's Most Excellent Majesty, 1895. p. 503-513.

Chairman/Président: E.F. Hansell.

Commissioner/Commissaire: C.F. Newcombe.

Also known as/Également connue sous le nom de: Royal Commission, Asylum for the Insane.

Loc.: BVA, BVAU, BVIP, BVIV, OOA, OONL, OOP, OTMCL, OTU, QMM, QQL, SRL, SSU

452 **Royal Commission on Charges Preferred Against Captain N. Fitzstubbs.**
Report. In British Columbia. Legislative Assembly. *Sessional papers.* 7th Parliament, 1st Session. Victoria: R. Wolfenden, Printer to the Queen's Most Excellent Majesty, 1895. p. 497-498.

Commissioner/Commissaire: H.P.P. Crease.

Loc.: BVA, BVAU, BVIP, BVIV, OOA, OONL, OOP, OTMCL, OTU, QMM, QQL, SRL, SSU

453 **1898**

Commission Appointed to Hold an Enquiry for the Purpose of Ascertaining the Truth of Matter Alleged in a Letter from Mrs. Harry Thompson Regarding the Conduct of Warden Armstrong or Guard Calbick of the Provincial Gaol at New Westminster.
Report. 1898. 5 p. (typescript)

Commissioner/Commissaire: E. Harrison, Jr.

Loc.: BVIPA

454 **Commission Appointed to Hold an Inquiry into Matters Affecting the Provincial Gaol, Kamloops.**
Report. 1898. 4 p. (typescript)

Commissioner/Commissaire: A.E. Beck.

Loc.: BVIPA

455 **Commission in the Matter of the "Public Inquiries Act" and of an Investigation under the Said Act as to the Truth of Certain Allegations of Mal-administration in the Department of Lands and Works.**
Report. 1898. 2 p. (typescript)

Commissioner/Commissaire: G.A. Walkem.

Loc.: BVIPA

456 **1899**

Commission of Enquiry into the Management of the Fire and Water Departments of the Corporation of the City of New Westminster, more Especially with Reference to the Fire which Occurred on the Night of the 10th, and the Morning of the 11th, of September 1898.
Report. Nanaimo, B.C., 1899. 15 *l*. (typescript)

Commissioner/Commissaire: E. Harrison.

Loc.: BVIP, OONL

457 **Royal Commission, re Parliament Buildings.**
Report. In British Columbia. Legislative Assembly. *Sessional papers.* 8th Parliament, 1st Session. Victoria: R. Wolfenden, Printer to the Queen's Most Excellent Majesty, 1899. p. 1351-1354.

Commissioner/Commissaire: A.J. McColl.

Also known as/Également connue sous le nom de: Commission re Parliament Buildings Contract.

Loc.: ACU, BNND, BVA, BVAU, BVIP, BVIV, NSHL, OOA, OONL, OOP, OPET, OTMCL, OTU, QMM, QQL, SRL, SSU

458 **1900**

Special Commission under the Provisions of the "Bennett-Atlin Commission Act, 1899", and the "Public Inquiries Act".
Report. In British Columbia. Legislative Assembly. *Sessional papers.* 9th Parliament, 1st Session. Victoria: R. Wolfenden, Printer to the Queen's Most Excellent Majesty, 1900. p. 495-496.

Commissioner/Commissaire: P.A. Irving.

Also known as/Également connue sous le nom de: Bennett-Atlin Commission.

Loc.: ACU, BNND, BVA, BVAU, BVIP, BVIV, NSHL, OOA, OONL, OOP, OPET, OTMCL, OTU, OWTU, QMM, QQL, SRL, SSU

459 **1901**

Commission Appointed to Inquire into and Concerning all Matters Connected with the General Administration of the Hospital for the Insane at New Westminster.
Report. In British Columbia. Legislative Assembly. *Sessional papers*. 9th Parliament, 2nd Session. Victoria: R. Wolfenden, Printer to the King's Most Excellent Majesty, 1901. p. 229-235.

Commissioner/Commissaire: C.K. Clarke.

Loc.: ACU, BNND, BVAU, BVIP, BVIV, NSHL, OLU, OOA, OONL, OOP, OPET, OTMCL, OTU, QMM, QQL, SRL, SSU

460 **Commission Appointed to Inquire into the Grievances of the Settlers within the Tract of Lands Granted to the Esquimalt and Nanaimo Railway Company.**
Report. In British Columbia. Legislative Assembly. *Sessional papers*. 9th Parliament, 3rd Session. Victoria: R. Wolfenden Printer to the King's Most Excellent Majesty, 1901. p. 337-368.

Commissioner/Commissaire: E. Harrison.

Also known as/Également connue sous le nom de: Inquiry into Grievances of Settlers, E. & N. Railway Lands.

Loc.: ACU, BNND, BVAU, BVIP, BVIV, NSHL, OLU, OOA, OONL, OOP, OPET, OTMCL, OTU, QMM, QQL, SRL, SSU

461 **Commission to Enquire into the Conduct of Affairs at the Provincial Gaol at New Westminster.**
Report. 1901. 29 p. (typescript)

Commissioner/Commissaire: E. Harrison, Jr.

Loc.: BVIPA

462 **Porcupine-Chilkat Districts.**
Report under the Porcupine District Commission Act, 1900, by the Honourable Archer Martin, Special Commissioner with observations on the P. and C. Districts. Victoria: R. Wolfenden, Printer to the King's Most Excellent Majesty, 1901. 13 p.

Commissioner/Commissaire: A. Martin.

Loc.: BVAU, BVIP, OONL, OOU

463 **1903**

Commission to Inquire into the Administration of the "Liquor Licence Act, 1900", in the Fort Steele Licence District in East Kootenay.
Report. In British Columbia. Legislative Assembly. *Sessional papers.*
9th Parliament, 4th Session. Victoria: R. Wolfenden, Printer to the King's Most Excellent Majesty, 1903. p. J27.

Commissioner/Commissaire: W.H. Bullock-Webster.

Loc.: ACU, BNND, BVA, BVAS, BVAU, BVIP, BVIV, NBFL, NSHL, OOA, OONL, OOP, OTMCL, OTU, QMM, QQL, SRL, SSU

464 **Special Commission Appointed to Inquire into the Causes of Explosion in Coal Mines.**
Report. In British Columbia. Legislative Assembly. *Sessional papers.*
9th Parliament, 4th Session. Victoria: R. Wolfenden, Printer to the King's Most Excellent Majesty, 1903. p. J9-J16.

Commissioners/Commissaires: T. Boyce, J. Bryden, P.S. Lampman.

Also known as/Également connue sous le nom de: Commission on Coal Mines Explosions.

Loc.: ACU, BNND, BVA, BVAS, BVAU, BVIP, BVIV, NBFL, NSHL, OOA, OONL, OOP, OTMCL, OTU, QMM, QQL, SRL, SSU

465 **1904**

Commission in the Matter of the Conduct of Archibald Dick as Inspector of Mines.
Report. 1904. 1 p. (typescript)

Commissioner/Commissaire: W.W. Spinks.

Loc.: BVIPA

466 **Commission to Make Inquiry into all Matters Concerning the Management of the Provincial Home at Kamloops, B.C.**
Report. In British Columbia. Legislative Assembly. *Sessional papers.*
10th Parliament, 1st Session. Victoria: R. Wolfenden, Printer to the King's Most Excellent Majesty, 1904. p. G35-G37.

Commissioner/Commissaire: S.A. Fletcher.

Also known as/Également connue sous le nom de: Provincial Home Inquiry.

Loc.: ACU, BNND, BVA, BVAS, BVAU, BVIP, BVIV, NBFL, NSHL, OOA, OONL, OOP, OTMCL, OTU, QMM, QQL, SRL, SSU

467 **Special Commission to Inquire into the Administration of Justice in the City of Phoenix, the Discharge of Duties Devolving on the Police Magistrate, and the Police and Licence Commissioners of that City.**
Report. 1904. 13 p. (typescript)

Commissioner/Commissaire: H.A. Maclean.

Loc.: BVIPA

468 **1905**

Commission for the Purpose of Inquiring into and Reporting upon the Operation of the "Assessment Act, 1903", with respect to its Practical Bearings on the Financial Requirements of the Province.
Report. In British Columbia. Legislative Assembly. *Sessional papers.* 10th Parliament, 2nd Session. Victoria: R. Wolfenden, Printer to King's Most Excellent Majesty, 1905. p. F27-F30.

Commissioners/Commissaires: J. Buntzen, F. Carter-Cotton, D.R. Ker, R.G. Tatlow.

Loc.: ACU, BNND, BVA, BVAU, BVIP, BVIV, NBFL, NSHL, OOA, OONL, OOP, OTU, QMM, QQL, SRL, SSU

469 **Commission in the Matter of the Union Club, the Elks Club, Eureka Club, Chess Club, Playgoers Club and the Railway Porters Club.**
Report. 1905. 11 p. (typescript)

Commissioner/Commissaire: H.A. Maclean.

Loc.: BVIPA

470 **Commission on the Inquiry into the Conduct of Hugh Hunter in his Capacity as an Officer of the Provincial Government.**
Report. 1905. 2 p. (typescript)

Commissioner/Commissaire: R.F. Tolmie.

Loc.: BVIPA

471 **1906**

Commission Concerning the Action of the Department of Lands and Works in Connection with the Notice Dated September 22nd, 1905, Inviting Tenders for the Purchase of Government Property, Situated at Laurel Point, Victoria Harbour, Known as Lot 570B, Victoria City.
Report. 1906. 11 p. (typescript)

Commissioner/Commissaire: F. Peters.

Also known as/Également connue sous le nom de: Pendray Commission.

Loc.: BVIPA

472 **Commission re South Park School Drawing Books.**
Report. 1906. 33 p. (typescript)

Commissioner/Commissaire: P.S. Lampman.

Loc.: BVIPA

473 **1907**

Commission to Inquire into the Standing of the Liquor Licence Granted to (James) Hill, One of the Proprietors of the Cecil Hotel in the City of Ladysmith, B.C., and into the Conduct of the Licence Commissioners for the City of Ladysmith or Any of Those in Connection with the Said Licence.
Report. Victoria, 1907. 5 *l.* (typescript)

Commissioner/Commissaire: W.C. Moresby.

Loc.: BVIP, OONL

474 **1908**

Commission to Inquire into the Irrigation of Land in the Province of British Columbia.
Report. In British Columbia. Legislative Assembly. *Sessional papers.* 11th Parliament, 2nd Session. Victoria: R. Wolfenden, Printer to the King's Most Excellent Majesty, 1908. p. D1-D13.

Chairman/Président: F.J. Fulton.

Commissioner/Commissaire: L.G. Carpenter.

Also known as/Également connue sous le nom de: Irrigation Commission.

Loc.: BNND, BVA, BVAS, BVAU, BVIP, BVIV, NBFL, NSHL, OOA, OONL, OOP, OTU, QMM, QQL, SRL

475 **1908**

Commission to Make an Enquiry into the Claims of Certain Persons Who Had Entered upon the Crown Lands in the district of, Kootenay, under Reserve for Reclamation Purposes, with a View to Effecting an Adjustment of such Claims.
Report. Victoria, 1908. 4 *l.* (typescript)

Commissioner/Commissaire: W.F. Teetzel.

Loc.: BVIP, OONL

476 **1910**

Commission to Enquire into all Actions of the Commissioners of Police for the City of Victoria for the Year 1910, in Connection with Their Public Duties.
Report. 1910. 13 p. (typescript)

Commissioner/Commissaire: P.S. Lampman.

Loc.: BVIPA

477 **Royal Commission of Inquiry on Timber and Forestry.**
Final report. Victoria: R. Wolfenden, Printer to the King's Most Excellent Majesty, 1910. 116 p.

Chairman/Président: F.J. Fulton.

Commissioners/Commissaires: A.C. Flumerfelt, A.S. Goodeve.

Loc.: BVAS, BVAU, BVIV, OKQ, OLU, OOAG, OOG, OONL, OOP

478 **1911**

Commission to Select a Site for the University of British Columbia.
Report. In British Columbia. Legislative Assembly. *Sessional papers.* 12th Parliament, 2nd Session. Victoria: R. Wolfenden, Printer to the King's Most Excellent Majesty, 1911. p. M13-M14.

Commissioners/Commissaires: G. Dauth, C.C. Jones, W.C. Murray, O.D. Skelton, R.C. Weldon.

Also known as/Également connue sous le nom de: University Site Commission.

Loc.: BNND, BVA, BVAU, BVIP, BVIV, NSHL, OOA, OONL, OOP, OPET, OTU, QMM, QQL, SRL, SSU

479 **Fire Insurance Commission.**
Report. In British Columbia. Legislative Assembly. *Sessional papers.* 12th Parliament, 2nd Session. Victoria: R. Wolfenden, Printer to the King's Most Excellent Majesty, 1911. p. B1-B49.

Chairman/Président: R.S. Lennie.

Commissioners/Commissaires: A.B. Erskine, D.H. Macdowall.

Loc.: BNND, BVA, BVAU, BVIP, BVIV, NSHL, OOA, OONL, OOP, OPET, OTU, QMM, QQL, SRL, SSU

480 **1912**

Commission Appointed for the Purpose of Inquiring into all Questions Relating to the Proposed Incorporation into a City Municipality under the Name of the City of Alberni of Certain Parcels of Land Situate in the Alberni District, Vancouver Island.
Report. 1912. 8 p. (typescript)

Commissioner/Commissaire: T. Fell.

Loc.: BVIPA

481 **Commission re Vancouver General Hospital.**
Report. 1912. 92 p. (typescript)

Commissioner/Commissaire: R.W. Hannington.

Loc.: BVIPA

482 **1912**

Royal Commission on Municipal Government, 1912.
Report. Victoria: W.H. Cullin, Printer to the King's Most Excellent Majesty, 1912. 18 p.

Chairman/Président: W.H. Keary.

Commissioners/Commissaires: A.E. Bull, H.A. Maclean.

Loc.: BVAU, OON, OTYL

483 **Royal Commission on Taxation.**
Synopsis of report and full report. Victoria: W.H. Cullin, Printer to the King's Most Excellent Majesty, 1912. 38 p.

Chairman/Président: P. Ellison.

Commissioners/Commissaires: C.H. Lugrin, A.E. McPhillips, W.H. Malkin.

Loc.: BVAS, BVAU, MWU, OOAG, OONL, OTP, OTYL, SSU

484 **1913**

Commission re Board of School Trustees of the City of Nelson.
Report. 1913. 14 p. (typescript)

Commissioner/Commissaire: P.S. Lampman.

Loc.: BNND, BVIPA

485 **Royal Commission into the Administration of School Affairs in the District of South Vancouver, and Municipal Investigation.**
Report. Vancouver, 1913. 19 *l.* (typescript)

Commissioner/Commissaire: W.J. Crehan.

Loc.: BVIP, OONL

486 **Royal Commission on Matters Relating to the Sect of Doukhobors in the Province of British Columbia.**
Report. Victoria: W.H. Cullin, Printer to the King's Most Excellent Majesty, 1913. 66 p.

Commissioner/Commissaire: W. Blakemore.

Loc.: ACG, AE, BVAU, BVI, BVIPA, OONL

487 **Royal Commission on Milk-Supply in British Columbia.**
Report. Victoria: W.H. Cullin, Printer to the King's Most Excellent Majesty, 1913. 29 p.

Chairman/Président: A.P. Procter.

Commissioners/Commissaires: F.J. Coulthard, A. Knight.

Loc.: BNND, BVA, BVAS, BVAU, BVIP, BVIV, NBFL, NSHL, OONL, OOP, QMM, QQL, SRL, SSU

488 **1914**

Commission for the Purposes of Inquiring Fully into all Matters Affecting the Values of Lands Forming Part of the Former Songhees Reserve and Apportioned to the Esquimalt and Nanaimo Railway Company and the Canadian Northern Railway Company for the Purpose of the Said Railways.
Report. 1914. 6 p. (typescript)

Commissioner/Commissaire: F.W. Howay.

Loc.: BVIPA

489 **Commission re Timber Lease of Lot 439, Group 2, New Westminster District.**
Report. Victoria, 1914. 7 *l.* (typescript)

Commissioner/Commissaire: F.W. Howay.

Loc.: BVIP, OONL

490 **Commission to Inquire into all Matters in Connection with the Application for the Incorporation under the "Municipalities Incorporation Act" of Certain Lands Situated in Comox District, in the County of Nanaimo, to be Known as Courtenay, B.C.**
Report. 1914. 3 p. (typescript)

Commissioner/Commissaire: H.E.A. Robertson.

Loc.: BVIPA

491 **Commission to Enquire into all Matters in Connection with the Proposed Severance of Shaughnessy Heights from the Municipality of Point Grey and its Incorporation as a Separate Municipality and any other Matter that May Be Included in or Relevant to the Bill Intituled An Act to Incorporate Shaughnessy Municipality now before the Legislative Assembly of British Columbia.**
Report. [Victoria, 1914] 29 *l.* (typescript)

Commissioner/Commissaire: H.W.R. Moore.

Also known as/Également connue sous le nom de: Point Grey Commission or Shaughnessy Heights Investigation.

Loc.: BVIP, OONL

492 **Inquiry into the Affairs of the Present Board and Past Boards of School Trustees of the City of Vancouver.**
Report. [1914] 15 p. (typescript)

Commissioner/Commissaire: H.O. Alexander.

Loc.: BVIPA

493 **Royal Commission on Agriculture.**
Full report. Victoria: W.H. Cullin, Printer to the King's Most Excellent Majesty, 1914. ix, 398 p.

Chairman/Président: W.H. Hayward.

Commissioners/Commissaires: J.J. Campbell, W. Duncan, J. Kidston, A. Lucas, S. Shannon.

Loc.: BVA, BVAS, BVAU, BVI, OOAG, OONL, OOP, OTNY, SSU

494 **Royal Commission on Labour.**
Report. Victoria: W.H. Cullin, Printer to King's Most Excellent Majesty, 1914. v, 28 p.

Chairman/Président: H.G. Parson.

Commissioners/Commissaires: A.M. Harper, J. Jardine, J.A. MacKelvie, R.A. Stoney.

Loc.: BVA, BVAS, BVAU, BVIP, BVIV, OOL, OONL, OOP, OTYL

495 **Royal Commission Re Coal in British Columbia.**
Report. Victoria: W.H. Cullin, Printer to the King's Most Excellent Majesty, 1914. 30 p.

Commissioner/Commissaire: W.E. Burns.

Loc.: BNND, BVA, BVAU, BVIP, BVIV, NSHL, OONL, OOP, QQL, SRL, SSU

496 **1915**

Commission on Explosion in B. North Mine, Coal Creek.
Report. 1915. 9 p. (typescript)

Commissioner/Commissaire: J. Stewart.

Loc.: BVIPA

497 **Electoral Redistribution Commission.**
Reports. [Vancouver, 1915] various pagings (typescript)

Commissioners/Commissaires: W.A. MacDonald, A. Morrison.

Loc.: BVIP, OONL

498 **Inquiry into the Cause of and Responsibility for the Accident which Occurred on the 9th February, 1915, in the No. 1 Slope of the South Wellington Coal Mines.**
Report. 1915. 48 p. (typescript)

Commissioner/Commissaire: D. Murphy.

Loc.: BVIPA

499 **1916**

Commission to Inquire into the Sale by Public Auction in November 1909 of the Lands Specified in the Minute.
Report. 1916. 57 p. (typescript)

Commissioner/Commissaire: R.W. Harris.

Loc.: BVIPA

500 **Returned Soldiers Aid Commission.**
Report. Victoria: W.H. Cullin, Printer to the King's Most Excellent Majesty, 1916. 15 p.

Chairman/Président: H.E. Young.

Members/Membres: A.C. Burdick, R.H. Gale, A.W. Gray, E.W. Hamber, A.E. Planta, A. Stewart.

Loc.: BVAU, BVIP, BVIV, OONL

501 **1917**

Commission Appointed for the Purpose of Making Certain Inquiries Regarding the By-Election Held in the City of Vancouver, B.C. on the 26th of February 1916.
Report. In *Victoria Daily Times*, Saturday, August 18, 1917, p. 14.

Chairman/Président: W.A. Galliher.

Commissioners/Commissaires: W.A. Macdonald, D. Murphy.

Loc.: BVAS, BVAU, BVIP, OONL

502 **Commission Appointed to Investigate the Overseas Vote in Connection with the British Columbia Prohibition Act.**
Report. [Victoria: W.H. Cullin, Printer to the King's Most Excellent Majesty, 1917] 6 p.

Chairman/Président: D. Whiteside.

Commissioners/Commissaires: C.F. Nelson, F.A. Pauline.

Loc.: BVIP, OONL

503 **Commission in the Matter of the Fort George Election Inquiry Act and in the Matter of an Investigation and Inquiry under the Said Act.**
Report. [Victoria? 1917] 43 *l.* (typescript)

Commissioner/Commissaire: F.M. Young.

Loc.: BVIP, OONL

504 **Commission Investigating the Economic Conditions and Operations of The British Columbia Electric Railway Company and Subsidiary Companies.**
Report. [Vancouver: British Columbia Electric Railway Company] 1917? 61 p.

Commissioner/Commissaire: A. Shortt.

Loc.: BVAU, BVIP, BVIPA, BVIV, OKQ, OONL, OTMCL, OTP

505 **Commission to Enquire into the Charge Made by the Sixth Member for the City of Vancouver in the Legislative Assembly on the 17th Day of April, 1917, John Sedgwick Cowper Did Charge "that the Sum of $25,000 Was Placed in the Safe of the Hotel Vancouver by, or on Behalf of the Canadian Northern Railway on the Night of the 13th of September Last, and that the Same Money Was Received or Taken Away the Next Morning by a Person Who Was a Liberal Candidate at the By-election of February 26, 1916, and also at the General Election of September 14, 1916".**
Report. [Victoria] 1917. 5 *l.* (typescript)

Commissioner/Commissaire: F.B. Gregory.

Loc.: BVIPA, OONL

506 **1919**

Commission to Inquire into all Claims for Compensation for Injury, Either to Person or Property, Arising out of and in the Course of the Riots or Disorders which Occurred During the Coal-Miners' Strike on Vancouver Island in the Years 1913 and 1914.
Report. In British Columbia. Legislative Assembly. *Sessional papers.* v. 1. 14th Parliament, 3rd Session. Victoria: W.H. Cullin, Printer to King's Most Excellent Majesty, 1919. p. F1-F15.

Commissioner/Commissaire: F.B. Gregory.

Also known as/Également connue sous le nom de: Commission on Vancouver Island Riots, 1913-1914.

Loc.: BVA, BVAS, BVAU, BVIP, BVIV, NSHL, OONL, OOP, QMM, QQL, SRL, SSU

507 **1920**

Commission on Health Insurance.
Report on mother's pensions. Victoria: W.H. Cullin, Printer to the King's Most Excellent Majesty, 1920. 16 p.

Chairman/Président: E.S.H. Winn.

Commissioners/Commissaires: T.B. Green, D. McCallum, C. Spofford.

Loc.: BVAS, BVAU, BVIP, OOIN, OONL, OOP, OTU

508 **Commission to Enquire into the Question of Compensation in Respect of Losses Alleged to Have Been Sustained by Persons, Firms and Corporations by Reason of the Operation of the British Columbia Prohibition Act.**
Report. Vancouver, 1920. 2 *l.* (typescript)

Commissioner/Commissaire: A. Morrison.

Loc.: BVIP, OONL

509 **1921**

Coal Commission.
Report. 1921. 20 p. (typescript)

Commissioner/Commissaire: A. Henderson.

Loc.: BVIPA

510 **Commission to Enquire as to the Laws Relating to the Subject of Maternity Insurance in Force in other Countries.**
Report. Vancouver, 1921. 22 *l.* (typescript)

Commissioners/Commissaires: T.B. Green, E.S.H. Winn.

Also known as/Également connue sous le nom de: Commission on Maternity Insurance, 1921.

Loc.: BVIP, OONL

511 **Commission to Enquire as to the Laws Relating to the Subjects of Mothers' Pensions, Maternity Insurance, Health Insurance and Public Health Nursing, which Are in Force in other Countries.**
Report. Vancouver, 1921. 108 *l.* (typescript)

Chairman/Président: E.S.H. Winn.

Commissioners/Commissaires: T.B. Green, D. McCullum, C. Spofford.

Also known as/Également connue sous le nom de: Health Insurance Commission.

Loc.: BVIP

512 **1922**

Royal Commission re Albert Richard Baker, Chairman of Game Conservation Board.
Report. In British Columbia. Legislative Assembly. *Sessional papers.* v. 2. 15th Parliament, 2nd Session. Victoria: W.H. Cullin, Printer to the King's Most Excellent Majesty, 1922. p. V17-V21.

Commissioner/Commissaire: H.C. Shaw.

Loc.: BVA, BVAS, BVAU, BVIP, BVIV, OONL, OOP, QMM, QQL, SRL, SSU

513 **1924**

Commission re the Pacific Great Eastern Railway.
Report. In British Columbia. Legislative Assembly. *Sessional papers.* v. 2. 16th Parliament, 1st Session. Victoria: C.F. Banfield, Printer to the King's Most Excellent Majesty, 1924. p. M4-M21.

Commissioner/Commissaire: W.A. Galliher.

Also known as/Également connue sous le nom de: Royal Commission on Pacific Great Eastern Railway.

Loc.: BVA, BVAU, BVIP, BVIV, NSHL, OONL, OOP, QMM, QQL, SRL, SSU

514 **1927**

Commission re Allegations of Frank Carlow.
Report. [Victoria] 1927. 15 *l.* (typescript)

Commissioner/Commissaire: A. Morrison.

Loc.: BVIPA, OONL

515 **Commission under the United Church of Canada Act.**
Report. 1927. 11 p.

Commissioners/Commissaires: W.L. Clay, W.W. Fraser, J.S. Henderson, T. Humphries, R.G. MacBeth, E. McGougan, W.H. MacInnes, A.E. Mitchell, J.G. Robson, G.A. Wilson.

Loc.: BVIPA

516 **1927-1928**

Royal Commission on Mental Hygiene.
Report. Victoria: C.F. Banfield, Printer to the King's Most Excellent Majesty, 1927. 54 p.

Loc.: BVAS, BVIP, BVIV, OOA, QQL

———.
Final report. Victoria: C.F. Banfield, Printer to the King's Most Excellent Majesty, 1928, 20 p.

Chairman/Président: P.P. Harrison.

Commissioners/Commissaires: R. Hayward, W.A. McKenzie, V.W. Odlum.

Loc.: BVA, BVAU, BVIP, QQA, SRL

517 **Royal Commission re Campaign Funds.**
Findings. [Vancouver, 1927] 10 *l.* (typescript)

Commissioners/Commissaires: J.S. Henderson, W.H. Malkin, A. Morrison.

Loc.: BVIP, OONL

518 **Royal Commission to Inquire into the Truth of Certain Allegations Contained in a Declaration Made by One John A. Gauthier, Sworn in Seattle, Washington, U.S.A., on the 11th Day of February, 1927.**
Interim and final reports. Victoria, 1927. 17 *l.* (typescript)

Commissioner/Commissaire: A. Morrison.

Loc.: BVIP, OONL

519 **1928**

Commission on the Economic Conditions in Certain Irrigation Districts in the Province.
Report. Victoria: C.F. Banfield, Printer to the King's Most Excellent Majesty, 1928. 107 p.

Commissioner/Commissaire: W.G. Swan.

Loc.: BVAS, BVIP, OONL

520 **1929**

Kelowna Police Enquiry.
Report. Victoria, 1929. 11 *l.* (typescript)

Commissioner/Commissaire: L. Crease.

Loc.: BVIP, OONL

521 **Milk Inquiry Commission, 1928.**
Report. Victoria: C.F. Banfield, Printer to the King's Most Excellent Majesty, 1929. 112 p.

Chairman/Président: F.M. Clement.

Commissioners/Commissaires: G.E. Hancox, H.W. Hill.

Loc.: BVA, BVAU, OLU, OOAG, OONL, OOP, OTU

522 **Royal Commission Appointed to Inquire into Certain Allegations Against John L. Barge, of Queen Charlotte City, Province of British Columbia.**
Report. 1929. 1 p. (typescript)

Commissioner/Commissaire: W.E. Fisher.

Loc.: BVIPA

523 **Royal Commission re Saanich Secession.**
Report. 1929. 15 p. (typescript)

Commissioner/Commissaire: P.S. Lampman.

Loc.: BVIPA

524 **Sumas Dyking District Relief Commission.**
Final report. New Westminster, B.C., 1929. 6 *l.* (typescript)

Chairman/Président: B. Dixon.

Commissioners/Commissaires: W.L. Macken, D. Whiteside.

Loc.: BVIP, OONL

525 **1930-1932**

Royal Commission on State Health Insurance and Maternity Benefits.
Progress report. Victoria: C.F. Banfield, Printer to the King's Most Excellent Majesty, 1930. 30 p.

———.
Final report. Victoria: C.F. Banfield, Printer to the King's Most Excellent Majesty, 1932. 63 p.

Chairman/Président: C.F. Davie.

Commissioners/Commissaires: L.E. Borden, J.J. Gillis, W.F. Kennedy, G.S. Pearson.

Also known as/Également connue sous le nom de: State Health Insurance and Maternity Benefits Commission.

Loc.: BVA, BVAS, BVAU, BVIP, OOAG, OOIN, OONH, OOP

526 **1930-1931**

Royal Commission Investigating the Fruit Industry (and Interrelated Conditions) of the Districts Territorially Known as the Okanagan, Kootenay, and Kettle River of the Province of British Columbia.
Report. Victoria: C.F. Banfield, Printer to the King's Most Excellent Majesty, 1930-1931. 2 v.

Commissioner/Commissaire: W.S. Evans.

Loc.: BVA, BVAU, BVAS, BVIP, BVIV, OOAG, OONL, OTY

527 **1931**

Royal Commission re Mount Douglas Park.
Report. 1931. 7 p. (typescript)

Commissioner/Commissaire: O.C. Bass.

Loc.: BVIPA

528 **1932**

Royal Commission on Chiropractic and Drugless Healing.
Report. Victoria: C.F. Banfield, Printer to King's Most Excellent Majesty, 1932. 11 p.

Commissioner/Commissaire: D. Murphy.

Loc.: BVAU, BVIP, BVAU, OONL

529 **1934**

The Municipal Taxation Commission.
Report. Vancouver, 1934. 90 p. (typescript)

Chairman/Président: A.M. Harper.

Commissioner/Commissaire: A.D. Paterson.

Loc.: BVA, BVAS, BVAU, BVIP, OOAG, OOB, OONL, OTYL, SRL

530 **1937-1938**

Coal and Petroleum Products Commission.
The petroleum industry. Victoria: C.F. Banfield, Printer to the King's Most Excellent Majesty, 1937. xxvi, 332 p. (Report of the Coal and Petroleum Products Commission; v. 1)

———.

The coal industry. Victoria: C.F. Banfield, Printer to the King's Most Excellent Majesty, 1937. xl, 422 p. (Report of the Coal and Petroleum Products Commission; v. 2)

———.

Paragraph 3 of the terms of the Commission. Victoria: C.F. Banfield, Printer to the King's Most Excellent Majesty, 1938. xxxv, 500 p. (Report of the Coal and Petroleum Products Commission; v. 3)

Commissioner/Commissaire: M.A. Macdonald.

Also known as/Également connue sous le nom de: Royal Commission re Petroleum Products. Royal Commission re Coal Industry.

Loc.: ACG, BVA, BVAU, BVIP, MWU, NSHPL, OKQ, OLU, OOB, OOG, OOL, OOM, OONE, OONL, OOP, OOUM, QQLA, SRL, SSU

531 **Royal Commission re Beban Mine Disaster.**
Report. 1937. 6 p. (typescript)

Commissioner/Commissaire: R.R. Wilson.

Loc.: BVIPA

532 **Royal Commission re Labour Dispute between Burns and Company, Limited, and its Employees.**
Report. [1937?] 9 p.

Commissioner/Commissaire: J.C. McIntosh.

Loc.: BVIPA

533 **Royal Commission re Projectionists and Kinematographs.**
Report. 1937. 20 p. (typescript)

Commissioner/Commissaire: J.M. Coady.

Loc.: BVIPA

534 **Royal Commission re the Home of the Friendless.**
Report. 1937. 24 p. (typescript)

Commissioner/Commissaire: H.I. Bird.

Loc.: BVIPA

535 **1942**

Commission Appointed to Inquire into the Police Administration of the Corporation of the City of New Westminster.
Report. 1942. 19 p. (typescript)

Commissioner/Commissaire: F.W. Howay.

Loc.: BVIPA

536 **Commission Appointed to Specifically Investigate and Report Upon the Various Schemes Established under the Authority of the "Natural Products Marketing (British Columbia) Act".**
Report. Victoria: C.F. Banfield, Printer to the King's Most Excellent Majesty, 1942. 72 p.

Commissioner/Commissaire: A.M. Harper.

Loc.: BVA, BVIP, OKQ, OONL

537 **1943**

Commission Relating to The Workmen's Compensation Board.
Report. Victoria: C.F. Banfield, Printer to the King's Most Excellent Majesty, 1943. 245 p.

Commissioner/Commissaire: G.M. Sloan.

Also known as/Également connue sous le nom de: Workmen's Compensation Board Inquiry.

Loc.: BVA, BVAS, BVAU, BVIP, OKQL, OOL, OONL, OOP

538 **Commission to Inquire into the Administration of Mount View High School.**
Report. [Ashcroft, B.C., 1943] 29 *l.* (typescript)

Commissioner/Commissaire: J.O. Wilson.

Loc.: BVIP, OONL

539 **1945**

Commission of Inquiry into Educational Finance.
Report. Victoria: C.F. Banfield, Printer to the King's Most Excellent Majesty, 1945. 108 p.

Commissioner/Commissaire: M.A. Cameron.

Loc.: AEU, BVAS, BVAU, BVI, BVIP, MWU, OOB, OOCC, OOF, OONL, OTC, OTP, OTYL

540 **Commission Relating to the Forest Resources of British Columbia.**
Report. Victoria: C.F. Banfield, Printer to the King's Most Excellent Majesty, 1945. 195 p.

Commissioner/Commissaire: G.M. Sloan.

Also known as/Également connue sous le nom de: Forest Inquiry.

Loc.: ACU, BVAS, BVI, BVIP, MWP, OOB, OONL, SRL

541 **1946**

Commission Relating to the "Chiropody Act".
Report. Victoria: C.F. Banfield, Printer to the King's Most Excellent Majesty, 1946. 23 p.

Commissioner/Commissaire: A.M. Harper.

Also known as/Également connue sous le nom de: "Chiropody Act" Inquiry.

Loc.: BVIP, OONL, OOP

542 **1947**

Dyking, Drainage, and Irrigation Commission.
Irrigation districts. Victoria: D. McDiarmid, Printer to the King's Most Excellent Majesty, 1947. 103 p. (Report of the Dyking, Drainage, and Irrigation Commission; v. 1)

Dyking and drainage districts. Victoria: D. McDiarmid, Printer to the King's Most Excellent Majesty, 1947. p. 111-150. (Report of the Dyking, Drainage, and Irrigation Commission; v. 2)

Commissioner/Commissaire: F.M. Clement.

Loc.: BVAS, BVAU, BVIP, OONL, OOT, SRL

543 **Provincial-Municipal Relations in British Columbia.**
Report. Victoria: D. McDiarmid, Printer to the King's Most Excellent Majesty, 1947. 190 p.

Commissioner/Commissaire: H.C. Goldenberg.

Loc.: BVA, BVAS, BVAU, BVI, BVIP, BVIPA, MWP, OKQ, OOB, OOCC, OOF, OOL, OONL, OOP, OOS, OTLS, OTYL, SRL

544 **The Royal Commission Appointed to Inquire into Health and Accident Insurance Associations Operating in the Province of British Columbia.**
Report. Victoria: D. McDiarmid, Printer to the King's Most Excellent Majesty, 1947. 47 p.

Commissioner/Commissaire: J.A. Grimmett.

Loc.: BVA, BVAU, BVI, BVIP, OOIN, OONL, OOP, OTP, SRL

545 **The Royal Commission on Societies which Pay a Death Benefit Derived in Whole or in Part from Assessment.**
Report. Victoria: D. McDiarmid, Printer to the King's Most Excellent Majesty, 1947. 95 p.

Commissioner/Commissaire: A.J. Cowan.

Loc.: BVA, BVIP, OKQ, OOIN, OONL, OOP, OTP, OTYL, SRL

546 **1948**

Commission on School Taxation.
Report. [Victoria, 1948] 46, 7 *l.* (typescript)

Chairman/Président: H.A. Maclean.

Commissioners/Commissaires: B.C. Bracewell, J.T. Clark, R.C. Grant, R.R.F. Sewell, J.A. Stewart.

Loc.: BVIP, OONL

547 **Royal Commission on Doukhobor Affairs.**
Interim report. New Westminster, B.C., 1948. 106 *l.* (typescript)

Commissioner/Commissaire: H.J. Sullivan.

Loc.: BVIP, OONL

548 **1951**

Commission to Inquire into all the Circumstances Surrounding the Incarceration of the said Sanger from the Time of his Arrest up to his Reception in Oakalla Prison Farm, and Including his Transportation from Victoria to Oakalla Prison Farm.
Re Daniel LeRoy Sanger: report. Victoria, 1951. 15 *l.* (typescript)

Commissioner/Commissaire: H.H. Shandley.

Loc.: BVIP, OONL

549 **Commissioner Appointed under the "Public Inquiries Act" by a Commission Dated the 19th Day of April, 1951.**
Report. 1951. 6 p. (typescript)

Commissioner/Commissaire: H.S. Wood.

Loc.: BVIP

550 **1952**

Commission Relating to The Workmen's Compensation Act and Board.
Report. Victoria: D. McDiarmid, Printer to the Queen's Most Excellent Majesty, 1952. 443 p.

Commissioner/Commissaire: G.M. Sloan.

Also known as/Également connue sous le nom de: Workmen's Compensation Board Inquiry.

Loc.: BVA, BVAU, BVI, BVIP, MWP, OKQL, OOAG, OOCC, OOL, OONL, OOP, OTLS, OTYL

551 **Hospital Insurance Inquiry Board.**
Report. Victoria: D. McDiarmid, Printer to the Queen's Most Excellent Majesty, 1952. 107 p.

Chairman/Président: S.J. Smith.

Members/Membres: D.C. Brown, W. Hendricks, A.W. Lundell, D.J. Proudfoot, R.C. Steele, H.J. Welch, H.E. Winch.

Loc.: BVA, BVAM, BVAS, BVIP, BVIV, OFF, OONH, OONL, OOP, SRL

552 **Industrial Conciliation and Arbitration Inquiry Board.**
Report. Victoria: D. McDiarmid, Printer to the Queen's Most Excellent Majesty, 1952. 27 p.

Chairman/Président: A.J.R. Ash.

Members/Membres: A.J. McDonell, B.M. MacIntyre, J.D. McRae, A.J. Turner.

Loc.: BVA, BVI, BVIP, MWP, OOL, OONL

553 **1953**

British Columbia Liquor Inquiry Commission.
Report. Victoria: D. McDiarmid, Printer to the Queen's Most Excellent Majesty, 1953. 31 p.

Chairman/Président: H.H. Stevens.

Commissioners/Commissaires: G. Home, D.C. Swanson.

Loc.: BVA, BVAU, BVI, BVIP, OONL

554 **1954**

Inquiry Pursuant to the "Public Inquiries Act" into the Circumstances of Landslides at Whatshan.
Report. [Vancouver, 1954] 50, 2, 9 *l.* (typescript)

Commissioner/Commissaire: J.V. Clyne.

Also known as/Également connue sous le nom de: Whatshan Dam Inquiry.

Loc.: BVI, BVIP, MWP, OONL

555 **1955**

British Columbia Royal Commission on Milk.
Interim report on the inquiry into the production, marketing and distribution of whole milk in the Province of British Columbia.
Vancouver, 1955. 4 *l.* (typescript)

Loc.: BVIP, OONL

———.

Report. Victoria: D. McDiarmid, Printer to the Queen's Most Excellent Majesty, 1955. xiii, 214 p.

Commissioner/Commissaire: J.V. Clyne.

Loc.: BVA, BVAS, BVAU, BVI, BVIP, BVIV, MWHP, OOAG, OOF, OONL, OPET, OTU, OWAL

556 **1955-1965**

Commission Appointed to Inquire into the Allotment of Doukhobor Lands in the Province of British Columbia.
Interim report. [Vancouver, 1955] 4 *l.* (typescript)

———.

Second interim report. [Vancouver, 1956] 4 *l.* (typescript)

———.

Third interim report. [Vancouver, 1956] 2 *l.* (typescript)

———.

Fourth interim report. [Vancouver, 1957] 7 *l.* (typescript)

———.

Fifth interim report. [Vancouver, 1959] 18 *l.* (typescript)

Loc.: BVIP, OONL, OTU

———.
Final report. [Vancouver, 1965] 4 *l.* (typescript)

Commissioner/Commissaire: A.E. Lord.

Loc.: BVA, BVIP, BVIV, MWP, OONL

557 **Commission of Inquiry Pursuant to the "Public Inquiries Act" into Allegations of Impropriety in Connection with the Issuance of Forest Management Licences.**
Report. [Vancouver, 1955] 4 *l.* (typescript)

Commissioner/Commissaire: A.E. Lord.

Loc.: BVIP, OONL

558 **Inquiry in the Matter of the Public Inquiries Act and in the Matter of Lots in the Sub-Division of Lot 1476, Sayward District, Plan 8255.**
Report. [Nanaimo, B.C.] 1955. 8 *l.* (typescript)

Commissioner/Commissaire: L.A. Hanna.

Loc.: BVIP, OONL

559 **1955-1956**

Vancouver City Police Force Inquiry.
Interim report. [Vancouver] 1955. 161 p. (typescript)

Loc.: BVIP, OONL

———.
Final report. [Vancouver] 1956. 221, 40 p. (typescript)

Commissioner/Commissaire: R.H. Tupper.

Loc.: BVA, BVIP, OONL, OTP

560 **1957**

Commission Relating to the Forest Resources of British Columbia.
Report. Victoria: D. McDiarmid, Printer to the Queen's Most Excellent Majesty, 1957. 2 v.

Commissioner/Commissaire: G.M. Sloan.

Also known as/Également connue sous le nom de: Forest Inquiry.

Loc.: BVA, BVAS, BVAU, BVIP, OOB, OOF, OONL, OORD, OOS, OTP, OTU, QMG, SRL

561 **1958**

Industrial Inquiry Commission to Inquire into the Circumstances and Merits of the Dispute between the International Woodworkers of America and the Companies Represented by the Forest Industrial Relations.
Report. Victoria, 1958. 1 p. (typescript)

Commissioner/Commissaire: G.M. Sloan.

Loc.: BVIP, OONL

562 **Royal Commission on the Tree-Fruit Industry of British Columbia.**
Report. [Victoria] D. McDiarmid, Printer to the Queen's Most Excellent Majesty in right of the Province of British Columbia, 1958. 810 p.

Commissioner/Commissaire: E.D. MacPhee.

Loc.: BVAS, BVAU, BVI, BVIP, BVIV, OOAG, OOFF, OONL, OTNY, QMAC, QMU

563 **Royal Commission, Second Narrows Bridge Enquiry.**
Report. [Victoria] D. McDiarmid, Printer to the Queen's Most Excellent Majesty, 1958. v. 1

Commissioner/Commissaire: S. Lett.

Loc.: AEU, BVA, BVAU, BVI, BVIP, MWU, NSHPL, OKQ, OONL, OTLS, OTP

564 **Royal Commission to Inquire into the Circumstances and Merits of the Disputes Between the Plumbing and Pipe-fitting Industry and the Electrical Industry, and Various Employers, Employers' Associations, Employees and Unions.**
Report. Victoria, 1958. unpaged (typescript)

Chairman/Président: H.C. Goldenberg.

Commissioners/Commissaires: L.G. Crampton, E.A. Jamieson, G.A. Wilkinson.

Loc.: BVIP, OONL

565 **1959**

British Columbia Civil Service Act.
Report of a board of reference. Victoria, 1959 [Printed 1972] 70 p.

Commissioner/Commissaire: G.M. Sloan (1957-1958), A.W.R. Carrothers (1958- 1959).

Loc.: BVA, BVAS, BVAU, BVIP, BVIV, MWU, NSHPL, OLU, OONL, OOP, OTYL, QMML, QSHERU, SRL

566 **Commission in the Matter of a Tree-Farm Licence and in the Matter of Empire Mills Limited.**
Report. [Victoria, 1959] 20 *l.* (typescript)

Commissioner/Commissaire: C.W. Morrow.

Loc.: BVIP, OONL

567 **1959-1960**

Commission of Inquiry into Road-User Charges.
Report. [Victoria: D. McDiarmid, Printer to the Queen's Most Excellent Majesty in right of the Province of British Columbia, 1959] 72 p.

Loc.: BVAS, BVAU, BVIP, BVIV, MWP, OOF, OONL, OOT, OTYL

―――――.

Report of the 1960 (Second) Commission of Inquiry into Road-User Charges. [Victoria] 1960. 38, xvi *l.* (typescript)

Chairman/Président: H.F. Angus.

Commissioners/Commissaires: A.J. Bowering, G. Lindsay, W.F. Veitch.

Loc.: BVA, BVIP, OONL

568 **Royal Commission in the Matter of the British Columbia Power Commission.**
Report. In British Columbia Government News, v. 7, no. 8, September 1959. 24 p.

Chairman/Président: G.M. Shrum.

Commissioners/Commissaires: W.M. Anderson, J. Dunsmuir.

Loc.: BVAS, BVAU, BVIP, OONL, OOP, OTU

569 **1960**

Commission on Tree Farm Licences.
Report on Project III. [Victoria, 1960] ii, 62, 6 p. (typescript)

Commissioner/Commissaire: C.W. Morrow.

Loc.: BVIP, OONL

570 **Juvenile Delinquency Inquiry Board.**
Report. [Victoria: D. McDiarmid, Printer to the Queen's Most Excellent Majesty in right of the Province of British Columbia, 1960] 31 p.

Chairman/Président: E.C.F. Martin.

Members/Membres: B.H. Brown, H.J. Bruch, D.R.J. Campbell, G.H. Dowding, P.A. Gibbs, G.L. Gibson, L.M. Haggen, R. Harding, L.R. Peterson, B. Price, W.C. Speare, J.D. Tisdalle.

Loc.: AEU, BVAS, BVIP, OONL, OTLS, OTYL

571 **Royal Commission on Education.**
Report. [Victoria: D. McDiarmid, Printer to the Queen's Most Excellent Majesty in right of the Province of British Columbia, 1960] xviii, 460 p.

Chairman/Président: S.N.F. Chant.

Commissioners/Commissaires: J.E. Liersch, R.P. Walrod.

Loc.: ACU, AE, AEU, BNND, BVAS, BVI, BVIP, MWP, MWU, NBFU, NSHPL, OLU, OOCC, OOCU, OOL, OONL, OPET, OPAL, OTCT, OTER, OTP, OTU, OWA, QMM, QQL, SRU, SSU

572 **1961**

Inquiry into Marriages Entered into and Solemnized in Accordance with the Rites and Ceremonies of the Doukhobour Faith or Creed.
Interim report. [Nelson, B.C., 1961] 12 *l.* (typescript)

Commissioner/Commissaire: W. Evans.

Loc.: BVIP, OONL

573 **1962**

Puntledge River Inquiry.
Report. Vancouver, 1962. 33 *l.* (typescript)

Commissioner/Commissaire: H.F. Angus.

Loc.: BVIP

574 **1964**

British Columbia Royal Commission on Expropriation.
Report. [Victoria] 1964. various pagings

Commissioner/Commissaire: J.V. Clyne.

Loc.: BVA, BVAS, BVAU, BVI, BVIP, MWP, MWU, OKQL, OONL, OOP, OTLS, OTU, OWA, SRL

575 **1966**

Commission of Inquiry into Redefinition of Electoral Districts.
Report. [Victoria] 1966. 165 p.

Chairman/Président: H.F. Angus.

Commissioners/Commissaires: F.H. Hurley, K.L. Morton.

Also known as/Également connue sous le nom de: The Provincial Redistribution Commission.

Loc.: AEU, BVA, BVAS, BVAU, BVIP, BVIPA, BVIV, MWP, OKQ, OONL, OOP, OTLS, OTYL, OWTU

576 **Commission of Inquiry Workmen's Compensation Act.**
Report. [Victoria] A. Sutton, Printer to the Queen's Most Excellent Majesty in right of the Province of British Columbia, 1966. 451 p.

Commissioner/Commissaire: A.C. DesBrisay (1962-1964), C.W. Tysoe (1964-1966).

Loc.: AC, BVA, BVAM, BVAS, BVIV, MWP, MWU, OKQL, OLU, OOCW, OONL, OTLS, OTY, QMHE, QSHERU, SSU

577 **1966**

Royal Commission on Gasoline Price Structure.
Report relating to the fairness of the price structure of gasoline at the refinery, wholesale and retail levels in the Province of British Columbia. Victoria, 1966. 164 p. (typescript)

Commissioner/Commissaire: C.W. Morrow.

Loc.: AC, AEU, BVA, BVAU, BVIP, BVIV, MWP, NSHPL, OKQL, OOB, OOEC, OOF, OONL, OTP, OTY, OTYL, QMU, QQERE, QQL

578 **1967**

Commission of Inquiry into Invasion of Privacy.
Report. [Vancouver] 1967. 56 *l.* (typescript)

Commissioner/Commissaire: R.A. Sargent.

Loc.: AEU, BVA, BVAS, BVAU, BVIP, MWP, NSHPL, OKQL, OLU, OOC, OONL, OOP, OOSG, OTLS, OTU, OTYL, QMML, QMU, QQL, SRL

579 **1968**

Royal Commission on Automobile Insurance.
Report. [Victoria] 1968. 2 v.

Chairman/Président: R.A.B. Wootton.

Commissioners/Commissaires: P.A. Lusztig, C.E.S. Walls.

Loc.: AC, AEU, BVA, BVAS, BVAU, BVI, MWP, MWU, OKQL, OLU, OONL, OOP, OTLS, OTYL, OWTU, QMU, QQL, QSHERU, SRL, SSU

580 **1970**

British Columbia Liquor Inquiry Commission.
Report. [Victoria] A. Sutton, Printer to the Queen's Most Excellent Majesty in right of the Province of British Columbia, 1970. 165 p.

Chairman/Président: C.W. Morrow.

Commissioners/Commissaires: M.M. Johnson, E.M. Lawson.

Loc.: AEU, BVA, BVAS, BVAU, BVIP, MWP, NFSM, OLU, OOCI, OOF, OONL, OOP, OTLS, OTYL, OWAL, QQL

581 **1971**

Public Inquiry into the Circumstances of the Disturbance which Occurred on a Saturday Night, August 7, 1971, in that Part of the City of Vancouver known as "Gastown".
Report. [Vancouver, 1971] 17 *l.* (typescript)

Commissioner/Commissaire: T.A. Dohm.

Also known as/Également connue sous le nom de: Gastown Inquiry.

Loc.: BVIP, OONL

582 **1972**

Commission of Inquiry into Employer-Employee Relations in the Public Service of British Columbia.
Making bargaining work in British Columbia's public service: report. [Victoria] 1972. v, 112 p.

Chairman/Président: R.D. Higgins.

Commissioners/Commissaires: J.L. Fryer, N.T. Richards, N.J. Ruff, G.L. Tomalty.

Loc.: BVA, BVAS, BVAU, BVIV, MWP, NFSM, OOCI, OOL, OONL, OOPS, OTMCL, OTU, QSHERU, SRL

583 **1973**

Royal Commission Concerning the Preparation and Tendering of Bids Pertaining to the Construction of an Addition to the Campbell River and District General Hospital.
Report. Vancouver, 1973. 24 *l.* (typescript)

Commissioner/Commissaire: H.L. Purdy.

Loc.: BVIP, OONL

584 **Royal Commission on Post Secondary Education in the Kootenay Region.**
Report. [Victoria?] 1973. xviii, 133 p. (typescript)

Chairman/Président: I. McTaggart-Cowan.

Commissioners/Commissaires: G.C. Andrew, T.C. Byrne, L.S. Gansner, R. Hughes, J. Patterson, E.E. Wallach.

Loc.: AEU, BVAS, BVAU, BVIP, BVIV, NFSM, OOCU, OONL, OTER, OTMCL, OTY

585 **1974**

Inquiry, Jericho Hill School.
Report. [Vancouver] 1974. various pagings

Commissioner/Commissaire: B. Chud.

Loc.: AEU, BVA, BVAS, BVAU, BVI, BVIP, OONL, OTMCL

586 **Public Inquiry re the Corporation of the District of Surrey.**
Report. [Vancouver, 1974] 120 *l.* (typescript)

Commissioner/Commissaire: D.S. White.

Loc.: BVA, NFSM, OONL, OTYL

587 **1974-1976**

Royal Commission on Family and Children's Law.
Unified family court pilot project. Vancouver, 1974. various pagings (Report of the Royal Commission of Family and Children's Law; 1)

———.

The use of lay panels in the unified family court. Vancouver, 1974. 6, 3 *l.* (Report of the Royal Commission on Family and Children's Law; 2)

———.

The role of the family advocate. Vancouver, 1974. 4 *l.* (Report of the Royal Commission on Family and Children's Law; 3)

———.

The family, the courts, and the community. Vancouver, 1975. various pagings (Report of the Royal Commission on Family and Children's Law; 4)

―――――.
Children and the law: the legislative framework. Vancouver, 1975. 14 p. (Report of the Royal Commission on Family and Children's Law; 5.1)

―――――.
Children and the law: the status of children born to unmarried parents. Vancouver, 1975. 95, 20, 3 p. (Report of the Royal Commission on Family and Children's Law; 5.2)

―――――.
Children and the law: children's right. Vancouver, 1975. 26, 2 p. (Report of the Royal Commission on Family and Children's Law; 5.3)

―――――.
Children and the law: special needs of special children. Vancouver, 1975. 34, 2, 2 p. (Report of the Royal Commission on Family and Children's Law; 5.4)

―――――.
Children and the law: the protection of children (child care). Vancouver, 1975. various pagings (Report of the Royal Commission on Family and Children's Law; 5.5)

―――――.
Children and the law: custody, access, and guardianship. Vancouver, 1975. 39, 4 p. (Report of the Royal Commission on Family and Children's Law; 5.6)

―――――.
Children and the law: adoption. Vancouver, 1975. various pagings (Report of the Royal Commission on Family and Children's Law; 5.7)

―――――.
The Children's Act, 1976: a supplement to the fifth report of The Family and Children's Law Commission: draft model act for discussion purposes only. [Vancouver] 1975. various pagings (typescript)

―――――.
Report on matrimonial property. Vancouver, 1975. 94 p. (Report of the Royal Commission on Family and Children's Law; 6)

―――――.
Family maintenance. Vancouver, 1975. 68, 2 p. (Report of the Royal Commission on Family and Children's Law; 7)

―――――.
Preparation for marriage. Vancouver, 1975. various pagings (Report of the Royal Commission on Family and Children's Law; 8)

———.

Artificial insemination. Vancouver, 1975. 34 p. (Report of the Royal Commission on Family and Children's Law; 9)

———.

Native families and the law. Vancouver, 1975. 89, 3 p. (Report of the Royal Commission on Family and Children's Law; 10)

———.

Change of name. Vancouver, 1975. 2, 14 p. (Report of the Royal Commission on Family and Children's Law; 11)

———.

The medical consent of minors. Vancouver, 1975. 2, 18, 18 *l.* (Report of the Royal Commission on Family and Children's Law; 12)

———.

The Commission and the community compiled and prepared by Deanna Sylvester. Vancouver, 1975. various pagings (Report of the Royal Commission on Family and Children's Law; 13)

———.

Supplementary report of the Royal Commission on Family and Children's Law: summary of recommendations. Vancouver, 1976. 57 p. (typescript)

Chairman/Président: T.R. Berger.

Members/Membres: R.D. Collver, R.T. MacDonald, S. Segal, M. Vadasz.

Also known as/Également connue sous le nom de: The Family and Children's Law Commission.

Loc.: AEU, BVIP, BVIV, NFSM, OLU, OONL, OOP, OTYL, SRU

588 **1975**

Commission of Inquiry into Redefinition of Electoral Districts under the Public Inquiries Act.
Report. [Vancouver] 1975. vii, 151 p.

Chairman/Président: T.G. Norris.

Commissioners/Commissaires: F. Bowers, L.J. Wallace.

Loc.: AEU, BVA, BVAS, BVAU, BVI, BVIPA, MWP, NFSM, OONL, OOP, OTMCL, OTY, OWAL, QQL

589 **Forest Industry Labour Disputes Commission.**
Report. Vancouver, 1975. 38 *l.* (typescript)

Special Mediator/Médiateur spécial: H.E. Hutcheon.

Loc.: BVIP, OONL

590 **Public Inquiry Commission Appointed to Examine Certain Aspects of Vancouver Community College.**
Report. [Vancouver] 1975. vii, 85 p.

Chairman/Président: G. Suart.

Commissioners/Commissaires: J. Pritchard, M. Scott.

Loc.: AEU, BVA, BVAS, BVAU, BVIP, NFSM, OONL, OOP, OTMCL

591 **Royal Commission of Inquiry into the Use of Pesticides and Herbicides.**
Final report. [Vancouver] 1975. 3 v. in 4

Chairman/Président: C.J.G. Mackenzie.

Commissioners/Commissaires: W.K. Oldham, W.D. Powrie.

Loc.: AEU, BVA, BVAU, BVAS, BVIF, BVIP, MWP, NFSM, OLU, OOAG, OOFF, OONL, OOP, OTB, OTYL

592 **1976**

Commission of Inquiry on Property Assessment and Taxation.
Preliminary report. [Vancouver] 1976. various pagings

Chairman/Président: R.A. McMath.

Commissioners/Commissaires: R.M. Clark, S.W. Hamilton, A. Mackenzie, R.G. Marks, B. Meyer, S. Thompson.

Loc.: AEU, BVA, BVAS, BVAU, BVIP, BVIPA, MWU, OKQL, OLU, OONL, OOP, OTMCL, OTYL, OWAL

593 **Royal Commission on Forest Resources.**
Timber rights and forest policy in British Columbia: report. Victoria: [K.M. MacDonald, Printer to the Queen's Most Excellent Majesty in right of the Province of British Columbia] 1976. 2 v.

Commissioner/Commissaire: P.H. Pearse.

Loc.: AEU, BVAS, BVAU, BVIF, BVIP, MWP, MWU, OKQL, OLU, OOCI, OOEC, OOF, OONL, OOP, OTMCL, OTY, OWAL, QQT, SRL

594 **1977**

Commission in the Matter of the Public Inquiries Act and in the Matter of A.E. Filmer and G.D. McKinnon.
Report. [New Westminster, B.C., 1977] 8 *l.* (typescript)

Commissioner/Commissaire: T.K. Fisher.

Loc.: BVIP, OONL

595 **Commission of Inquiry Concerning the Education and Training of Practical Nurses and Related Hospital Personnel.**
Report. Vancouver, 1977. 16 *l.* (typescript)

Commissioner/Commissaire: N.A. Hall.

Loc.: BVIP, OONL

596 **Commission of Inquiry into the Grizzly Valley Natural Gas Pipeline.**
Report. Vancouver, 1977. 24 *l.* (typescript)

Commissioner/Commissaire: W.K. Smith.

Loc.: BVAU, BVIP, OONL, OOP

597 **Commission on Vocational, Technical, and Trades Training in British Columbia.**
Report. [Burnaby, B.C.] 1977. various pagings

Chairman/Président: D.H. Goard.

Commissioners/Commissaires: A.J. Blakeney, B. McCaffery, B. McDonald, C. Stairs, T.W. Trineer.

Loc.: BVAS, BVAU, BVIP, BVIV, NFSM, OOCU, OONL, OOP, OTC, OTMCL, OTY

598 **1977-1979**

Royal Commission on British Columbia Railway.
Interim report on affairs of Railwest Railcar manufacturing plant.
[Vancouver] 1977. 10, 20 *l.* (typescript)

Loc.: MWP, OONL

———.

Interim report on the future of the Fort Nelson extension. [Vancouver] 1977. 76 *l.* (typescript)

Loc.: BVA, BVIP, MWP, OONL

———.

Report. [Victoria: K.M. MacDonald, Queen's Printer] 1978. 4 v.

Loc.: BVA, BVIP, OONL

———.

Report: addendum XI. Statutory revision. [Victoria: K.M. MacDonald, Queen's Printer] 1979. 138 p.

Chairman/Président: L.G. MacKenzie.

Commissioners/Commissaires: D.H. Chapman, S.W. Welsh.

Loc.: BVIP, OONL

599 **1978-1979**

Royal Commission on Electoral Reform, 1978.
Interim report on the redefinition of electoral districts for the Province of British Columbia.
[Vancouver] 1978. various pagings

Loc.: BVA, BVIPA, BVIP, OONL, OOP, OTMCL

———.

Final report. [Vancouver] 1979. 6 v.

Commissioner/Commissaire: L.S. Eckardt.

Loc.: AEU, BVIP, NSHPL, OONL, OOP, OTY, QMML

600 **Royal Commission on the Incarceration of Female Offenders.**
Report. [Vancouver] 1978. 176 p.

Commissioner/Commissaire: P.M. Proudfoot.

Loc.: BVA, BVIP, OKQL, OONL, OOSG, OTMCL, OWAL, QQL

601 **1979**

Commission of Inquiry into and Concerning an Allegation by His Honour Judge Govan Made on May 9th 1979 that the Deputy Attorney-General, Mr. Richard Vogel, or Some Unnamed Person in the Ministry of the Attorney-General, Had Pursued a Course of Conduct with Respect to Matters Coming Before His Honour Judge Govan in his Capacity as a Judge of the Provincial Court from which He Inferred that his Independence as a Judge of the Provincial Court Was Being Interfered With.
Report. Victoria, 1979. 61 p. (typescript)

Commissioner/Commissaire: P.D. Seaton.

Loc.: BVIP, OONL

602 **1980**

Royal Commission of Inquiry, Health and Environmental Protection, Uranium Mining.
Report. [Victoria: Queen's Printer] 1980. 3 v.

Chairman/Président: D.V. Bates.

Commissioners/Commissaires: J.W. Murray, V. Raudsepp.

Loc.: BVA, BVAM, BVAWC, BVIP, BVIPA, MPW, NSHD, OCKA, OOAECB, OONL, OOP, OORD, SSU

603 **1982**

Public Inquiry Under the Inquiry Act into Electoral Representation in the Province of British Columbia.
Report. [Vancouver] 1982. iv, 48, 17 *l.* (typescript)

Commissioner/Commissaire: D.T. Warren.

Also known as/Également connue sous le nom de: Royal Commission on Electoral Representation.

Loc.: BVA, BVIPA, OONL, OOP

PRINCE EDWARD ISLAND/ ÎLE-DU-PRINCE-ÉDOUARD

604 **1876-1877**

Commission Appointed to Examine into the Accounts and Working of the Public Lands Office.
Preliminary report. In Prince Edward Island. House of Assembly. *Journal.* 26th General Assembly, 4th Session. Charlottetown: J.W. Mitchell, 1876. (Appendix Z)

———.

Final report. In Prince Edward Island. House of Assembly. *Journals.* 27th General Assembly, 1st Session. Charlottetown: J.W. Mitchell, 1877. (Appendix K)

Commissioners/Commissaires: H.J. Cundall, T. Desbrisay, W.H. Shanks.

Loc.: BVAU, BVIP, BVIV, NBFU, NFSM, OHM, OONL, OPET, OTL, OTMCL, OTNY, PCU

605 **1882**

Commission Appointed to Enquire into the Administration and Management of the Prince Edward Island Hospital for the Insane.
Report. In Prince Edward Island. House of Assembly. *Journal.* 28th General Assembly, 4th Session. Charlottetown: S.G. Lawson, 1882. (Appendix O)

Commissioners/Commissaires: C.C. Gardiner, G.W. Hodgson, A.A. Macdonald.

Loc.: BVAU, BVIP, BVIV, MWP, NBFU, NFSM, OHM, OONL, OPET, OTL, OTMCL, OTNY, PCU, QQL

606 **1891**

The Commission Appointed to Examine into and Investigate the Accounts, Transactions, and Management of the Department of Crown and Public Lands of this Province.
Final report. Charlottetown: Examiner Officer, 1891. 105 p.

Commissioners/Commissaires: F.H. Arnaud, L. Carvell.

Loc.: OOA

607 **1910**

Commission on Education in Prince Edward Island.
Report. Charlottetown: G.W. Gardiner, King's Printer, 1910. various pagings

Chairman/Président: D.C. McLeod.

Commissioner/Commissaire: F.G. Buote.

Loc.: OTER, PC, PCU

608 **1930**

Royal Commission on Education in the Province of Prince Edward Island.
Report. Charlottetown: Patriot Job Print, 1930. 55 p.

Chairman/Président: C. MacMillan.

Commissioners/Commissaires: D.S. McInnis, N. MacLeod.

Loc.: OONL, OTC, OTY, PC

609 **1960**

The Commission on Educational Finance and Related Problems in Administration.
Report. Charlottetown, 1960. 102 p.

Commissioner/Commissaire: M.E. LaZerte.

Loc.: NFSM, OKQ, OOCU, OOF, OOL, OONL, OOS, OTCT, OTER, PC, SRU

610 **1962**

Royal Commission To Inquire into and Concerning all Matters Relating to the Election of Members to the Legislative Assembly.
Report. [Charlottetown, 1962] 15, 37 *l.*

Chairman/Président: J.S. DesRoches.

Members/Membres: P.M. MacCaull, F. MacKinnon, F.L. MacNutt, L. O'Connor.

Also known as/Également connue sous le nom de: Royal Commission on Electoral Reform.

Loc.: BVAS, BVAU, NSHDL, OONL, OTYL, PC, SSU

611 **1965**

Royal Commission on Higher Education for Prince Edward Island.
Report. [Charlottetown] 1965. various pagings (typescript)

Chairman/Président: J.S. Bonnell.

Commissioners/Commissaires: N.A.M. MacKenzie, J.A. McMillan.

Loc.: AEU, BVIV, OKQ, OOCU, OONL, OOS, OTCT, OTER, PC

612 **1968**

Commission to Make Full Inquiry into and Concerning all Matters Relating to the Dairy Industry in the Province of Prince Edward Island.
Report. Charlottetown, 1968. 15 *l.* (typescript)

Commissioner/Commissaire: W.T. Murchie.

Loc.: OONL, PCA, PCPL

613 **1969**

The Commission of Inquiry into Matters Pertaining to Bathurst Marine Limited and Gulf Garden Foods Limited.
Report. [Charlottetown] 1969. 91, 18 p. (typescript)

Chairman/Président: C. St. Clair Trainor.

Commissioners/Commissaires: I.M. MacKeigan, A.E. Pierce.

Also known as/Également connue sous le nom de: The Commission of Inquiry, Georgetown Industries.

Loc.: OONL, OOP, PC

614 **1973**

Royal Commission on Land Ownership and Land Use.
Interim report. Charlottetown, 1973. x, 31 p.

Loc.: ACU, AEU, NSHDL, OOP, OOTC, OWAL, QMML, SRL

Report. Charlottetown, 1973. 98 p. (typescript)

Chairman/Président: C.W. Raymond.

Commissioners/Commissaires: C. Jones, J. Wells.

Loc.: AEU, BVAS, BVAU, MWP, NFSM, NSHDL, OKQL, OLU, OONL, OORD, OOSC, OTU, OTY, PC, QQL, SRL, SSU

615 **1974**

Commission of Inquiry into the Purchase of Gregors By-The-Sea Property by the Prince Edward Island Land Development Corporation and Sixty-Three (63) Acres of Land in East Royalty by the Prince Edward Island Housing Authority.
Report. Charlottetown, 1974. 70 p.

Commissioner/Commissaire: C. St. Clair Trainor.

Loc.: BVAU, BVIV, MWP, OONL, OOP, PC

616 **Commission of Inquiry Respecting Aspects of the Dairy Industry in Prince Edward Island.**
Report. [Charlottetown, 1974] various pagings (typescript)

Commissioner/Commissaire: E.J. Brennan.

Loc.: MWP, OTMCL, PC

617 **1976**

Commission of Inquiry into Matters Pertaining to Georgetown Shipyard.
Report. Charlottetown: Queen's Printer, 1976. vi, 202 p.

Commissioner/Commissaire: F.A. Large.

Loc.: AEU, MWP, OKQL, OONL, OTU, OTYL, QMML, QMU, PC

618 **The Commission of Inquiry into Matters Pertaining to the Queens County Jail.**
Report. Charlottetown, 1976. 119 p. (typescript)

Commissioner/Commissaire: A.K. Scales.

Loc.: MWP, OONL, OOP, OTU, OWAL, PC, QMML

619 **1977**

Commission of Inquiry into Matters Pertaining to the Charlottetown Police Force.
Report. Charlottetown: G.W.K. Auld, Queen's Printer, 1977. v, 126 p.

Commissioner/Commissaire: M.J. McQuaid.

Loc.: MWP, OONL, OOP, PC

620 **1980**

The Prince Edward Island Commission of Inquiry on Shopping Centres and Retail Stores.
Report. Charlottetown, 1980. iii, 304 p.

Chairman/Président: F.J. McNeill.

Members/Membres: E.G. Fullerton, G. Handrahan, M. Reeves, D. White.

Loc.: NBS, NSHDIP, NSHL, OONL, OOP, PC

621 **1981**

Commission of Inquiry into the P.E.I. Fishery.
Report. [Charlottetown] 1981. 2 v.

Commissioner/Commissaire: E.P. Weeks.

Loc.: OONL, OOP, PC

622 **1982**

Commission of Inquiry into the Cost of Electric Power to the Residents of Prince Edward Island.
Report. [Charlottetown] 1982. various pagings (typescript)

Commissioner/Commissaire: M.J. McQuaid.

Loc.: OOFF, OONL, OOP, PCU

ALBERTA

623 **1908**

Royal Commission on the Coal Mining Industry in the Province of Alberta, 1907.
Report. Edmonton, [1908?] 11 *l.* (typescript)

Chairman/Président: A.L. Sifton.

Commissioners/Commissaires: W. Haysom, L. Stockett.

Loc.: AEA, AEP, AEU, OOL, OONL

624 **1909**

Commission on the Pork Industry in the Province of Alberta, 1908.
Report. Edmonton: J.W. Jeffery, Government Printer, 1913 [1909] 24 p.

Chairman/Président: R.A. Wallace.

Commissioners/Commissaires: J. Bower, A.G. Harrison.

Loc.: ACG, AEP, OONL

625 **1910**

Royal Commission on the Alberta and Great Waterways Railway Company.
Report. [Edmonton, 1910] 58 p.

Commissioners/Commissaires: N.D. Beck, H. Harvey, D.L. Scott.

Loc.: AE, AEA, AEP, AEU, OONL, OOP

626 **1915**

Commission Appointed for the Investigation and Enquiry into the Cause and Effect of the Hillcrest Mine Disaster.
Report. In Alberta. Dept. of Public Works. Mines Branch. *Annual report, 1914.* Edmonton: J.W. Jeffery, Government Printer, 1915. p. 160-169.

Commissioner/Commissaire: A.A. Carpenter.

Loc.: AEA, AEP, BVAG, BVAU, OKQ, OOG, OONL, OOSS

627 **Commission Appointed to Consider the Granting of Degree-Conferring Powers to Calgary College.**
Report. Edmonton: J.W. Jeffery, Government Printer, 1915. 17 p. (Sessional paper no. 1, 1915)

Chairman/Président: R.A. Falconer.

Commissioners/Commissaires: A.S. MacKenzie, W.C. Murray.

Loc.: AEA, AEP, OONL

628 **1918**

Inquiry into and Concerning Compensation for Injuries Received by Workmen in Alberta.
Report of investigation regarding workmen's compensation. [Edmonton] 1918. *l* ix p.

Chairman/Président: J.T. Stirling.

Commissioners/Commissaires: J.A. Kinney, W.T. McNeill.

Loc.: AEP, OOL, OONL

629 **1919**

Coal Mining Industry Commission.
Report. [Edmonton: J.W. Jeffery, King's Printer] 1919. 13 p.

Chairman/Président: J.T. Stirling.

Commissioners/Commissaires: J. Loughran, W.F. McNeill, H. Shaw, W. Smitten.

Loc.: AC, ACG, AEA, AEMM, AEP, OOAG, OOL, OONL

630 **1922**

Commission on Banking and Credit with Respect to the Industry of Agriculture in the Province of Alberta.
Report. [Edmonton?] 1922. 49 *l.* (typescript)

Commissioner/Commissaire: D.A. McGibbon.

Loc.: AEA, AEP, AEU, OOA, OOAG, OOCC, OONL, OTMCL

631 **The Survey Board for Southern Alberta.**
Report. Edmonton: King's Printer, 1922. 44 p.

Chairman/Président: C.A. Magrath.

Commissioners/Commissaires: A.A. Carpenter, W.H. Fairfield, G.R. Marnoch.

Loc.: AC, ACG, ACU, AEP

632 **1925**

Commission to Inquire into and Concerning the Circumstances Attending the Reception at the Provincial Gaol at Lethbridge of One Edward Moore.
Report. 1925. 28 *l.* (typescript)

Commissioner/Commissaire: W.L. Walsh.

Also known as/Également connue sous le nom de: Lethbridge Gaol Inquiry.

Loc.: AEA, AEP

633 **1926**

Alberta Coal Commission, 1925.
Report. Edmonton: W.D. McLean, Acting King's Printer, 1926. vii, 391 p.

Chairman/Président: H.M.E. Evans.

Commissioners/Commissaires: R.G. Drinnan, F. Wheatley.

Loc.: AC, ACG, AEA, AEP, AEU, MWP, OOG, OOL, OOM, OONL, OOP

634 **Commission Appointed to Enquire into, Report on and Make Recommendations in Regard to Matters Affecting the Welfare of that Part of the Province of Alberta Generally Known as the Tilley East Area.**
Report. Edmonton, 1926. 2, 22 *l.* (typescript)

Chairman/Président: E.J. Fream.

Commissioners/Commissaires: Z. McIlmoyle, J.W. Martin, V. Meek.

Loc.: AEA, AEP, OONL

635 **1927**

Commission Appointed to Inquire into the Advisability of the Establishment of a Forty-Eight Hour Working Week in Alberta.
Majority report. [*Minority report*] [Edmonton, 1927] 11, 3 *l.* (typescript)

Chairman/Président: A.A. Carpenter.

Commissioners/Commissaires: N. Hindsley, E.E. Roper.

Loc.: AEA, AEP, OONL

636 Commission to Investigate any Cases in which Difficulties, Differences of Opinion or Hardships Were Alleged to Have Arisen as Affecting Minorities of Either the United Church of Canada, the Presbyterian Church in Canada, the Methodist Church or the Congregational Churches.
Report. 1927. 20 *l.* (typescript)

Chairman/Président: J.E.A. Macleod.

Commissioners/Commissaires: S.H. McCuaig, D.G. McQueen, H.J. Montgomery, A.S. Tuttle, C.E. Wilson.

Loc.: AEA, AEP, OONL

637 **1927**

Commission to Make an Inquiry for the Purpose of Ascertaining as Far as Possible the Cause of an Explosion which Occurred on the 23rd Day of November, 1926, in a Coal Mine Operated by the McGillivray Creek Coal and Coke Company at Coleman.
Report. [Edmonton, 1927] 18 *l.* (typescript)

Commissioner/Commissaire: H. Harvey.

Loc.: AEA, AEP, OONL

638 **1928**

Commission of Inquiry as to the Equipment, Maintenance, Supervision, Control and Management of the Innisfail Municipal Hospital.
Report. [Calgary, Alta, 1928] 22 *l.* (typescript)

Commissioner/Commissaire: W.L. Walsh.

Loc.: AEA, AEP, OONL

639 **1929**

Commission Appointed to Investigate the Provincial Training School at Red Deer, Provincial Mental Institute at Oliver, Provincial Mental Hospital at Ponoka.
Report. Toronto, 1929. 59 *l.* (typescript)

Commissioners/Commissaires: C.B. Farrar, C.M. Hincks.

Loc.: AEA, AEP

640 **1930**

Commission Appointed to Report on the Lethbridge Northern and Other Irrigation Districts of Alberta.
Report. Edmonton: King's Printer 1930. 42 p.

Chairman/Président: M.L. Wilson.

Members/Membres: L.C. Charlesworth, W.H. Fairfield.

Loc.: AEA, AEP, AEU

641 **1931**

Inquiry into Certain Matters Pertaining to the Administration of the Affairs of the Municipal District of Inga, No. 520.
Report. 1931. 50 *l.* (typescript)

Commissioner/Commissaire: T.M.M. Tweedie.

Loc.: AEA, AEMA, AEP

642 **1934**

Commission Regarding Administration of Justice.
Report. [Edmonton, 1934] 9 *l.* (typescript)

Commissioner/Commissaire: H. Harvey.

Loc.: AEA, AEP, OONL

643 **1935**

Alberta Taxation Inquiry Board on Provincial and Municipal Taxation.
Preliminary report. 1935. 87 p. (typescript)

Loc.: AEA, AEP, OOF

———.
Report. Edmonton: A. Shnitka, King's Printer, 1935. 147 p.

Chairman/Président: J.F. Percival.

Commissioners/Commissaires: J.J. Duggan, J. Gair, W.D. Spence, J.C. Thompson.

Loc.: AC, ACG, AEA, AEP, AEU, OOB, SRL

644 **Royal Commission Respecting the Coal Industry of the Province of Alberta, 1935.**
Report. Edmonton: A. Shnitka, King's Printer, 1936. 103 p.

Commissioner/Commissaire: M. Barlow.

Loc.: AC, ACG, AEA, AEP, AEU, OOCI, OOL, OOM, OONL, OOP, QMU

645 **1936**

Enquiry into and Concerning the Problems of Health, Education and General Welfare of the Half-Breed Population of the Province.
Report. [Edmonton, 1936] 15 *l.* (typescript)

Commissioners/Commissaires: E.A. Braithwaite, J.M. Douglas, A.F. Ewing.

Loc.: ACG, AEA, AEP, OONL

646 **1937**

Commission Appointed in 1936 to Inquire into the Various Phases of Irrigation Development in Alberta.
Report. [Lethbridge, Alta] The Lethbridge Herald, 1937. 32 p.

Chairman/Président: A.F. Ewing.

Commissioners/Commissaires: R.W. Risinger, F.A. Wyatt.

Loc.: ACG, AEA, AEP, AEU, OOA, OOG, OONL, OOS

647 **Special Committee Appointed to Enquire into Fluid Milk and Cream Trade of the Province of Alberta.**
Departmental report. [Edmonton] 1937. 24 *l.* (typescript)

Chairman/Président: R. Sheppard.

Commissioners/Commissaires: W. King, D. Lush, W.E. Masson, W.L. White.

Loc.: AEA, AEP, OONL

648 **1938**

Enquiry Concerning the Construction and Re-construction and Maintenance of the Highway between the City of Edmonton and the City of Wetaskiwin, in the Province of Alberta, and the Highway between the City of Edmonton and the Town of Jasper, in the Province of Alberta.
Report. [Edmonton, 1938] 117 *l.* (typescript)

Commissioner/Commissaire: H.W. Lunney.

Loc.: AEA, AEP

649 **1939**

Commission Appointed to Inquire into Alleged Irregularities in the Conduct and the Management of the Business and Affairs of the Eastern Irrigation District.
Report. [Lethbridge, Alta, 1939] 5 *l.* (typescript)

Commissioner/Commissaire: J.A. Jackson.

Loc.: AEA, AEP, OONL

650 **1940**

Royal Commission Appointed to Inquire into Matters Connected with Petroleum and Petroleum Products.
Alberta's oil industry: the report. Calgary, Alta: [Imperial Oil Limited] 1940. 278 p.

Chairman/Président: A.A. McGillivray.

Commissioner/Commissaire: L.R. Lipsett.

Loc.: AC, ACG, AE, AEP, AEU, BVAS, BVAU, MW, MWP, NBFU, NBSAM, NBSM, NFSM, NSHPL, OH, OKQ, OLU, OOB, OOCC, OOF, OOFF, OOG, OOM, OONE, OONL, OOP, OOSH, OOU, OTH, OTP, OTY, OWAL, QMG, QQL

651 **1942**

Commission Appointed to Inquire into a Disaster which Occurred at the Mine of Brazeau Collieries Limited at Nordegg, Alberta, on October 31st, A.D. 1941.
Report. [Edmonton, 1942?] 34 *l.* (typescript)

Commissioner/Commissaire: A.F. Ewing.
Loc.: AEA, AEP, OOL, OONL

652 **1948**

Commission of Inquiry to Investigate Charges, Allegations and Reports Relating to the Child Welfare Branch of the Department of Public Welfare.
Report. [Edmonton, 1948] 96 *l.* (typescript)

Chairman/Président: W.R. Howson.

Commissioners/Commissaires: E.B. Feir, J.W. McDonald.

Loc.: AC, ACG, AEA, AEHSD, AEP, AEU, OOL, OONL, OOP, OOSC, OTLS, SRL

653 **Royal Commission on Taxation.**
Report. Edmonton: A. Shnitka, King's Printer, 1948. 101 p. (Sessional paper no. 71)

Commissioner/Commissaire: J.W. Judge.

Loc.: AC, ACG, ACU, AEA, AEMA, AEMM, AEP, AET, AEU, BVA, BVAU, NSHPL, OOB, OOF, OOG, OOL, OONL, OTCT, SRL

654 **1949**

Natural Gas Commission.
Enquiry into reserves and consumption of natural gas in the Province of Alberta: report. Edmonton: A. Shnitka, King's Printer, 1949. 127, xv p.

Chairman/Président: R.J. Dinning.

Commissioners/Commissaires: R.C. Marler, A. Stewart.

Loc.: AC, ACSP, AEA, AEMM, AEP, AER, AET, AEU, OONL

655 **1952**

Commission to Conduct an Inquiry into Causes and Conditions Contributing to Floods in the Bow River at Calgary.
Report. 1952. 55 *l.* (typescript)

Chairman/Président: W.J. Dick.

Commissioners/Commissaires: D.W. Hayes, A. McKinnon.

Loc.: AEEN, AEP

656 **1956**

Royal Commission on the Metropolitan Development of Calgary and Edmonton.
Report. Edmonton: A. Shnitka, Printer to the Queen's Most Excellent Majesty, 1956. various pagings

Chairman/Président: G.F. McNally.

Commissioners/Commissaires: G.M. Blackstock, P.G. Davies, C.P. Hayes, I.C. Robison.

Loc.: AC, ACG, ACU, AEA, AEHSD, AEHT, AEMA, AEP, AET, AEU, BVA, BVAU, BVIP, OH, OOCM, OOF, OOGB, OONL, OTU, OTY, OTYL, SRL, SSU

657 **Royal Commission to Investigate the Conduct of the Business of Government.**
Report. Edmonton, 1956. 88, 229 p. (typescript)

Chairman/Président: H.J. Macdonald (1955-1956), J.C. Mahaffy (1956).

Commissioners/Commissaires: M.L. Brown, J.D. Dower, J.H. Galbraith, G.H. Villett.

Also known as/Également connue sous le nom de: Royal Commission Appointed to Investigate Certain Charges and Allegations Made during the Provincial Election Campaign of 1955.

Loc.: AC, AEA, AEP, BVA, OONL, OTP

658 **1958**

Royal Commission on the Development of Northern Alberta.
Report. Edmonton: [Commercial Printers] 1958. xiii, 115 p.

Chairman/Président: J.G. MacGregor.

Commissioners/Commissaires: R.C. Marler, J.O. Patterson.

Loc.: AC, ACG, ACSP, AE, AEA, AEMA, AEP, AEU, BVAS, BVAU, BVIP, OH, OOAG, OOFF, OOG, OORD, OOTC, OTP, OTU

659 **Royal Commission on the Feasibility of Establishing a Scale or Scales of Salaries for Teachers in the Province of Alberta and Allied Matters.**
Report. Edmonton, 1958. 134 *l.* (typescript)

Chairman/Président: G.M. Blackstock.

Commissioners/Commissaires: J. Harvie, H.E. Smith.

Loc.: AC, AE, AEA, AEP, BVAU, MWP, OONL, OTER, OTU, OW

660 **1959**

Royal Commission on Education in Alberta.
Report. Edmonton: L.S. Wall, Printer to the Queen's Most Excellent Majesty, 1959. xxiii, 451 p.

Chairman/Président: D. Cameron.

Commissioners/Commissaires: J.S. Cormack, N.W. Douglas, D.A. Hansen, G.L. Mowat, W.C. Taylor.

Loc.: AC, ACG, AEP, AEU, BVA, BVAS, BVAU, BVI, BVIP, BVIV, MWP, MWU, NFSM, NSHPL, OKQ, OLU, OOCC, OOCU, OOL, OONL, OOP, OOSS, OPET, OSTCB, OTC, OTLS, OTP, OTV, OTY, OWA, OWTU, QMM, QMU, QQL, QQLA, SRL, SSU

661 **1963**

The Royal Commission on Prearranged Funeral Services.
Report. Edmonton, 1963. v, 21 p. (typescript)

Commissioner/Commissaire: C.C. McLaurin.

Loc.: AEA, AESHD, NSHPL, OONL, OTLS, OTYL, SRL

662 **1965**

Inquiry into the Administration, Management and Financial Affairs of the Lethbridge Central Feeder's Association Limited, and the General Operation in Respect to the Participation of the Members Therein.
Report. 1965. 2 v.

Commissioner/Commissaire: L.S. Turcotte.

Loc.: AEA, AEP

663 **1966**

Public Inquiry into the Appointment by the Minister of Education of an Official Trustee for Fort Vermilion School Division No. 52.
Report. 1966. 45 p. (typescript)

Commissioner/Commissaire: N.V. Buchanan.

Loc.: AEA, AEP

664 **1967**

Alberta Royal Commission on Juvenile Delinquency.
Report. [Edmonton] 1967. 62 *l.* (typescript)

Loc.: AC, ACMR, AE, AEA, AEE, AEHSD, AEP, BVA, BVAS, BVAU, BVIP, NFSM, NSPL, OKQL, OLU, OONL, OOP, OOU, OTP, OTU, OTYL, OWAL, QMML, QSHERU, SRU, SSU

———.

Supplementary report on juvenile delinquency in Alberta submitted by Jean Clyne Nelson. [Edmonton] 1967. 107, 2 *l.* (typescript)

Chairman/Président: F.H. Quigley.

Commissioners/Commissaires: J.C. Nelson, F. Kennedy.

Also known as/Également connue sous le nom de: The Provincial Commission on Juvenile Delinquency.

Loc.: AC, ACMR, AE, AEA, AEE, AEHSD, AEP, BVAS, NSHPL, OONL, OTLS, OTU, OWAL, QSHERU

665 **Public Inquiry into the Adequacy of the Provisions of the Mechanics Lien Act, 1960.**
Report. 1967. 193 p. (typescript)

Commissioner/Commissaire: N.V. Buchanan.

Loc.: AC, AEP

666 **1968**

Prairie Provinces Cost Study Commission.
Report. Regina: L. Amon, Queen's Printer, 1968. xxxi, 463 p.

Chairman/Président: M.J. Batten.

Commissioners/Commissaires: W. Newbigging, S.M. Weber.

Also known as/Également connue sous le nom de: Royal Commission on Consumer Problems and Inflation.

Loc.: AC, ACU, AEA, AEP, AEU, BVI, MWA, MWP, OOAG, OONL, SRL, SRPC, SSU

667 **Royal Commission Respecting the Use or Attempted Use by the Honourable Alfred J. Hooke of his Office as a Member of the Executive Council of Alberta, and the Use or Attempted Use by Edgar W. Hinman of his Office as a Member of the Executive Council of Alberta.**
Report. [Edmonton, 1968] 362 p. (typescript)

Commissioner/Commissaire: W.J.C. Kirby.

Loc.: AC, AEP, OONL, OOP

668 **1970**

Commission to Investigate the Services to Single Transient Men in the City of Edmonton, the Methods of Providing such Services and to Assess Allegations of Mistreatment.
Report. [Edmonton] 1970. 14 *l.* (typescript)

Commissioner/Commissaire: M.B. O'Byrne.

Loc.: AEA, AEHSD, AEP, OONL

669 **Inquiry on the Operations of the Edmonton Real Estate Board Co-operative Listing Bureau Limited.**
Report. [Calgary, Alta, 1970] 24 *l.* (typescript)

Commissioner/Commissaire: C.C. McLaurin.

Loc.: AEP, OONL

670 **1971**

Inquiry into the Conduct of Public Business of the Municipality of Calgary.
Interim report with respect to the Police Commission. Yellowknife, N.W.T., 1971. 30 *l.* (typescript)

———.

Report. Yellowknife, N.W.T., 1971. 156 *l.* (typescript)

Commissioner/Commissaire: W.G. Morrow.

Loc.: AC, AEP, AEU

671 **1972**

Commission on Educational Planning.
A future of choices, a choice of futures: report. [Edmonton: L.S. Wall, Queen's Printer for the Province of Alberta, 1972] 325 p.

Commissioner/Commissaire: W.H. Worth.

Loc.: AC, ACG, AEA, AEAG, AEE, AEECA, AEML, AEOM, AEP, AEU, BVA, BVAS, BVAU, MW, MWP, NBFU, NBSU, NSHPL, OKQL, OOC, OOF, OONL, OOP, OOS, OOSH, OOU, OPAL, OTB, OTER, OTU, OTYL, OWTU, QMBM, QMMLS, QMMN, QMU, QQLA, SRL, SSM

672 **1972**

The Red Deer College Inquiry.
Report. Edmonton, 1972. 107 p.

Commissioner/Commissaire: T.C. Byrne.

Loc.: AEAE, AEE, AEIC, AEP, AET, AEU

673 **1973**

Grande Cache Commission.
Final report. [Emonton, 1973] 160 p. (typescript)

Chairman/Président: N.R. Crump.

Commissioners/Commissaires: D. Graham, T.H. Patching.

Loc.: AC, AEFIA, AEHSD, AEHT, AEP, AEU, BVA, BVAS, MWP, OONL, OOP, OOSS, OTYL

674 **Inquiry into the Alleged Excessive Use of Force at the Calgary Correctional Institute.**
Report. [Calgary, Alta, 1973?] unpaged (typescript)

Commissioner/Commissaire: A.M. Harradance.

Loc.: AEP, AEU, BVAS, BVAU, OONL, OOSG, OTYL

675 **1974-1978**

Board of Review, Provincial Courts.
Administration of justice in the provincial courts of Alberta: the coroner system in Alberta. [Edmonton: Queen's Printer for the Province of Alberta, 1974] xix, 23 p. (Report of the Board of Review, Provincial Courts; no. 1)

———.
Administration of justice in the provincial courts of Alberta. Edmonton, 1975. xiii, 222 *l.* (Report of the Board of Review, Provincial Courts; no. 2)

———.
The juvenile justice system in Alberta. [Edmonton, 1977] x, 104 p. (Report of the Board of Review, Provincial Courts; no. 3)

———.
Native people in the administration of justice in the provincial courts of Alberta. [Edmonton, 1974] ix, 88 p. (Report of the Board of Review, Provincial Courts; no. 4)

Chairman/Président: W.J.C. Kirby.

Members/Membres: J.E. Bower, M. Wyman.

Loc.: AC, AEP, AEU, BVAU, MWU, NFSM, OKQL, OLU, OONL, OOP, OOSC, OOSG, OOU, OTMCL, OTUL, OTYL, QMML, QQL, QSHERU

676 **Inquiry Made into Matters Concerning Establishment, Operation and Failure of the Cosmopolitan Life Assurance Company and PAP Holdings Ltd.**
Report. Edmonton, 1974. 137, 72 *l.* (typescript)

Commissioner/Commissaire: R.P. Kerans.

Loc.: AECA, AEP, OONL, OOP, OOU, OTYL, OWAL

677 **1975**

Inquiry Made into Matters Concerning a Grant or Sale of Bull Semen to the Government of Brazil between the 1st Day of January, 1973 and the 28th Day of May, 1975.
Report. [Edmonton, 1975?] 39 *l.* (typescript)

Commissioner/Commissaire: S.V. Legg.

Loc.: AEP, OONL, OTY

678 **Royal Commission to Inquire into the Affairs of the Alberta Housing Corporation.**
Report. [Calgary, Alta, 1975] 160 p.

Commissioner/Commissaire: J.M. Cairns.

Loc.: AEA, AEP, NFSM, OKQL, OONL, OTYL

679 **1978**

Commission of Inquiry into the Affairs and Activities in the Province of Alberta of Royal American Shows Inc.
Royal American Shows Inc. and its activities in Alberta: report. [Edmonton] 1978. various pagings.

Commissioner/Commissaire: J.H. Laycraft.

Loc.: AC, AEP, OOCI, OONL, QMML

Royal Commission to Ascertain Whether any Confidential Information in Possession of the Government of Alberta in Connection with the Annexation of Certain Lands to the City of Edmonton as Provided for in Order in Council 538/81 of June 11, 1981, or in Connection with a Proposed Land Assembly by the Government of Alberta within the Area to be Annexed Was Improperly Made known to any Person, or Whether any Former Member of the Executive Council Made Representations Affecting the Said Annexation and Land Assembly Decisions.
Report. Calgary, Alta, 1982. 60 *l.* (typescript)

Commissioner/Commissaire: W.R. Brennan.

Also known as/Également connue sous le nom de: Brennan Inquiry.

Loc.: OONL, OOP

SASKATCHEWAN

681 **1907**

Commission Appointed to Inquire into and Report upon the Municipal System of the Province of Saskatchewan.
Report. [Regina, 1907] 24 p.

Chairmen/Présidents: P. Ferguson (Rural Section), J.W. Smith (Urban Section).

Commissioners/Commissaires: W. Andrew, H.H. Campkin (Rural Section), A. Whyte (Urban Section).

Also known as/Également connue sous le nom de: Municipal Commission.

Loc.: OONL, OTYL, SRL

682 **1910**

Elevator Commission of the Province of Saskatchewan.
Report. Regina: J.A. Reid, Government Printer, 1910. 141 p.

Chairman/Président: R. Magill.

Commissioners/Commissaires: F.W. Green, G. Langley.

Loc.: OKQ, OOCC, OONL, OOP, OTP, SRL, SSU

683 **1913**

Agricultural Credit Commission of the Province of Saskatchewan.
Report. Regina: J.W. Reid, Government Printer, 1913. 224, iii p.

Chairman/Président: J.H. Haslam.

Commissioners/Commissaires: C.A. Dunning, E.H. Oliver.

Also known as/Également connue sous le nom de: Royal Commission of Inquiry into Agricultural Credit.

Loc.: OKQ, OOAG, OONL, OOP, OTMCL, SSU

684 **1914**

Grain Markets Commission of the Province of Saskatchewan.
Report. Regina: J.W. Reid, Government Printer, 1914. 150, iii p.

Chairman/Président: J.H. Haslam.

Commissioners/Commissaires: C.A. Dunning, G. Langley.

Also known as/Également connue sous le nom de: Royal Commission of Inquiry into Grain Markets.

Loc.: AEU, OKQ, OOAG, OONL, OTMCL, SRL, SSU

685 **1915**

Commission Appointed to Inquire into the Conditions of the Live Stock Industry in the South-Western Portion of the Province.
Final report of Live Stock Commission. In Saskatchewan. Dept. of Agriculture. *Tenth annual report, 1914*. Regina: J.W. Reid, Government Printer, 1915. p. 313-314. (Appendix B)

Chairman/Président: T.R. Brown.

Commissioners/Commissaires: C.M. Hamilton, J.D. Simpson.

Loc.: OOAG, OONL, OOS, OTP, OTY, SRL

686 **Farm Machinery Commission of the Province of Saskatchewan.**
Report. Regina: J.W. Reid, Government Printer, 1915. 41 p.

Chairman/Président: H.W. Newlands.

Commissioners/Commissaires: J.H. Lamont, J.A. Maharg, W.R. Motherwell, W.F.A. Turgeon.

Also known as/Également connue sous le nom de: Royal Commission of Inquiry into Sale of Farm Machinery.

Loc.: OOAG, OONL, SRL

687 **Saskatchewan Educational Commission on Agricultural and Industrial Education, Consolidation of Schools, Training and Supply of Teachers, Courses of Study, Physical and Moral Education, with Recommendations.**
Report. Regina: J.W. Reid, Government Printer, 1915. 208 p.

Chairman/Président: D.P. McColl.

Commissioners/Commissaires: D. McIntyre, W.A. McIntyre, T.E. Perrett, W.J. Rutherford.

Also known as/Également connue sous le nom de: Commission on Agricultural and Industrial Education.

Loc.: AEU, OLU, OONL, SRL, SSU

688 **1917-1918**

Commission Appointed to Inquire into and Investigate the Marketing of Live Stock and Live Stock Products of the Province.
Interim report. Regina: J.W. Reid, King's Printer, 1917. 92 p.

Loc.: ACG, OONL, SRL, SSU

―――――.
Final report. Regina: J.W. Reid, King's Printer, 1918. 110 p.

Chairman/Président: W.C. Sutherland.

Commissioners/Commissaires: J.D. McGregor, W.R. Motherwell, J.G. Rutherford, O.D. Skelton.

Also known as/Également connue sous le nom de: Livestock Commission.

Loc.: SRL

689 **1921**

Royal Commission of Inquiry into Farming Conditions.
Report. Regina: J.W. Reid, King's Printer, 1921. 70 p.

Chairman/Président: W.J. Rutherford.

Commissioners/Commissaires: J. Bracken, N. McTaggart, H.O. Powell, G. Spence.

Also known as/Également connue sous le nom de: Better Farming Commission.

Loc.: ACG, BVAS, NFSM, OOA, OOAG, OODF, QMU, SRL, SSU

690 **1922**

Saskatchewan Anti-Tuberculosis Commission.
Report. Regina: J.W. Reid, King's Printer, 1922. 94 p.

Chairman/Président: A.B. Cook.

Commissioners/Commissaires: J.F. Cairns, R.G. Ferguson.

Loc.: OONL, SRL

691 **1928**

Saskatchewan Power Resources Commission.
Report. Regina: J.W. Reid, King's Printer, 1928. 190 p.

Chairman/Président: L.A. Thornton.

Commissioners/Commissaires: A.R. Greig, A. Hitchcock.

Loc.: ACG, OOAG, OONL, OOP, QQL, SRPC, SSU

692 **1929**

Royal Commission Appointed to Enquire into Workmen's Compensation for Saskatchewan.
Report. Regina: J.W. Reid, King's Printer, 1929. 30 p.

Chairman/Président: P.M. Anderson.

Commissioners/Commissaires: A.W. Heise, L.D. McTavish, F.M. Still, H. Perry.

Loc.: OOL, OONL, OTYL, SRL

693 **Royal Grain Inquiry Commission.**
Reports. Regina: J.W. Reid, King's Printer, 1929. 157 p.

Chairman/Président: J.T. Brown.

Commissioners/Commissaires: W.J. Rutherford, J.A. Stoneman.

Also known as/Également connue sous le nom de: Commission Appointed to Inquire into the Grading, Mixing, Handling and Marketing of Western Canada Grain.

Loc.: AEP, BVAU, BVIP, OOAG, OOCC, OOCI, OH, OONL, OTP, OTY, SRL

694 **1930**

Public Service Inquiry Commission.
Report. Regina, 1930. 54, 29 p. (typescript)

Chairman/Président: M.J. Coldwell.

Commissioners/Commissaires: J.F. Bryant, A. Hayworth.

Loc.: OONL, OOP, SRL

695 **Saskatchewan Royal Commission on Immigration and Settlement, 1930.**
Report. Regina: R.S. Garrett, King's Printer, 1930. 206 p.

Chairman/Président: W.W. Swanson.

Commissioners/Commissaires: T. Johnston, G.C. Neff, A.R. Reusch, P.H. Shelton.

Loc.: ACG, BVAU, OH, OOAG, OOCC, OOG, OONL, OTP, OWTU, SRL, SSU

696 **1931**

Royal Commission to Inquire into Statements Made in Statutory Declarations and Other Matters, 1930.
Report. Regina: R.S. Garrett, King's Printer, 1931. 180 p.

Chairman/Président: J. McKay.

Commissioners/Commissaires: J.F.L. Embury, P.E. Mackenzie.

Loc.: OONL, OOP, OTMCL, OTYL, SRL

697 **1934**

Royal Milk Inquiry Commission, 1933.
Report. [Regina, 1934] 42 p. (typescript)

Commissioner/Commissaire: W. Allen.

Also known as/Également connue sous le nom de: Milk Inquiry Commission.

Loc.: OKQ, OOAG, OOCI, OONL, OTP, SRL, SSU

698 **1935**

Royal Commission on the Coal Mining Industry in the Province of Saskatchewan.
Report. Regina: T.H. McConica, King's Printer, 1935. 46 p.

Commissioner/Commissaire: W.F.A. Turgeon.

Loc.: OLU, OOCI, OOM, OONL, OTP, SRL, SSU

699 **1936**

Commission of Inquiry into Provincial and Municipal Taxation.
Report. Regina: T.H. McConica, King's Printer, 1936. 196 p.

Chairman/Président: N.H. Jacoby.

Members/Membres: H.H. Christie, L. Johnson, C.E. Little, J.J. McGurran.

Also known as/Également connue sous le nom de: Taxation Commission.

Loc.: BVAS, BVAU, MWU, NSHS, OOB, OOF, OONL, OOS, OTP, OTY, SRL, SSU

700 **1938**

Royal Commission to Inquire into and Make Recommendations Concerning the Advisability of Providing Standard Forms of Mortgage, Crop Payment Leases, Agreements for Sale, Chattel Mortgages, Lien Notes and Conditional Sale Agreements for Use in the Province.
Report. [Regina] 1938. 47 *l*. (typescript)

Commissioner/Commissaire: W.M. Martin.

Loc.: OONL, OTYL, SRL

701 **1943**

Commission on Employer-Employee Relations.
Report. [Regina?] 1943. 64, 3 *l*. (typescript)

Commissioners/Commissaires: H.Y. MacDonald, W.M. Martin.

Loc.: OONL, OTYL, SRL

702 **1944**

> **Health Services Survey Commission.**
> *Report.* Regina: T.H. McConica, King's Printer, 1944. 14 p.
>
> **Commissioner/Commissaire:** H.E. Sigerist.
>
> Loc.: MWP, OOB, OONH, OONL, OTP, QMMM, SRL, SSU

703 **1946**

> **Commission on Little Manitou Lake.**
> *Report.* [Regina?] 1946. 25 l. (typescript)
>
> **Chairman/Président:** O. Wingrove.
>
> **Commissioners/Commissaires:** B. Brachman, W.P. Johns, J.G. Rempel.
>
> Loc.: OONL, OTP, SRL

704 **1947**

> **Royal Commission on Forestry Relating to the Forest Resources and Industries of Saskatchewan.**
> *Report.* Regina: T.H. McConica, King's Printer, 1947. 150 p.
>
> **Chairman/Président:** F. Eliason.
>
> **Commissioners/Commissaires:** W. Bayliss, D. Galbraith, J.C.W. Irwin, J. Mitchell.
>
> Also known as/Également connue sous le nom de: Saskatchewan Royal Commission on Forestry.
>
> Loc.: ACG, BVAU, OLU, OOB, OOFP, OONL, OOS, SRL

705 **Royal Commission on the Fisheries of the Province of Saskatchewan.**
Report. Regina: [T.H. McConica, King's Printer for Saskatchewan] 1947. 131 p.

Chairman/Président: W.A. Clemens.

Commissioners/Commissaires: H. McAllister, A.H. MacDonald, A. Mansfield, D.S. Rawson.

Loc.: ACG, BVAU, MWU, NBFU, OLU, OOF, OON, OONL, OTP, OWTU, SRL, SSU

706 **1949**

Commission to Investigate the Penal System of Saskatchewan.
Report. [Regina: T.H. McConica, King's Printer, 1949] iv, 116 p.

Chairman/Président: S.R. Laycock.

Commissioners/Commissaires: C. Halliday, W.H. Holman.

Also known as/Également connue sous le nom de: The Saskatchewan Penal Commission.

Loc.: ACU, AEU, BVIV, MWU, NSHDL, OKQL, OONL, OOP, OOSG, OTYL, QMU, SSU

707 **1950**

Royal Commission on the Coal Industry of Saskatchewan.
Report. Regina: T.H. McConica, King's Printer, 1950. 79 p.

Chairman/Président: J.E.L. Graham.

Commissioners/Commissaires: R.C. Carter, R.D. Howland.

Loc.: BVA, BVAU, NSHPL, OLU, OOF, OOL, OON, OONL, OOTC, OTU, QQL, SRL, SSU

708 **1953**

Royal Commission on Public Accountancy in Saskatchewan, 1953.
Report. [Regina?] 1953. 44 *l.* (typescript)

Chairman/Président: H.F. Thomson.

Commissioners/Commissaires: F.C. Cronkite, T.H. McLeod.

Loc.: MWP, OOB, OOCC, OONL, OTU, OTYL, SRL, SSU

709 **1954-1958**

Royal Commission on Agriculture and Rural Life.
Crown land settlement in North-Eastern Saskatchewan; interim report.
Regina, 1954. 52 l. *(typescript)*

Loc.: BVAU, MWP, OOGB, OONL, OTU, SRL, SSU

The scope and character of the investigation. Regina: L. Amon, Printer to the Queen's Most Excellent Majesty, 1955. xiii, 122 p. (Report of the Royal Commission on Agriculture and Rural Life; no. 1)

Mechanization and farm costs. Regina: L. Amon, Printer to the Queen's Most Excellent Majesty, 1955. xv, 175 p. (Report of the Royal Commission on Agriculture and Rural Life; no. 2)

Agriculture credit. Regina: L. Amon, Printer to the Queen's Most Excellent Majesty, 1955. xiii, 131 p. (Report of the Royal Commission on Agriculture and Rural Life; no. 3)

Rural roads and local government. Regina: L. Amon, Printer to the Queen's Most Excellent Majesty, 1955. xix, 320 p. (Report of the Royal Commission on Agricultural and Rural Life; no. 4)

Land tenure: rights and responsibilities in land use in Saskatchewan. Regina: L. Amon, Printer to the Queen's Most Excellent Majesty, 1955. xiv, 194 p. (Report of the Royal Commission on Agriculture and Rural Life; no. 5)

Rural education. Regina: L. Amon, Printer to the Queen's Most Excellent Majesty, 1956. xxii, 438 p. (Report of the Royal Commission on Agriculture and Rural Life; no. 6)

Movement of farm people. Regina: L. Amon, Printer to the Queen's Most Excellent Majesty, 1956. xvii, 210 p. (Report of the Royal Commission on Agriculture and Rural Life; no. 7)

Agricultural markets and prices. Regina: L. Amon, Printer to the Queen's Most Excellent Majesty, 1956. xvi, 251 p. (Report of the Royal Commission on Agriculture and Rural Life; no. 8)

Crop insurance. Regina: L. Amon, Printer to the Queen's Most Excellent Majesty, 1956. xii, 143 p. (Report of the Royal Commission on Agriculture and Rural Life; no. 9)

The home and family in rural Saskatchewan. Regina: L. Amon, Printer to the Queen's Most Excellent Majesty, 1956. xiv, 198 p. (Report of the Royal Commission on Agriculture and Rural Life; no. 10)

———.
Farm electrification. Regina: L. Amon, Printer to the Queen's Most Excellent Majesty, 1957. xii, 100 p. (Report of the Royal Commission on Agricultural and Rural Life; no. 11)

———.
Service centers. Regina: L. Amon, Printer to the Queen's Most Excellent Majesty, 1957. xiii, 154 p. (Report of the Royal Commission on Agriculture and Rural Life; no. 12)

———.
Farm income. Regina: L. Amon, Printer to the Queen's Most Excellent Majesty, 1958. xx, 451 p. (Report of the Royal Commission on Agriculture and Rural Life; no. 13)

———.
A program of improvement. Regina: L. Amon, Printer to the Queen's Most Excellent Majesty, 1957. x, 149 p. (Report of the Royal Commission on Agriculture and Rural Life; no. 14)

Chairman/Président: W.B. Baker.

Commissioners/Commissaires: N. Adams, T.H. Bourassa, H.L. Fowler, C.W. Gibbings, J.L. Phelps.

Loc.: ACG, AEU, BVAS, MWU, NFSM, NSHPL, OKQL, OOA, OOB, OONL, OOP, OTP, OTY, OWA, QMHE, QMM, QMU, QQL, SRL, SSU

710 **1958**

Royal Commission on Certain Mineral Transactions, 17th December, 1958.
Report. [Regina, 1958] 78 *l*.

Chairman/Président: R.T. Graham.

Members/Membres: F.C. Cronkite, T. Lax.

Loc.: BVAU, OONL, OTU, SRL

711 **1963**

Commission in the Matter of The Mechanics' Lien Act.
Report. [Regina] 1963. 53, 49 *l*. (typescript)

Commissioner/Commissaire: H.F. Thomson.

Also known as/Également connue sous le nom de: Royal Commission on Mechanics' Liens.

Loc.: AEU, BVA, BVAU, MWU, NSHD, OONL, OTYL, OWAL, SRL, SSU

712 **1963**

Inquiries into Hospital Staff Appointments.
Report. Regina, 1963. vii, 104 *l.* (typescript)

Commissioner/Commissaire: M. Woods.

Loc.: ACG, AE, MWP, OONL, OOP, OTP, SRL

713 **1965**

Royal Commission on Government Administration.
Report. Regina: L. Amon, Printer to the Queen's Most Excellent Majesty, 1965. 1040 p.

Chairman/Président: F.W. Johnson.

Commissioners/Commissaires: L.I. Barber, J.M. Rowand.

Loc.: ACG, ACU, AE, AEU, BVA, BVAU, BVIV, MW, OLU, OOAG, OOCC, OOF, OONL, OOP, OOPW, OORD, OTMCL, OTP, QMHE, SRL, SSU

714 **1965**

Royal Commission on Taxation.
Report. Regina: L. Amon, Printer to the Queen's Most Excellent Majesty, 1965. xv, 225. p.

Chairman/Président: T.H. McLeod.

Commissioners/Commissaires: K.L. George, E.G. Miller.

Loc.: ACU, AEU, BVAS, BVAU, BVIV, NFSM, NSHDIP, OOCC, OONL, OOS, OOU, OTP, OTU, OTY, OWA, QMML, QMU, SRL, SSU

715 **1966**

Public Accountancy Commission.
Report. Regina: L. Amon, Printer to the Queen's Most Excellent Majesty, 1966. 54 p.

Chairman/Président: M.J. Batten.

Commissioners/Commissaires: J.P. Pringle, L. Wilkinson.

Loc.: BVAS, BVIV, OONL, SRL

716 **Royal Commission on Surface Rights and Pipeline Easements.**
Report. Regina, 1966. various pagings (typescript)

Commissioner/Commissaire: J.E. Friesen.

Loc.: AE, AEU, BVA, BVAU, MWU, NSHDL, OONL, OOP, OTUL, OTYL, OWAL, QMML, SRPC, SSU

717 **1967**

Library Inquiry Committee.
Library service in Saskatchewan: the report of the Library Inquiry Committee (a survey with recommendations). Regina: The Library Inquiry Committee, 1967. 134 p.

Chairman/Président: J.H. Maher.

Members/Membres: R.H. Macdonald, W.A. Riddell.

Loc.: AC, AE, AEU, BVA, BVAS, BVAU, BVIP, BVIV, MW, MWP, OLUS, OOC, OONH, OONL, OOP, OOU, OTP, OTULS, OW, QMMLS, QMU, SRL, SRP, SRU, SSU

1968

Prairie Provinces Cost Study Commission.

see/voir

Alberta. Prairie Provinces Cost Study Commission.
(no. 666)

718 **1973**

Royal Commission on University Organization and Structure.
Report. [Regina?] 1973. iii, 48 *l*. (typescript)

Chairman/Président: E. Hall.

Members/Membres: S. Nicks, G. South.

Loc.: AEU, BVAS, BVAU, OONL, OOSS, OPET, OTY, OWA, QMG, QSHERU, SRL, SSU

719 **1977**

Royal Commission Appointed to Inquire into the Wilderness Challenge Camps as Proposed and Operated by the Ranch Ehrlo Society.
Report. [Saskatoon, Sask., 1977] 90 *l.* (typescript)

Commissioner/Commissaire: J.H. Maher.

Loc.: OONL, SRL, SSU

720 **1978**

The Cluff Lake Board of Inquiry.
Final Report. Regina, 1978. xii, 429 p.

Chairman/Président: E.D. Bayda.

Members/Membres: A. Groome, K. McCallum.

Loc.: AEU, BVA, BVAWC, BVI, MWP, NSHPL, OKF, OOAECB, OOF, OOFF, OON, OONHBR, OONL, OOP, OOTC, QMHE, SRL, SSU

NEWFOUNDLAND/TERRE-NEUVE

721 **1950**

The Royal Commission on the Cost of Living in Newfoundland.
Report. St. John's, 1950. xv, 111 *l.*

Chairman/Président: F.S. Grisdale.

Commissioners/Commissaires: L.H.M. Ayre, C.C. Janes.

Loc.: MWP, NFSG, NFSM, OKF, OOB, OOCI, OOF, OOL, OONL, OOP, OTP

722 **1955**

Royal Commission on Forestry.
Report. St. John's: D.R. Thistle, Printer to the Queen's Most Excellent Majesty, 1955. 240 p.

Chairman/Président: H. Kennedy.

Commissioners/Commissaires: D.R. Cameron, R.C. Goodyear.

Loc.: BVAU, MWP, NFSG, NFSM, OH, OOB, OOF, OOFF, OONL, OTP, OTU, QQL, QQLA

723 **1956**

Commission of Enquiry into the Questions Relating to the Imposition of the School Tax at Corner Brook.
Report. St. John's, 1956. 72 *l.*

Commissioners/Commissaires: B.J. Abbott, C. Sheppard, B. White.

Loc.: MWP, NFSG, NFSM, OONL

724 **Royal Commission on Agriculture.**
Report. St. John's: D.R. Thistle, Printer to the Queen's Most Excellent Majesty, 1956. 391 p.

Chairman/Président: A.M. Shaw.

Commissioners/Commissaires: W.M. Drummond, P.J. Murray.

Loc.: BVA, BVAU, BVIV, NBSAM, NFSG, NFSM, NSHPL, OOAG, OOB, OOF, OONL, OOP, OOTU, QQL

725 **1957**

The Newfoundland Royal Commission for the Preparation of the Case of the Government of Newfoundland for the Revision of the Financial Terms of the Union.
Report. St. John's, 1957. 2 v.

Chairman/Président: P.J. Lewis.

Members/Membres: G.S. Doyle, P. Gruchy, A.B. Perlin, C.C. Pratt.

Loc.: BVAU, NFSG, NFSM, OOB, OONL, OOP

726 **1960**

Commission of Enquiry on the Logging Industry.
Report. [St. John's] 1960. 61, xviii p.

Chairman/Président: B. Dunfield.

Commissioners/Commissaires: A. Bugden, R. Leith.

Loc.: BVA, BVAU, NFSG, NFSM, NSHPL, OOB, OOL, OONL, OTU

727 **Royal Commission on Pensions, 1960.**
Report. St. John's, 1960. viii, 263, 39 *l.* (typescript)

Chairman/Président: G.W.D. Allen.

Commissioners/Commissaires: F.R. Clark, J.G. O'Grady.

Loc.: NFSG

728 **1962**

The Royal Commission on Truck Transportation.
Report. [St. John's] Guardian Limited, 1962. 71 p.

Chairman/Président: A. Johnson.

Commissioners/Commissaires: R.R. Costigan, G.C. Rowe.

Loc.: NFSG, NFSM, OOFF, OONL, OOTC, OTLS, QQL, QQLA

729 **1964**

Commission of Enquiry on House Construction Costs in the City of St. John's, Newfoundland.
Report. St. John's, 1964. 1 v.

Chairman/Président: P.H. White.

Member/Membres: J.W. Conway, R. Manning, M.O. Morgan, H.T. Renouf.

Loc.: NFSG, NFSM

730 **1966**

Commission of Enquiry into the Practice of Public Accounting.
Report. [St. John's] 1966. 36 p.

Commissioner/Commissaire: B. Dunfield.

Loc.: MWP, NFSG, NFSM, OONL, OOP

731 **The Royal Commission on Electrical Energy.**
Report. [St. John's] 1966. 108 *l.*

Chairman/Président: G.C. Rowe.

Commissioners/Commissaires: W.G. Adams, W. Andrews, H. Baird, M. Blackmore, R. Cheeseman, C. Eaton, G.I. Hill, H.K. Joyce, P.D. Lewis, F.J. O'Leary, J. Parker.

Loc.: NFSG, NFSM, NSHPL, OOF, OONE, OONL, OOP

732 **Royal Commission on Health.**
Report. [St. John's] 1966. 3 v.

Commissioner/Commissaire: W.R. Brain.

Loc.: BVAS, MWHP, MWU, NFSM, NFSMM, NSHPL, OLUM, OOF, OONH, OONL, OOP, OTU, OTY, QMM

733 **Royal Commission on Pensions.**
Report. St. John's, 1966. 2 v. (typescript)

Chairman/Président: G.T. Dyer.

Members/Membres: J.V. Ralph, F.D.R. Woolgar.

Loc.: NFSG, NFSM, OOF, OONL

734 **The Royal Commission on Transportation.**
Report. [St. John's] 1966. 91 p.

Chairman/Président: P.J. Lewis.

Commissioners/Commissaires: W. Atkinson, F. Ayre, H. Collingwood, R. Cook, A. Crosbie, W. Hann, N. Hutton, E. Miller, J. Molloy, F. Noseworthy, U. Strickland, E. Winsor.

Loc.: NFSG, NFSM

735 **1967-1968**

Royal Commission on Education and Youth.
Report. [St. John's] 1967-1968. 2 v.

Chairman/Président: P.J. Warren.

Commissioners/Commissaires: C. Abbott, L.H.M. Ayre, P.D. Bowring, T.J. Dalton, T.M. Doyle, T.M. Hopkins, G. LeGrow, H.D. Macgillivray, G.B. March, J.J. Murphy, C.C. Pratt.

Loc.: AEU, BVAU, MWU, NFSG, NFSM, OKQM, OLU, OOCU, OOCW, OONF, OONL, OOSS, OTP, OTU, OTY, OWA, QQLA, SSU

736 **Royal Commission on the Economic State and Prospects of Newfoundland and Labrador.**
Report. St. John's: Creative Printers & Publishers, Office of the Queen's Printer, 1967. 498 p.

Chairman/Président: G.F. Pushie.

Commissioners/Commissaires: J.D. Fraser, J.D. Grubb, A.R. Lundrigan, A.M. Martin, J.C. McCarthy, H. Mifflin, F.D. Moores, J.R. O'Dea, A.B. Perlin, C.A. Pippy, H.D. Roberts, N.H. Smith, L.B. Stead.

Loc.: BVA, NFSG, NFSM, OOB, OOF, OOFI, OONE, OONL, OOS, OTCT, OTP, OWAL, QQL, QQLA, SSU

737 **1968**

Royal Commission on Food and Drug Prices.
Report. St. John's, 1968. 2, 167 *l.* (typescript)

Chairman/Président: W.G. Adams.

Commissioners/Commissaires: H. Allen, T.J. Dalton, J. O'Brien.

Loc.: NFSG, NFSM, NSHPL, OONL, OTYL

738 **Royal Commission on Minimum Wages.**
Report. St. John's, 1968. vii, 86 *l.* (typescript)

Chairman/Président: J.D. Higgins.

Commissioners/Commissaires: L.J. Dobbin, P.J. Gardiner.

Loc.: NFSG

739 **1969**

Commission of Enquiry into the Cost of Home Construction and Housing in the Province of Newfoundland and Labrador.
Report. [St. John's] 1969. 2 v.

Commissioner/Commissaire: L.W. Kostaszek.

Loc.: BVAU, NFSG, NFSM, OONL, QSHERU

740 **1969-1970**

Royal Commission on the City of St. John's Act.
Interim report. [St. John's] 1969. various pagings (typescript)

Loc.: MWP, NFSG, NFSM, OONL, OTYL, QQL

Final report. [St. John's] 1970. 3, 2, 14 *l.* (typescript)

Chairman/Président: E.J. Phelan.

Commissioners/Commissaires: D.W.K. Dawe, G. Stirling.

Loc.: NFSG, NFSM, OONL, QQL

741 **Royal Commission Respecting Radiation, Compensation & Safety at the Fluorspar Mines St. Lawrence, Nfld.**
Report. [St. John's] 1969. 341 p.

Chairman/Président: F.J. Aylward.

Members/Membres: F. Gover, H.B. Murphy, W.D. Parsons.

Loc.: NFSG, NFSM, OOL, OOM, OONL, OOP

742 **1970**

Royal Commission on Forestry.
Report. St. John's, 1970. 63 p.

Chairman/Président: L.Z. Rousseau.

Commissioners/Commissaires: H.J. Hodgins, R.E. McArdle.

Loc.: AEU, BVAS, BVAU, NFSM, OOFF, OONL

743 **1972-1973**

Royal Commission of Enquiry into Blackhead Road Urban Renewal Scheme.
Final report, part-I: summary of findings and recommendations. St. John's, 1972. various pagings

Loc.: AEU, MWP, OONL, NFSG, NFSM, QQL

———.

Interim report, part-II: urban renewal plan. Rev. ed. St. John's, 1973. various pagings

———.

Interim report, part-III: land acquisition and compensation. St. John's, 1973. various pagings

———.

Interim report, part-IV: municipal services. St. John's, 1972. various pagings

———.

Interim report, part-V: administration and cost. St. John's, 1972. various pagings

Interim report, part-VI: social and community development. St. John's, 1972. various pagings

Commissioner/Commissaire: L.M. Kostaszek.

Loc.: NFSG, NFSM

744 **The Royal Commission on Labour Legislation in Newfoundland and Labrador.**
Report. St. John's: Office of the Queen's Printer, 1972. 1(50), 561 p.

Commissioner/Commissaire: M. Cohen.

Loc.: BVA, BVAS, MWP, NFSG, NFSM, NSHPL, OLU, OOEC, OOF, OONL, OOP, OOSC, OOUD, OTY, OWAL, QMU, QQLA

745 **Royal Commission on St. John's Harbour Arterial Route.**
Report. St. John's, 1972. various pagings (typescript)

Commissioner/Commissaire: T.G. Dalton.

Loc.: NFSM, OONL, OOTC

746 **Royal Commission on Taxation and Revenue of the City of St. John's.**
Report. St. John's, 1972. xiv, 321 p.

Commissioner/Commissaire: J.D. Fraser.

Loc.: NFSG, NFSM, OONL, OOP, OTU, OTYL, QMML

747 **Royal Commission to Enquire into the Leasing of Premises for the Use and Occupancy of the Newfoundland Liquor Commission.**
Report. [St. John's] 1972. 47, lvii p.

Chairman/Président: F. O'Dea.

Commissioner/Commissaire: J.D. Wilson.

Loc.: AEU, MWP, MWU, NFSG, NFSM, OOF, OONL, OOP, OTYL, OWAL, QQL

748 **1973**

The Royal Commission on Illegal Work Stoppages.
Report. [St. John's] 1973. xv, 82 p.

Commissioner/Commissaire: E.A. Neary.

Loc.: AEU, BVA, BVAS, MWP, MWU, NFSG, NFSM, OONL, OOP, OTMCL, OTYL, OWAL, QMML, QQL, SRL, SSU

749 **The Royal Commission on Matters Pertaining to the Relationships of the Workmen's Compensation Board with the Employees.**
Report. [St. John's, 1973?] vii, 32 p.

Commissioner/Commissaire: H. O'Neill.

Loc.: BVA, BVAS, NFSG, NFSM, OLU, OOL, OONL, OOP, OTMCL, OTYL, OWAL, QMML, QQL, SRL, SSU

750 **Royal Commission to Enquire into the Amount of Social Assistance Received by Frederick Thompson and Ruth Thompson of Bauline Line, St. John's.**
Report. [St. John's] 1973. 56, xliv *l.* (typescript)

Commissioner/Commissaire: G.W. Seabright.

Loc.: NFSG, NFSM, OONL, OOP

751 **Royal Commission to Enquire into the Magistracy of Newfoundland and Labrador.**
Report. [St. John's] 1973. 423 p.

Commissioner/Commissaire: G.L. Steele.

Loc.: AEU, OONL, OOP, QMML

752 **1974**

The Commission of Enquiry into Certain Matters Pertaining to Welfare and the Disposition of DOSCO Assets, on Bell Island, Newfoundland.
Report: part I, welfare. St. John's, 1974. vii, 110 *l.* (typescript)

Commissioner/Commissaire: A.S. Mifflin.

Loc.: MWP, NFSG, NFSM, QQL, SRL

753 **1974-1976**

Commission of Enquiry into the St. John's Urban Region Study.
First interim report. St. John's, 1974. 2 v.

Loc.: NFSM, NSHDIP, OONL, OOP

———.
Second interim report. St. John's, 1975. viii, 86 p.

Loc.: MWP, NFSM, NSHDIP, OONL, OOP, QQL

———.
Third and final report. St. John's, 1976. xiii, 317 p.

Chairman/Président: A.G. Henley.

Commissioners/Commissaires: M.G. Andrews, H.B. Morgan.

Loc.: AEU, BVIP, NFSM, OONL, OOP, QQL

754 **Royal Commission on Labrador.**
Social services. [St. John's] 1974. iii, 297 p. (Report of the Royal Commission on Labrador; v. 1)

———.
Social services. [St. John's, 1974] iv, 298-532 p. (Report of the Royal Commission on Labrador; v. 2)

———.
Economic factors. [St. John's, 1974] vi, 533-772 p. (Report of the Royal Commission on Labrador; v. 3)

———.
Economic factors. [St. John's, 1974] vii, 772A-1079 p. (Report of the Royal Commission on Labrador; v. 4)

———.
Other matters: status of women, population, isolation. [St. John's, 1974] ii, 1080-1165 p. (Report of the Royal Commission on Labrador; v. 5)

———.
The role of government. [St. John's, 1974] iv, 1166-1412 p. (Report of the Royal Commission on Labrador; v. 6)

Chairman/Président: D. Snowden.

Commissioners/Commissaires: C. Goodyear, F. Hettasch, R. Snell.

Loc.: AEU, BVAS, BVAU, MWP, NFSM, OOFF, OONL, OORD, OOTC, OTMCL, OTY, OWAL, SRL

755 **Royal Commission on Mineral Revenue.**
Report. St. John's, 1974. various pagings (typescript)

Commissioners/Commissaires: G.K. Goundrey, W.H. Maher, L.A. Martin.

Loc.: AEU, MWP, MWU, NFSG, NFSM, OKQL, OONL, OOP, OOTC, OTYL, QMML, QQL, SRL

756 **Royal Commission on Municipal Government in Newfoundland and Labrador.**
Report. St. John's, 1974. 711 p.

Chairman/Président: H.J. Whalen.

Commissioners/Commissaires: H.G. Harnett, T.M. Hopkins, C.W. Powell.

Loc.: BVIP, MWP, NBSU, NFSG, NSHPL, OONL, OOP, OTY, QQL, SRL

757 **Royal Commission on Nursing Education.**
Report. [St. John's] 1974. various pagings (typescript)

Commissioner/Commissaire: L.A. Miller.

Loc.: BVAU, BVAS, NFSM, OOCN, OONL, OOP, OTMCL, OTU, QQL, SRL

758 **1975**

Commission of Inquiry into the Closing of Upper Gullies School.
Final report. [St. John's, 1975] 126 p. (typescript)

Commissioner/Commissaire: T.J. Corbett.

Loc.: NFSG, NFSM, OONL, OOP

759 **1977**

Commission Appointed to Enquire into the Purchase and Delivery of a Television Set, Worth in Excess of $1,000.00, to the Honourable Frank D. Moores, Premier of Newfoundland, by A.B. Walsh Electrical Limited.
Report. [St. John's, 1977] 10 *l.* (typescript)

Commissioner/Commissaire: R.S. Furlong.

Loc.: NFSG, OONL, OOP

760 **1978**

Commission of Enquiry into all Matters Relating to the Acquisition of Land for, in Connection with or Incidental to the Development of Gros Morne National Park.
Report. [St. John's] 1978. various pagings (typescript)

Commissioner/Commissaire: H.H. Cummings.

Loc.: NFSG, NFSM, OONL, OOP

761 **Commission of Enquiry into the Chafe's Nursing Home Fire, Dec. 26, 1976 and into the Safety Standards and Quality of Care in Homes for Special Care and Welfare Institutions in the Province of Newfoundland.**
Report. St. John's, [1978?] iv, 252 *l.* (typescript)

Commissioner/Commissaire: J.R. Gushue

Also known as/Également connue sous le nom de: Chafe's Nursing Home Public Inquiry.

Loc.: MWP, NFSG, NFSM, OONL, OOP, QQL

762 **1979**

Public Enquiry into Release and Publication of Police Reports into Fire at Elizabeth Towers, St. John's.
First report. [Corner Brook, Nfld., 1979] 47 *l.* (typescript)

Commissioner/Commissaire: P.L. Soper.

Loc.: NFSG, OONL, OOP

763 **1979-1981**

Royal Commission into the Cause or Causes of Three Industrial Accidents Involving Death which Occurred in January and February, 1977, within the Mines and Property of the Iron Ore Company of Canada Situated near Labrador City and into the Circumstances Surrounding the Same.
Report. St. John's, 1979-1981. 2 v.

Commissioner/Commissaire: V.P. McCarthy.

Loc.: OONL, OOP

764 **1980-1981**

Royal Commission to Inquire into the Inshore Fishery of Newfoundland and Labrador.
Report. St. John's, 1980-1981. 2 v.

Chairman/Président: B.V. Paddock.

Commissioners/Commissaires: D.E. Howley, A.J. Maloney.

Loc.: NFSG, NFSM, OOEC, OOF, OONL, OOP

765 **1981**

Commission of Inquiry into the Purchasing Procedures of the Department of Public Works and Services.
Report. St. John's, 1981. viii, 522 p. (typescript)

Commissioner/Commissaire: J.W. Mahoney.

Loc.: OONL, OOP

766 **Royal Commission of Enquiry into the Financial Losses of Marystown Shipyard Limited.**
Report. St. John's, 1981. vi, 201 p.

Chairman/Président: R.J. Olivero.

Commissioners/Commissaires: J.G. Day, F.W. Russell.

Loc.: OONL, OOP

767 **Royal Commission on Forest Protection and Management.**
Report. St. John's, 1981. 2 v.

Chairman/Président: C.F. Poole.

Commissioners/Commissaires: W.J. Carroll, A.T. Rowe.

Loc.: BVIF, OOFF, OONL, OOP, SRL

INDEX TO CHAIRMEN AND COMMISSIONERS — INDEX DES PRÉSIDENTS ET COMMISSAIRES

A

Abbott, B.J., 723
Abbott, C., 735
Adami, J.G., 302
Adams, N., 709
Adams, W.G., 731, 737
Ahern, M.J., 302
Aikins, J.A.M., 369, 372
Akerley, I.W., 100
Alexander, H.O., 492
Allen, G.W.D., 727
Allen, H., 737
Allen, W., 697
Alleyn, R., 343
Allison, G.A., 357
Amos, W.A., 169
Amyot, W., 307
Anderson, P.M., 692
Anderson, W.M., 568
Andrew, G.C., 584
Andrew, W., 681
Andrews, A.E., 27
Andrews, M.G., 753
Andrews, W., 731
Anglin, T.W., 119, 121, 122, 126
Angus, H.F., 567, 573, 575
April, N., 346
Archibald, M.B., 65
Arès, R., 316
Arnaud, F.H., 606
Ash, A.J.R., 552
Asselin, L.N., 292, 293
Atkinson, W., 734
Auger, G., 319
Avery, W.H., 215
Aylen, J.O., 241
Aylesworth, A.B., 138
Aylsworth, J.B., 115
Aylward, F.J., 741
Ayre, F., 734
Ayre, L.H.M., 721, 735

B

Bélanger, M., 341
Baby, G., 297
Bain, J., Jr., 132
Bain, J.W., 152
Baird, H., 731
Baker, W.B., 709
Balcom, A.B., 61
Balcom, S.R., 96
Ball, F.A., 423
Ball, H.M., 440
Ballantyne, T., 115
Barber, L.I., 713
Barker, F.E., 5
Barlow, M., 644
Baron, D.R., 421
Barr, A., 349
Barrett, G., 389
Barron, J.A., 136
Barrow, A.I., 100
Barry, R.L., 375
Bartlett, C., 368
Bartlett, W.J., 374
Bass, O.C., 527
Bateman, J.D., 237
Bates, D.V., 602
Batten, M.J., 666, 715
Baxter, J.B.M., 17
Baxter, M., 53
Bayda, E.D., 720
Bayliss, W., 704
Bayly, G.H.U., 285
Beatteay, F.C., 13
Beaubien, A.S., 409
Beaudry, R., 358, 361
Beaulé, P., 306
Beaulieu, L.A., 271
Beck, A.E., 454
Beck, N.D., 625
Beer, G.F., 154
Begbie, M.B., 438, 439, 442, 447, 448, 449

Bélanger, M., 351
Bell, A., 139
Bell, F.H., 39
Bell, R., 120
Bellan, R.C., 432
Belleau, C., 355
Bennett, C.E., 242, 258
Berger, T.R., 587
Berman, W., 71
Bernier, T.A., 364
Bertram, J., 131
Best, W.L., 154
Betournay, L., 363
Bird, H.I., 534
Bird, W.J., 61
Black, N.J., 398
Black, R.M., 92
Black, W.J., 374
Blackmore, M., 731
Blackstock, G.M., 656, 659
Blakemore, W., 486
Blakeney, A.J., 597
Blois, E.H., 47, 48, 49
Blondin, M., 362
Blue, A., 120, 128
Bodie, J.L., 410
Bole, E.F., 408
Boles, A.T., 190
Bonnell, J.S., 611
Boothroyd, F., 426
Borden, L.E., 525
Bothwell, J.-A., 306
Bouchard, J.-M., 355
Bouchard, M., 326
Boudreau, A.J., 27
Boulter, U.W., 56
Bourassa, T.H., 709
Bourgeois, G., 302
Bourgeois, P., 348, 352
Bower, J., 624
Bower, J.E., 675
Bowering, A.J., 567
Bowers, F., 588

Provinces' accession numbers / Numéro d'entrée des provinces

1-36	New Brunswick/Nouveau-Brunswick	437-603	British Columbia/Colombie-Brtitannique
37-110	Nova Scotia/Nouvelle-Écosse	604-622	Prince Edward Island/Île-du-Prince-Édouard
111-288	Ontario	623-680	Alberta
289-362	Québec	681-720	Saskatchewan
363-436	Manitoba	721-767	Newfoundland/Terre-Neuve

Index to Chairmen and Commissioners — Index des Présidents et Commmissaires

Bowring, P.D., 735
Boyce, T., 464
Boyd, J.A., 129, 137
Boyer, L., 308
Boynton, C., 221
Bracewell, B.C., 546
Brachman, B., 703
Bracken, J., 405, 689
Brain, W.R., 732
Braithwaite, E.A., 645
Breckon, W., 221
Brennan, E.J., 616
Brennan, W.R., 680
Bridges, G.F.G., 20, 24
Brittain, H.L., 176, 209
Britton, B.M., 130
Brockway, Z.R., 113
Brodie, J.L., 299
Brooks, S.E., 428
Brooks, T., 129
Brosha, A., 72
Brossard, R., 332
Brousseau, E.-G., 306
Brown, B.H., 570
Brown, D.C., 551
Brown, J.T., 693
Brown, M.L., 657
Brown, S., 221
Brown, T.J., 45
Brown, T.R., 685
Brown, W., 115
Bruch, H.J., 570
Bruns, J.H., 407
Bryant, J.F., 694
Bryden, J., 464
Buchanan, N.V., 663, 665
Buchanan, R.J., 374
Bugden, A., 726
Bull, A.E., 482
Bullock-Webster, W.H., 463
Bulman, W.J., 388
Bunting, W.H., 133
Buntzen, J., 468
Buote, F.G., 607
Burbidge, G.W., 449
Burchell, G.B., 46
Burdick, A.C., 500
Burgoyne, D.J., 285
Burke, C.E., 223

Burland, J., 302
Burns, W.E., 495
Burritt, O.H., 392
Butler, M.J., 135
Butt, W., 241
Byrne, E., 115
Byrne, E.G., 27
Byrne, T.C., 584, 672

C

Cairns, J.F., 690
Cairns, J.M., 678
Cameron, D., 660
Cameron, D.R., 722
Cameron, J.D., 367, 372
Cameron, M.A., 539
Camp, D.K., 262
Campbell, A.D., 58
Campbell, A.J.C., 58
Campbell, A.M., 370
Campbell, C., 37
Campbell, D.L., 416
Campbell, D.R.J., 570
Campbell, J., 130
Campbell, J.J., 493
Campbell, J.S., 171
Campbell, M.A., 228
Campbell, R.L., 320
Campbell, V.A., 100
Campkin, H.H., 681
Cannon, L., 312
Cannon, L.J., 303
Carlhian, J.-P., 331
Carpenter, A.A., 626, 631, 635
Carpenter, L.G., 474
Carroll, H.G., 305
Carroll, W.F., 64, 66
Carroll, W.J., 767
Carrothers, A.W.R., 565
Carsley, C.F., 318
Carter-Cotton, F., 468
Carter, R.C., 707
Cartwright, J.R., 126
Carvell, L., 606
Casselman, A.C., 145
Casselman, W.H., 166
Castonguay, C., 345

Caswell, D.J., 241
Chabot, V., 317, 319, 327, 328
Chadwell, K., 426
Chambers, F.C., 374
Champagne, P., 318
Chant, S.N.F., 571
Chapman, A.V., 228
Chapman, D.H., 598
Charbonneau, J.H., 319
Charbonneau, M., 300
Charlesworth, L.C., 640
Charlton, J., 120
Cheeseman, R., 731
Cherrier, A.A., 372
Chevrette, G., 356
Chevrier, E.R.E., 216
Chipman, G.F., 388
Chouinard, J.B., 15, 16
Christensen, E., 26
Christie, G.I., 223
Christie, H.H., 699
Christie, M., 374
Chud, B., 585
Clark, F.R., 727
Clark, J.T., 546
Clark, R.M., 592
Clarke, C.K., 459
Clarke, L.O., 95
Clarke, W.H., 228
Clarkson, G.T., 186
Clay, W.L., 515
Clemens, W.A., 705
Clement, F.M., 521, 542
Clement, S.E., 381
Cliche, R., 356
Cloutier, B., 35
Clyne, J.V., 554, 555, 574
Coady, J.M., 533
Coatsworth, E., 159
Cochran, M.B., 221
Cody, H.J., 141, 154, 175, 197
Coe, W., 120
Cohen, M., 744
Coldwell, G.R., 374
Coldwell, M.J., 694
Collingwood, H., 734
Collver, R.D., 587
Collyer, F.J., 387
Colquhoun, A.H.U., 141

Provinces' accession numbers / Numéro d'entrée des provinces

1-36	New Brunswick/Nouveau-Brunswick	437-603	British Columbia/Colombie-Brtitannique
37-110	Nova Scotia/Nouvelle-Écosse	604-622	Prince Edward Island/Île-du-Prince-Édouard
111-288	Ontario	623-680	Alberta
289-362	Québec	681-720	Saskatchewan
363-436	Manitoba	721-767	Newfoundland/Terre-Neuve

Index to Chairmen and Commissioners — Index des Présidents et Commmissaires

Comeau, A.H., 43
Common, W.B., 206, 212
Conacher, L.P., 215
Connell, W.T., 197
Conquergood, C.R., 228
Conway, J.W., 729
Cook, A.B., 690
Cook, R., 734
Cooper, J.A., 145
Corbett, T.J., 758
Cordell, A.H., 287
Cormack, J.S., 660
Cormier, A.-J., 25
Cornwall, C.F., 443
Cossette-Trudel, A., 338
Costigan, R.R., 728
Côté, P.-M., 331
Coughlin, J.J., 209, 211
Coulter, A.R., 241
Coulthard, F.J., 487
Courchesne, G., 309
Cousineau, A., 333
Cousineau, R., 346
Cowan, A.J., 545
Coxe, D.G.M., 287
Craise, H., 221
Crampton, L.G., 564
Crawford, F.W., 404
Crease, H.P.P., 438, 439, 445, 446, 452
Crease, L., 520
Crehan, W.J., 485
Crocket, O.S., 14
Crofford, D.H., 423
Cromarty, J.D., 274
Cronkite, F.C., 708, 710
Cronyn, H., 52
Crosbie, A., 734
Cross, A.G., 305
Crossin, A.L., 397, 403
Crothers, T.W., 145
Crowe, G.R., 375
Crowe, W., 41
Crump, N.R., 673
Cuddy, J.A., 407
Cumming, L.R., 417
Cummings, H.H., 760
Cummings, H.L., 209
Cundall, H.J., 604

Cunningham, J.H., 63
Curran, C.F., 58
Curran, J.P., 378
Currier, G.W., 9

D

Dagnaud, P.M., 43
Dalton, T.G., 745
Dalton, T.J., 735, 737
Dandurand, R., 304
Dargaval, J.R., 147
Dauth, G., 478
Davidson, C.P., 297
Davie, A.E.B., 440
Davie, C.F., 525
Davies, P.G., 656
Dawe, D.W.K., 740
Dawson, R.M., 67
Day, J.G., 766
Deacon, T.R., 371
Dearness, J., 133
Deblois, E.J., 290
Décarie, V., 321
Defoy, J.A., 290
de la Chevrotière, J., 345
Delaney, J.H., 92, 96
DeLury, A.T., 154
Denison, W.W., 187
Dennis, C.D., 54
Deroche, A.P., 175
de Rome, Marie-Laurent, Sr., 330
DesBrisay, A.C., 576
Desbrisay, T., 604
Deschênes, J.-C., 352
Desjardins, L.G., 292, 293
Deslauriers, J., 350
Desmarais, C., 362
DesRoches, J.S., 610
Deutsch, J.J., 25, 401, 408
Dick, A., 40
Dick, O.J., 15, 16
Dick, W.J., 655
Dick, W.W.B., 35
Dickey, H.B., 98
Dickson, J., 128
Dickson, J.B., 11, 18, 24

Dickson, R.G.B., 420
Dinelle, J., 345
Dinning, R.J., 654
Dixon, B., 524
Dixon, H., 279
Doak, J.C., 414
Doane, F.W.W., 50
Dobbin, L.J., 738
Dohm, T.A., 581
Donnelly, J.F., 272
Donnelly, M.S., 416, 429
Donovan, W.J., 398
Dorion, A.A., 296
Doucet, M.J., 43
Douglas, J.M., 645
Douglas, N.W., 660
Douglas, R.A., 51
Dowding, G.H., 570
Dowell, C.H., 107
Dowell, H., 101
Dower, J.D., 657
Dowie, I.R., 256
Dowsley, J.K., 168
Doyle, G.S., 725
Doyle, T.M., 735
Doyon-Ferland, M., 353
Drake, M.W.T., 444, 447
Drinnan, R.G., 633
Drolet, J.-Y., 334
Drummond, R., 41
Drummond, W.M., 724
Drury, C., 121, 123
Dryden, J., 115
Dryden, J.C., 400
Dryden, W.A., 221
Dubé, J.E., 302
Dubord, R., 352
Duchesneau, J.A., 295
Dugas, E., 346
Duggan, J.J., 643
Dulmage, A.L., 424
Duncan, A.R., 52, 57
Duncan, W., 493
Dunfield, B., 726, 730
Dunlop, W.C., 99
Dunn, J., 217
Dunning, C.A., 683, 684
Dunsmuir, J., 568
Dyer, G.T., 733

Provinces' accession numbers / Numéro d'entrée des provinces	
1-36 New Brunswick/Nouveau-Brunswick	437-603 British Columbia/Colombie-Brtitannique
37-110 Nova Scotia/Nouvelle-Écosse	604-622 Prince Edward Island/Île-du-Prince-Édouard
111-288 Ontario	623-680 Alberta
289-362 Québec	681-720 Saskatchewan
363-436 Manitoba	721-767 Newfoundland/Terre-Neuve

Index to Chairmen and Commissioners — Index des Présidents et Commmissaires

Dyment, A.E., 217
Dymond, A.H., 115
Dysart, A.K., 391
Dyson, W.A., 345

E

Eaton, C., 731
Eckardt, L.S., 599
Edwards, M.H., 257
Eliason, F., 704
Elliott, A.C., 440
Ellison, P., 483
Embury, J.F.L., 696
Erskine, A.B., 479
Evans, H.M.E., 633
Evans, K., 150
Evans, W., 572
Evans, W.S., 526
Ewing, A.F., 645, 646, 651

F

Fahlgren, J.E.J., 281
Fairfield, W.H., 631, 640
Falconbridge, W.G., 137
Falconer, R.A., 627
Fallis, W.S., 382
Farmer, S.J., 400
Farrar, C.B., 639
Feir, E.B., 652
Fell, T., 480
Ferguson, P., 681
Ferguson, R.G., 690
Filion, G., 330
Filion, O., 314
Findlay, T.B., 410
Finlayson, J.N., 396
Fisher, R.G., 201
Fisher, T.K., 594
Fisher, W.E., 522
Fisher, W.S., 7, 8
Fiske, E.S., 4
Flavelle, J.W., 141
Fleming, J., 129
Fletcher, N.A., 221
Fletcher, R., 374

Fletcher, S.A., 466
Flumerfelt, A.C., 477
Ford, A.R., 197
Forke, R., 381
Forrest, W.D., 63
Fortier, G., 335, 337
Fortin, J.-A., 314
Fortin, L.-P., 320
Foster, J.T., 309
Fowler, H.L., 709
Fowler, R.M., 343
Fox, S.W., 400
Fox, W.S., 223
Francq, G., 306
Frankel, E.L., 236
Frankel, S.J., 31
Fraser, G.L., 229
Fraser, J.D., 736, 746
Fraser, J.F., 51
Fraser, J.J., 2
Fraser, W.W., 515
Fream, E.J., 634
Friesen, J.E., 716
Frigon, A., 310
Fryer, J.L., 582
Fulcher, E., 374
Fullerton, E.G., 620
Fulton, F.J., 474, 477
Fulton, W.J., 381
Furlong, R.S., 759

G

Gagné, A., 353
Gagnon, E., 348
Gagnon, E.D., 352
Gair, J., 643
Galbraith, D., 704
Galbraith, J.H., 657
Gale, R.H., 500
Galliher, W.A., 501, 513
Galloway, R., 241
Galt, A.C., 377, 379
Gansner, L.S., 584
Gardiner, C.C., 605
Gardiner, P.J., 738
Garigue, P., 321
Gash, N.B., 155

Gass, C.L., 21
Gauthier, D., 320
Gauthier, R., 350
Gauvin, J.-L., 355
Gendron, J.-D., 353
Geoffroy, J.-P., 343
George, K.L., 714
Gibbings, C.W., 709
Gibbons, J., 154
Gibbs, P.A., 570
Gibson, G.L., 570
Gibson, R., 115, 123
Gibson, T.W., 128, 156
Gillis, J.J., 525
Gilpin, E., Jr., 40
Gingras, J., 314
Glendinning, H., 123
Globensky, A., 301
Goard, D.H., 597
Godson, T.E., 191
Goldenberg, H.C., 28, 32, 33, 239, 244, 341, 397, 543, 564
Goodeve, A.S., 477
Goodyear, C., 754
Goodyear, R.C., 722
Gordon, C.B., 301
Gordon, J.L., 372
Gordon, J.R., 220
Gorman, T.W., 92
Gould, H., 347
Goundrey, G.K., 755
Gover, F., 741
Graham, D., 673
Graham, G.E., 35
Graham, J.E.L., 707
Graham, J.G., 102
Graham, R.T., 710
Graham, R.W., 221
Graham, W., 44
Grant, C., 243, 249, 255
Grant, H.C., 394
Grant, R.C., 546
Grant, R.M., 272
Gray, A.W., 500
Gray, J.H., 438, 439
Gray, K.C., 220
Green, F.W., 682
Green, M.G., 96
Green, N., 109

Provinces' accession numbers / Numéro d'entrée des provinces

1-36	New Brunswick/Nouveau-Brunswick	437-603	British Columbia/Colombie-Brtitannique
37-110	Nova Scotia/Nouvelle-Écosse	604-622	Prince Edward Island/Île-du-Prince-Édouard
111-288	Ontario	623-680	Alberta
289-362	Québec	681-720	Saskatchewan
363-436	Manitoba	721-767	Newfoundland/Terre-Neuve

232

Index to Chairmen and Commissioners — Index des Présidents et Commmissaires

Green, T.B., 507, 510, 511
Greenlay, C.E., 400
Gregory, F.B., 505, 506
Gregory, W.D., 176, 182
Greig, A.R., 691
Grierson, J., 401
Griesbach, F., 221
Griffith, F.E., 70
Grills, H., 386
Grimmer, W.C.H., 13, 15, 16
Grimmett, J.A., 544
Grisdale, F.S., 721
Groome, A., 720
Grubb, J.D., 736
Gruchy, P., 725
Guérard, J.-M., 324, 329
Guérin, G., 354
Guérin, J.J., 302
Guillemette, A.-M., 345
Guimont, P.-H., 316
Gundy, W.P., 154
Gunn, J.T., 163
Guptill, G.W., 83
Gurney, E.H., 223
Gushue, J.R., 761

H

Hafenbrak, I.F., 374
Hagey, J.G., 241
Haggen, L.M., 570
Haig, G.T., 434
Hale, T., 46
Haley, D.J., 287
Hall, E., 718
Hall, G.E., 236, 248
Hall, J.M., 199, 200
Hall, N.A., 595
Hall, W.L., 53
Halliday, C., 706
Halpenny, J., 381
Halse, G.H., 368, 369
Halter, G.S., 417
Ham, J.M., 270
Hamber, E.W., 500
Hamilton, C.C., 38
Hamilton, C.M., 685

Hamilton, J., 241
Hamilton, S.W., 592
Hancox, G.E., 521
Handrahan, G., 620
Haney, M.J., 182
Hann, W., 734
Hanna, L.A., 558
Hannington, R.W., 481
Hansell, E.F., 451
Hansen, D.A., 660
Hansen, S., 407
Hanway, J.A., 63
Harding, R., 570
Hardy, E., 246
Harkness, D.B., 381
Harnett, H.G., 756
Harper, A.M., 494, 529, 536, 541
Harradance, A.M., 674
Harris, E.C., 102
Harris, L., 182
Harris, R.W., 499
Harrison, A.G., 624
Harrison, E., 450, 456, 460
Harrison, E., Jr., 453, 461
Harrison, P.P., 516
Hartt, E.P., 281
Harvey, G.R., 237
Harvey, H., 625, 637, 642
Harvie, J., 659
Haslam, J.H., 683, 684
Hatfield, F., 26
Hattie, W.H., 47
Hawkins, C.G., 72
Haworth, J.C., 423
Hayes, C.P., 656
Hayes, D.W., 655
Haysom, W., 623
Hayward, R., 516
Hayward, W.H., 493
Hayworth, A., 694
Head, W.H., 374
Heaton, E.P., 181
Hedlin, R., 404
Heise, A.W., 692
Hellyer, A., 176
Henderson, A., 509
Henderson, E.F., 228
Henderson, J., 221

Henderson, J.S., 515, 517
Hendricks, W., 551
Henley, A.G., 753
Héon, G.-H., 315
Hervey, R.G., 124
Hettasch, F., 754
Hewak, B., 427
Hicks, C., 21
Hicks, R.V., 242
Higgins, J.D., 738
Higgins, R.D., 582
Hilbourn, E.H., 115
Hill, G.I., 731
Hill, H.W., 521
Hill, P.C., 37
Hincks, C.M., 639
Hindsley, N., 635
Hitchcock, A., 691
Hobson, J.I., 129
Hodge, W., 41
Hodgins, F.E., 158, 160, 189, 192
Hodgins, H.J., 742
Hodgson, G.W., 605
Hogg, T.H., 223, 402
Holgate, H., 9
Holland, J., 396
Holloway, G.T., 156
Holman, W.H., 706
Holmes, C., 221
Holt, C.M., 302
Home, G., 553
Hope, J.A., 228
Hopkins, T.M., 735, 756
Hoskin, J., 134
Houck, R.S., 228
Houston, W., 119
Howay, F.W., 488, 489, 535
Howland, R.D., 707
Howland, W.P., 113
Howley, D.E., 764
Howson, W.R., 652
Huffman, H., 221
Hughes, C.J.A., 36
Hughes, R., 584
Hughes, S.H.S., 254, 280
Humphries, I.A., 205
Humphries, T., 515
Hunt, J.M., 423

Provinces' accession numbers / Numéro d'entrée des provinces			
1-36	New Brunswick/Nouveau-Brunswick	437-603	British Columbia/Colombie-Brtitannique
37-110	Nova Scotia/Nouvelle-Écosse	604-622	Prince Edward Island/Île-du-Prince-Édouard
111-288	Ontario	623-680	Alberta
289-362	Québec	681-720	Saskatchewan
363-436	Manitoba	721-767	Newfoundland/Terre-Neuve

Hurley, F.H., 575
Hutcheon, H.E., 589
Hutton, N., 734

I

Inglis, R.E., 87
Innis, H.A., 60, 401
Irving, A., 122
Irving, P.A., 458
Irwin, H., 369, 374
Irwin, J.C.W., 704
Isbister, C.M., 269

J

Jackman, W.T., 387
Jackson, G.E., 154
Jackson, J.A., 649
Jacobson, S.S., 92
Jacoby, N.H., 699
James, R.A., 423
Jamieson, E.A., 564
Janes, C.C., 721
Jardine, J., 494
Jean, M., 362
Jeanneret, M., 262
Jessup, J.H., 220
Jetté, L.A., 297
Johns, E., 381
Johns, W.P., 703
Johnson, A., 728
Johnson, E., 441
Johnson, F.W., 713
Johnson, J.A., 279
Johnson, L., 699
Johnson, M.M., 580
Johnson, T.H., 381
Johnston, A.S., 60
Johnston, E.F.B., 119
Johnston, T., 695
Jonah, H.N., 35
Jones, C., 614
Jones, C.C., 478
Jones, J.H., 60
Jowsey, R.J., 220
Joyce, H.K., 731

Juba, S., 408
Judd, J.C., 142
Judge, J.W., 653
Juniper, A.B., 374
Jury, A.F., 121
Juteau, L., 358, 361

K

Kardash, W.A., 400
Keable, J.F., 360
Keary, W.H., 482
Keith, D.A., 253
Keith, J.C., 209
Kelly, A., 228, 245
Kelly, H.T., 157
Kelly, M.J., 4
Kelso, J.J., 123, 174
Kennedy, C.A., 368
Kennedy, C.F., 96
Kennedy, E.-J.-C., 304
Kennedy, F., 664
Kennedy, H., 224, 722
Kennedy, W.F., 525
Ker, D.R., 468
Ker, R., 437
Kerans, R.P., 676
Kidston, J., 493
Kierstead, W.C., 14
Kilburn, J., 5
Kilgour, J.F., 391
Killam, A.C., 366
Kilpatrick, J., 26
Kimball, J.W., 415
King, E., 26
King, O.P., 5
King, W., 647
Kingsmill, J.J., 130
Kingstone, A.C., 198
Kinney, J.A., 628
Kirby, W.J.C., 667, 675
Kirkland, A., 134
Kirkwood, A., 128, 131
Knight, A., 487
Kocsis, L.F., 423
Kostaszek, L.W., 739, 743
Krever, H., 256, 284
Kushner, C.N., 410

L

L'Heureux, P., 405
Lachaîne, G.A., 345
Lachapelle, E.P., 302
Lachapelle, L., 349
Lacroix, G., 340
Lagacé, G., 358
Laidlaw, T.W., 394
Lair, R., 320
Laliberté, J.-G., 359
LaMarsh, J.V., 271
Lamarsh, R., 127
Lamont, J.H., 686
Lamontagne, L., 331
Lampman, P.S., 464, 472, 476, 484, 523
Landry, A., 320
Landry, P.A., 6
Lane, W.F., 21
Lang, D.W., 202
Langelier, F., 300
Langley, G., 682, 684
Langmuir, J.W., 118, 121
Lanteigne, L., 35
Laplante, L., 347
Lapointe, E., 310
Lapointe, J., 330
Lapointe, L.-A., 318
Large, F.A., 617
Larocque, P., 330
Larue, A., 315
Latchford, F.R., 177, 204
Latter, J.R., 314
Laurent, E., 345
Lavoie, J.P., 295
Lawson, E.M., 580
Lawson, S., 218
Lax, T., 710
Laycock, S.R., 706
Laycraft, J.H., 679
LaZerte, M.E., 609
Leach, W.W., 265, 286
LeBel, A.M., 222
LeBel, L.A., 24
Leblanc, C.A., 289
Leblanc, W.M., 43
Leboeuf, Y., 348
Legault, G.-E., 342

Provinces' accession numbers / Numéro d'entrée des provinces

1-36	New Brunswick/Nouveau-Brunswick	437-603	British Columbia/Colombie-Brtitannique
37-110	Nova Scotia/Nouvelle-Écosse	604-622	Prince Edward Island/Île-du-Prince-Édouard
111-288	Ontario	623-680	Alberta
289-362	Québec	681-720	Saskatchewan
363-436	Manitoba	721-767	Newfoundland/Terre-Neuve

Index to Chairmen and Commissioners — Index des Présidents et Commmissaires

Legg, S.V., 677
Legris, J.H., 299
LeGrow, G., 735
Leitch, A., 221
Leith, R., 726
Lemay, M., 362
LeMay Warren, J.D., 345
Lennie, R.S., 479
Lennox, H.I.S., 161
Lespérance, J., 302
Lessard, A., 309
Letarte, P., 335, 337
Lett, S., 563
Levesque, J.-A., 22
Levin, E.A., 430
Lewis, P.D., 731
Lewis, P.J., 725, 734
Lick, R., 221
Liersch, J.E., 571
Limerick, R.V., 30
Lindsay, G., 567
Link, J.R., 107
Lippé, R., 342
Lipsett, L.R., 650
Lister, G.A., 374
Little, C.E., 699
Locke, C., 371, 375
Lord, A.E., 556, 557
Loughran, J., 629
Love, R.J., 19
Lucas, A., 493
Lucas, R.A., 124
Lugrin, C.H., 483
Lundell, A.W., 551
Lundrigan, A.R., 736
Lunney, H.W., 648
Lush, D., 647
Lusztig, P.A., 579
Lynch, P., 38
Lynk, J.R., 101

M

McAllister, H., 705
McAndrew, P.J., 237
McArdle, R.E., 742
McArthur, H., 241
McArthur, J.E., 34, 91

MacBeth, R.G., 515
Macbeth, T., 173
MacBride, M., 166
McCaffery, B., 597
McCague, G.A., 268
McCallum, A.F., 169
MacCallum, J.H., 74
McCallum, K., 720
McCarthy, J.C., 736
McCarthy, V.P., 763
MacCaull, P.M., 610
McClelan, A.R., 3
McCloskey, H.C., 220
McColl, A.J., 457
McColl, D.P., 687
McCoy, W.J., 185
McCrae, C.A., 405
McCuaig, S.H., 636
McCullum, D., 507, 511
McCutcheon, J.M., 193
Macdiarmid, F.G., 147
MacDonald, A., 50
MacDonald, A.A., 605
MacDonald, A.G., 43
MacDonald, A.H., 705
McDonald, B., 597
Macdonald, B.J.S., 273
McDonald, C., 4
McDonald, C., 287
MacDonald, D., 37
Macdonald, D.A., 376, 391
Macdonald, D.B., 141
McDonald, E.R., 14
McDonald, G.C., 310
MacDonald, H., 42
MacDonald, H.J., 376, 657
MacDonald, H.Y., 701
McDonald, J.W., 652
Macdonald, M.A., 530
Macdonald, R.H., 717
MacDonald, R.T., 587
MacDonald, W.A., 497, 501
Macdonald, W.J., 409
McDonell, A.J., 552
MacDonnell, H.J., 83
Macdonnell, I.M., 219, 230
Macdougall, F., 6
MacDougall, R.L., 34, 91
McDougall, S., 311

Macdowall, D.H., 479
McDowell, J., 409
MacEwan, H.R., 108
McFadden, V., 45
MacFarlane, R.O., 407
McGeorge, W.G., 127
McGibbon, D.A., 630
McGillivray, A.A., 650
McGillivray, G.A., 235, 247
Macgillivray, H.D., 735
McGorman, S.E., 209
McGougan, E., 515
McGregor, J.D., 688
MacGregor, J.G., 658
McGurran, J.J., 699
Machray, J.A., 372
McIlhone, J., 330
McIlmoyle, Z., 634
McInnes, D., 70, 79
McInnes, J.R., 416
McInnes, R., 82
MacInnes, W.H., 515
McInnis, D.S., 608
Macintosh, J.A., 179
McIntosh, J.C., 532
McIntyre, A., 127
MacIntyre, B.M., 552
McIntyre, D., 374, 388, 687
McIntyre, L.M., 106
McIntyre, W.A., 372, 687
McIvor, R.C., 246
McKay, A., 43
MacKay, A.D., 61
MacKay, A.H., 47
McKay, F., 401
McKay, J., 696
MacKay, J.K., 226
McKay, J.W., 53
McKay, K.W., 135
Mackay, P., 290
MacKay, W.A., 101, 104, 107, 110
McKechnie, A.S., 398
MacKeen, H.P., 93
McKeen, J., 48, 49
MacKeigan, I.M., 75, 613
MacKelvie, J.A., 494
Macken, W.L., 524
Mackenzie, A., 592

Provinces' accession numbers / Numéro d'entrée des provinces

1-36	New Brunswick/Nouveau-Brunswick	437-503	British Columbia/Colombie-Brtitannique
37-110	Nova Scotia/Nouvelle-Écosse	604-522	Prince Edward Island/Île-du-Prince-Édouard
111-288	Ontario	623-680	Alberta
289-362	Québec	681-720	Saskatchewan
363-436	Manitoba	721-767	Newfoundland/Terre-Neuve

Index to Chairmen and Commissioners — Index des Présidents et Commmissaires

McKenzie, A.S., 64
MacKenzie, A.S., 627
McKenzie, C., 236
Mackenzie, C.J.G., 591
McKenzie, D.G., 51
McKenzie, F.C., 362
MacKenzie, L.G., 598
MacKenzie, N.A.M., 611
Mackenzie, P.E., 696
McKenzie, W.A., 516
MacKenzie, W.H., 22
McKeown, H.A., 7, 8
McKibbin, J., 112
McKinney, A., 221, 248
McKinnon, A., 655
McKinnon, A.H., 77, 85
MacKinnon, F., 610
Macklem, T.C.S., 138
McLachlan, T., 79
McLaren, J.I., 164
McLaughlin, A.P.N., 24
McLaurin, C.C., 661, 669
Maclean, H.A., 467, 469, 482, 546
McLean, W.A., 153
McLellan, R.F., 71
Maclellan, W.E., 43
McLenaghen, J., 394
Maclennan, J., 135
McLennan, J.C., 197
McLeod, D.C., 607
MacLeod, H.A., 46
MacLeod, H.F., 15, 16
MacLeod, J.E.A., 636
MacLeod, N., 228
MacLeod, N., 608
McLeod, T.H., 708, 714
MacMahon, H., 135
MacMaster, D., 298
McMath, R.A., 592
MacMillan, C., 608
McMillan, J., 115
McMillan, J.A., 611
MacMillan, J.W., 57
MacMurchy, H., 174
Macnab, I.P., 62, 76
McNally, G.F., 656
McNaught, W.K., 154
McNeil, N., 154

McNeil, S.B., 41
McNeill, F.J., 620
McNeill, W.F., 629
McNeill, W.T., 628
MacNutt, F.L., 610
MacPhee, E.D., 562
McPherson, A.L., 187
Macpherson, D.M., 123
McPherson, E.A., 403
MacPherson, H.P., 52, 56, 57
Macpherson, T.H., 135
McPhillips, A.E., 483
McQuaid, M.J., 619, 622
McQueen, D.G., 636
McQueen, J., 10
McRae, J.D., 552
MacRitchie, J.J., 74
McRuer, J.C., 250
MacSween, R.J., 89
McTaggart-Cowan, I., 584
McTaggart, N., 689
McTague, C.P., 217
MacTavish, D.B., 136
McTavish, L.D., 692
McWhinney, E., 353
McWilliams, J.B., 131
Madden, J.E., 214
Madden, W. Jr., 40
Magee, J., 189
Magill, R., 42, 682
Magone, C.R., 215
Magrath, C.A., 153, 631
Mahaffy, J.C., 657
Maharg, J.A., 686
Maher, J.H., 717, 719
Maher, W.H., 755
Mahon, H.E., 55
Mahoney, J.W., 765
Major, W.S., 241
Malaher, W.G., 404
Malcolm, F., 115
Malkin, W.H., 483, 517
Maloney, A.J., 764
Malouf, A.H., 359
Mann, W.L., 399
Manning, H.W., 409
Manning, R., 729
Mansfield, A., 705
March, G.B., 735

Marion, J.-A., 315
Marks, R.G., 592
Marler, R.C., 654, 658
Marnoch, G.R., 631
Marois, G., 301
Marriott, G.P., 272
Marshall, B., 228
Martin, A., 462
Martin, A.M., 736
Martin, E.C.F., 570
Martin, J.-M., 331
Martin, J.W., 634
Martin, L.A., 755
Martin, R., 349
Martin, W.M., 700, 701
Mason, J.J., 129
Masson, D., 298
Masson, W.E., 647
Masten, C.A., 162
Mathers, A.T., 381
Mathers, T.G., 376
Mathieu, J.-M., 321
Mathieu, M., 298
Matte, N.M., 353
Mauro, A.V., 422
Maxwell, R.W., 25
Meagher, A.J., 81
Meek, V., 634
Mellish, H., 50
Menzies, A.F., 399
Mercier, L., 339
Meredith, W.R., 138, 141, 151, 157, 163, 165
Merritt, W.H., 120
Mersereau, L.A., 19
Messier, M., 338
Meyer, B., 592
Michaud, J., 331
Michener, R., 416
Middleton, A., 370
Middleton, W.E., 195
Mifflin, A.S., 752
Mifflin, H., 736
Miller, C.C., 414
Miller, E., 734
Miller, E.G., 714
Miller, J.S., 369
Miller, L.A., 757
Miller, W.G., 156

Provinces' accession numbers / Numéro d'entrée des provinces

1-36	New Brunswick/Nouveau-Brunswick	437-603	British Columbia/Colombie-Brtitannique
37-110	Nova Scotia/Nouvelle-Écosse	604-622	Prince Edward Island/Île-du-Prince-Édouard
111-288	Ontario	623-680	Alberta
289-362	Québec	681-720	Saskatchewan
363-436	Manitoba	721-767	Newfoundland/Terre-Neuve

Miller, W.W., 374
Mills, C.I., 21
Mills, J., 133
Milner, A.C., 75
Minville, E., 316, 321
Mitchell, A.E., 515
Mitchell, C.H., 169
Mitchell, G., 221
Mitchell, H., 40
Mitchell, J., 704
Mitchell, J., 124
Mitchell, L., 429
Moffatt, J., 45
Molloy, J., 734
Mombourquette, A.E., 43
Montgomery, H.J., 636
Montgomery, W., 221
Montpetit, A., 321
Montpetit, E., 309
Moore, H.W.R., 491
Moores, F.D., 736
Morand, D.R., 267
Morcel, R., 334
Morden, A.R., 112
Morden, K.G., 236
Moreira, A.R., 90, 97
Moresby, W.C., 473
Morgan, E., 132, 136
Morgan, H.B., 753
Morgan, M.O., 729
Morphy, H.B., 140
Morrison, A., 497, 508, 514, 517, 518
Morrison, G.M., 78, 80
Morrison, L.S., 12
Morrow, C.W., 566, 569, 577, 580
Morrow, W.G., 670
Morton, K.L., 575
Moseley, W.E., 103
Moss, C., 138
Motherwell, W.R., 686, 688
Mowat, G.L., 660
Muggah, A.D., 83
Mulroney, B., 356
Mulrooney, P.J., 241
Munroe, D., 330
Munson, J.H.D., 364
Murchie, W.T., 612

Murphy, D., 498, 501, 528
Murphy, G.H., 53
Murphy, H.B., 741
Murphy, J.J., 735
Murray, J.W., 602
Murray, P.J., 724
Murray, W.C., 388, 395, 478, 627
Musgrave, F., 76

N

Nadeau, U., 27
Nantel, G.A., 292, 293
Nason, H.M., 105
Naylor, C.A., 241
Neapole, C., 346
Neary, E.A., 748
Neelands, R.J., 228
Neff, G.C., 695
Nelson, C.F., 502
Nelson, J.C., 664
Nepveu, G., 345
New, H.I., 228
Newbigging, W., 666
Newcombe, C.F., 451
Newcombe, R.F., 72
Newlands, H.W., 686
Nickle, W.F., 147, 164
Nicks, S., 718
Norris, T.G., 588
Norton, W.E., 411
Noseworthy, F., 734
Nourse, C.G.K., 395
Noxon, J., 113
Nugent, R.A.L., 435

O

O'Brien, A., 430
O'Brien, J., 737
O'Byrne, M.B., 668
O'Connor, L., 610
O'Dea, F., 747
O'Dea, J.R., 736
Odlum, V.W., 516
O'Grady, J.G., 727

Oldham, W.K., 591
O'Leary, F.J., 731
Oliver, E.H., 683
Olivero, R.J., 766
O'Neill, H., 749
Orde, J.F., 188
O'Sullivan, D.A., 118
Ouellet, F., 350
Ouellet, J., 350
Outhit, W.D., 86

P

Paddock, B.V., 764
Pagnuelo, S., 298
Palmer, J., 4
Palmer, W.H., 283
Paquin, C.R., 302
Paradis, A., 350
Parent, A.-M., 330
Parent, H., 316, 318
Parenteau, R., 333
Parizeau, J., 342
Parker, J., 731
Parker, W.D., 252
Parson, H.G., 494
Parsons, S.R., 163
Parsons, W.D., 741
Patching, T.H., 673
Paterson, A.D., 529
Paterson, A.R.D., 382
Paterson, G., 380, 385
Patrick, W., 369
Patterson, C.S., 114
Patterson, G., 45
Patterson, J., 584
Patterson, J.A., 170
Patterson, J.O., 658
Pauline, F.A., 502
Pearce, J.S., 125
Pearse, P.H., 593
Pearson, G.S., 525
Pelletier, E., 302
Pelletier, J.-A., 349
Pepperdence, L.M., 17
Percival, J.F., 643
Perdue, W.E., 377
Perlin, A.B., 725, 736

Provinces' accession numbers / Numéro d'entrée des provinces

1-36	New Brunswick/Nouveau-Brunswick	437-603	British Columbia/Colombie-Brtitannique
37-110	Nova Scotia/Nouvelle-Écosse	604-622	Prince Edward Island/Île-du-Prince-Édouard
111-288	Ontario	623-680	Alberta
289-362	Québec	681-720	Saskatchewan
363-436	Manitoba	721-767	Newfoundland/Terre-Neuve

Index to Chairmen and Commissioners — Index des Présidents et Commmissaires

Perrault, C.-H., 341
Perreault, C., 362
Perrett, T.E., 687
Perrier, P., 304
Perrin, H., 45
Perry, H., 692
Perry, J.E., 349
Peters, F., 471
Peters, G.A., 180
Peterson, L.R., 570
Pettit, H., 178
Pettypiece, H.J., 139
Phelan, E.J., 740
Phelps, J.L., 709
Phillips, W.E., 223
Phinney, H.W., 56
Phipps, R.W., 128
Picard, G., 318
Pierce, A.E., 613
Pigott, J.M., 228
Pippy, C.A., 736
Planta, A.E., 500
Planta, J.P., 443
Plourde-Gagnon, S., 268
Pocock, E.A., 176
Poirier, G., 359
Poirier, R.P., 346
Pollock, C., 246
Pomerleau, C., 349
Poole, C.F., 767
Poole, J.S., 400
Porter, A., 268
Pottier, V.J., 69, 74
Powell, C.W., 756
Powell, H.O., 689
Powrie, W.D., 591
Praeger, E.A., 448
Pratt, A., 135
Pratt, C.C., 725, 735
Pratte, G., 311
Prefontaine, E., 400
Prendergast, J.E.P., 383
Prévost, J.A., 311
Prévost, Y., 347
Price, B., 570
Prince, S.H., 53, 58
Pringle, J.A., 266
Pringle, J.P., 715
Pritchard, J., 590

Procter, A.P., 487
Proudfoot, D.J., 551
Proudfoot, P.M., 600
Proudfoot, W., 117
Pruden, D.F., 431
Pulford, W.S., 124
Purdy, H.L., 583
Pushie, G.F., 736
Puttee, A.W., 371, 374, 382, 389
Pyne, A.R., 147

Q

Quigley, F.H., 664

R

Racine, A., 203, 210
Ralph, J.V., 733
Rand, C.R., 88
Rand, I.C., 251
Randolph, A.F., 1
Rankin, A.M., 153
Rankin, E., 355
Rankin, J.B., 127
Rankin, W., 148
Ransom, F.W., 388
Rathbun, E.W., 131
Raudsepp, V., 602
Rawson, D.S., 705
Raymond, C.W., 614
Rayson, L., 362
Read, H.T., 71
Reeves, M., 620
Régnier, A., 333
Reid, A., 241
Reid, L.H., 228
Rempel, J.G., 703
Renouf, H.A., 91, 94
Renouf, H.T., 729
Reusch, A.R., 695
Rhodes, W., 295
Richards, N.T., 582
Richey, A.S., 9
Riddell, W.A., 717
Riddell, W.R., 177, 196

Rigg, R.A., 374
Riley, H.J., 405
Riley, W.C., 409
Rioux, M., 350
Risinger, R.W., 646
Ritchie, A., 1
Roach, W.D., 213, 227, 231, 232, 240
Robarts, J.P., 276
Robb, D.W., 42
Robbins, R.H., 417
Roberts, H.D., 736
Robertson, A.R., 437
Robertson, H.E.A., 490
Robertson, J.G.A., 68
Robichaud, L.P.A., 19
Robicheau, J.L.P., 51
Robidoux, J.E., 291
Robins, S.L., 278
Robinson, C.B., 132
Robinson, J.B., 129
Robinson, M.M., 221
Robison, I.C., 656
Robson, H.A., 373, 377, 384
Robson, J.G., 515
Rocher, G., 330
Roddick, T.G., 302
Rohmer, R.H., 262
Ronayne, P., 83
Roper, E.E., 635
Roscoe, F.J., 437
Rosebrugh, A.M., 121
Ross, A.E., 166
Ross, D.C., 208, 211
Ross, H., 59
Ross, H.I., 324, 329
Ross, J.A., 182
Ross, J.F.W., 259
Ross, P.D., 193
Ross, R.A., 182
Rothstein, M.E., 436
Rousseau, A., 302
Rousseau, L.Z., 742
Routhier, A.B., 294
Routhier, R., 362
Rowand, J.M., 713
Rowat, J.P., 316
Rowe, A.T., 767
Rowe, F., 83, 84

Provinces' accession numbers / Numéro d'entrée des provinces		
1-36	New Brunswick/Nouveau-Brunswick	
37-110	Nova Scotia/Nouvelle-Écosse	
111-288	Ontario	
289-362	Québec	
363-436	Manitoba	
437-603	British Columbia/Colombie-Brtitannique	
604-622	Prince Edward Island/Île-du-Prince-Édouard	
623-680	Alberta	
681-720	Saskatchewan	
721-767	Newfoundland/Terre-Neuve	

Index to Chairmen and Commissioners — Index des Présidents et Commmissaires

Rowe, G.C., 728, 731
Roy, E., 306
Ruff, N.J., 582
Russell, B., 44
Russell, F.W., 766
Russell, T.A., 175
Rutherford, J.G., 688
Rutherford, W.J., 687, 689, 693
Rutledge, E.J., 400

S

St. Clair Trainor, C., 613, 615
Saint-Jacques, H., 228
St-Laurent, J., 334
Salvas, E., 324, 329
Sampson, H., 374
Sanderson, C.R., 228
Sargent, R.A., 578
Saunders, E., 126, 146, 149
Saunders, W., 115
Savage, A., 399
Savoy, G., 309
Sayles, E.R., 216
Scales, A.K., 618
Schultz, I., 400
Scott, A.F., 117
Scott, D.L., 625
Scott, F.G., 309
Scott, H., 221
Scott, M., 590
Scott, R.J., 221
Scovil, H.R., 34
Seabright, G.W., 750
Seal, G., 374
Seaton, P.D., 601
Sedgewick, G.H., 196
Segal, S., 587
Seheult, L.R., 29
Senkler, E.J., 117, 130
Sewell, R.R.F., 546
Sexton, F.H., 64
Shandley, H.H., 548
Shanks, W.H., 604
Shannon, S., 493
Shapiro, B.B., 282

Sharp, J., 164
Sharpe, G.E., 410
Sharpe, T., 389
Shaw, A.M., 724
Shaw, H., 629
Shaw, H.C., 512
Shaw, L.R., 96
Shaw, R.V., 81
Shelton, P.H., 695
Sheppard, C., 723
Sheppard, H.M., 228
Sheppard, R., 647
Shives, K., 4
Shortt, A., 139, 504
Shortt, E.M., 263
Shrum, G.M., 568
Sifton, A.L., 623
Sifton, C., 367
Sigerist, H.E., 702
Sigfusson, S., 394
Simard, A., 302
Simon, H., 241, 242
Simpson, H.C., 369
Simpson, J.D., 685
Sinclair, J.S., 118
Skelton, O.D., 478, 688
Slaven, T.P., 81
Slayter, W.B., 37
Sloan, G.M., 537, 540, 550, 560, 561, 565
Smith, A., 123
Smith, A.I., 336, 344
Smith, C.R., 429
Smith, G., 141
Smith, H.E., 659
Smith, H.G.H., 414
Smith, H.K., 124
Smith, J.W., 681
Smith, L.J, 246
Smith, N.H., 736
Smith, R., 204
Smith, S., 223
Smith, S.E., 228
Smith, S.J., 551
Smith, W., 38
Smith, W.K., 596
Smith, W.Y., 23
Smitten, W., 629
Snell, R., 754

Snider, C.G., 167, 183
Snow, A.J.R., 143, 144
Snowden, D., 754
Solandt, O.M., 261
Solomon, J.R., 400
Somerville, C.R., 175
Sommerville, N., 176
Soper, P.L., 762
South, G., 718
Southworth, T., 131
Spalding, J., 396, 403
Speare, W.C., 570
Spence, G., 689
Spence, W.D., 643
Spinks, W.W., 465
Spofford, C., 507, 511
Stairs, C., 597
Stapells, R.B., 246
Stead, L.B., 736
Steele, G.L., 751
Steele, R.C., 551
Sterne, E.T., 223
Stevens, H.H., 553
Stevens, H.L., 426
Stevenson, W.W., 268
Stewart, A., 500
Stewart, A., 654
Stewart, A.D., 124
Stewart, H.E., 279
Stewart, J., 496
Stewart, J.A., 546
Stewart, R.D., 22
Still, F.M., 692
Stinson, L., 400
Stirling, G., 740
Stirling, J.T., 628, 629
Stock, E., 115
Stock, T., 115
Stockett, L., 623
Stone, G.A., 12, 13, 15, 16
Stoneman, J.A., 693
Stoney, R.A., 494
Strachan, D., 154
Stratford, R.K., 223
Street, W.P.R., 138
Strickland, U., 734
Suart, G., 590
Sullivan, H.J., 547
Sullivan, J.G., 386

Provinces' accession numbers / Numéro d'entrée des provinces

1-36	New Brunswick/Nouveau-Brunswick	437-603	British Columbia/Colombie-Brtitannique
37-110	Nova Scotia/Nouvelle-Écosse	604-622	Prince Edward Island/Île-du-Prince-Édouard
111-288	Ontario	623-680	Alberta
289-362	Québec	681-720	Saskatchewan
363-436	Manitoba	721-767	Newfoundland/Terre-Neuve

Index to Chairmen and Commissioners — Index des Présidents et Commmissaires

Sutcliffe, H.W., 220
Sutherland, R.F., 157, 169
Sutherland, W.C., 688
Swadron, B.B., 288
Swailes, D., 400
Swan, W.G., 519
Swanson, D.C., 553
Swanson, W.W., 695
Sweeney, E.B., 17
Sweet, J.A., 234
Swindells, F.W., 56
Sylvestre, C.A., 335, 337
Symington, H.J., 381

T

Tallin, G.P.R., 418
Taraska, P., 430
Tatlow, R.G., 468
Taylor, A.H., 124
Taylor, T.W., 130, 364
Taylor, W.C., 660
Teed, A.I., 6
Teed, E.R., 12
Teetzel, W.F., 475
Tellier, J., 322, 323, 325
Tessier, A., 305
Thibeault, L., 320
Thinel, L., 351
Thivierge, P.N., 299
Thompson, E.W., 124
Thompson, G., 346
Thompson, J., 416
Thompson, J.C., 643
Thompson, J.M., 381
Thompson, S., 592
Thompson, S.O., 400
Thomson, H.F., 708, 711
Thomson, J.A., 386
Thornton, L.A., 691
Thorson, J.T., 397
Thorvaldson, G.S., 400
Thur, O., 351
Tisdalle, J.D., 570
Titus, F.E., 184, 194
Toal, J., 425
Tobin, S., 37
Todd, F., 1

Tolmie, J.C., 166
Tolmie, R.F., 470
Tomalty, G.L., 582
Tooke, A., 23
Tory, H.M., 56
Townshend, W.A., 228
Trahan, J., 348, 352
Trainor, O.C., 399
Tremblay, A., 320
Tremblay, G., 309
Tremblay, M., 346
Tremblay, O., 349
Tremblay, T., 316
Trenholm, B.M., 91
Trineer, T.W., 597
Tritschler, G.E., 413, 419, 433
Trueman, A.W., 401
Tupper, R.H., 559
Turcotte, L.S., 662
Turgeon, W.F.A., 395, 406, 686, 698
Turner, A.J., 552
Turner, H.M., 223
Tuttle, A.S., 636
Tweedie, T.M.M., 641
Tysoe, C.W., 576

U

Upshall, W.G., 287
Urquhart, M.C., 256
Urquhart, N.C., 220
Usick, R., 431

V

Vadasz, M., 587
Vadboncoeur, J., 338
Van Belleghem, J.G., 410
Vannini, I.A., 260
Veitch, W.F., 567
Villett, G.H., 657
Vissac, G.A., 70
Vroom, W.E., 3

W

Waines, W.J., 412
Waisberg, H., 264
Walkem, G.A., 455
Walker, B.E., 134, 141
Walker, J.A., 73
Wallace, J.A., 175
Wallace, L.J., 588
Wallace, R.A., 624
Wallace, R.C., 223
Wallace, W.B., 44
Wallach, E.E., 584
Wallbridge, L., 365
Walls, C.E.S., 579
Walrod, R.P., 571
Walsh, W.L., 632, 638
Walters, C.E., 102
Walters, C.S., 207
Ward, H.A., 172
Ward, R.S., 374
Wardle, R.A., 394
Warren, D.T., 603
Warren, P.J., 735
Watson, E., 166
Watson, J., 115
Watterworth, J., 125
Waugh, J., 174
Weber, S.M., 666
Weeks, E.P., 621
Weijs, J.H., 428
Welch, H.J., 203, 551
Weldon, R.C., 478
Wells, D.C., 225, 238
Wells, J., 614
Wells, W.W., 7, 8
Welsh, S.W., 598
Whalen, H., 26
Whalen, H.J., 756
Wheatley, F., 633
White, A., 128
White, B., 723
White, D., 620
White, D.S., 586
White, P.H., 729
White, W.L., 647
Whitebone, J.A., 24
Whiteford, J.L., 405
Whitelaw, W., 115

Provinces' accession numbers / Numéro d'entrée des provinces

1-36	New Brunswick/Nouveau-Brunswick	437-603	British Columbia/Colombie-Brtitannique
37-110	Nova Scotia/Nouvelle-Écosse	604-622	Prince Edward Island/Île-du-Prince-Édouard
111-288	Ontario	623-680	Alberta
289-362	Québec	681-720	Saskatchewan
363-436	Manitoba	721-767	Newfoundland/Terre-Neuve

Index to Chairmen and Commissioners — Index des Présidents et Commmissaires

Whitelock, W.L., 228
Whiteside, D., 502, 524
Whiteside, J.W., 275
Whitney, J.L., 241
Whitton, C., 390
Whyte, A., 681
Wickwire, J.C., 83, 92
Wilkie, D.R., 135
Wilkinson, G.A., 564
Wilkinson, L., 715
Williams, C.G., 220
Williams, D.C., 285
Williams, E.K., 393
Williamson, S.W., 58
Willis, E.F., 400
Willison, J.S., 154, 175
Wilmott, A.R., 233
Wilmott, J.H., 124
Wilson, A., 115
Wilson, C.E., 636
Wilson, C.N., 27

Wilson, G.A., 515
Wilson, G.B., 372
Wilson, H., 221
Wilson, J.D., 747
Wilson, J.O., 538
Wilson, J.T., 277
Wilson, M.L., 640
Wilson, R.R., 531
Wilton-Clark, H., 79
Winch, H.E., 551
Winchester, J., 116, 125
Winegard, W.C., 248
Wingrove, O., 703
Winn, E.S.H., 507, 510, 511
Winsor, E., 734
Wisdom, J.B., 48, 49
Wiser, J.P., 115
Wood, A.W., 431
Wood, E.B., 111
Wood, H., 407
Wood, H.S., 549

Wood, S.C., 115
Woods, M., 712
Woodsworth, J.S., 374
Woolgar, F.D.R., 733
Wootton, R.A.B., 579
Worth, W.H., 671
Wright, D.B., 76
Wright, D.M., 193
Wuhr, M., 23
Wyatt, F.A., 646
Wyman, M., 675

X - Y - Z

Young, C.R., 216, 223
Young, F.M., 503
Young, H.E., 500
Young, M., 156
Young, S.A., 271
Yuill, J., 374

Provinces' accession numbers / Numéro d'entrée des provinces

1-36	New Brunswick/Nouveau-Brunswick	437-603	British Columbia/Colombie-Brtitannique
37-110	Nova Scotia/Nouvelle-Écosse	604-622	Prince Edward Island/Île-du-Prince-Édouard
111-288	Ontario	623-680	Alberta
289-362	Québec	681-720	Saskatchewan
363-436	Manitoba	721-767	Newfoundland/Terre-Neuve

SUBJECT INDEX — INDEX DES SUJETS

A

A.B. Walsh Electrical Limited, 759
A.W. Mason Ltd., 20
Abitibi Power & Paper Company Limited, 217
Acadia Coal Company, 64
The Acadian Commission, 43
Accidents du travail, 301, 306
Accounting, 708, 715, 730
Adams, Frederick, 457
Administration municipale, 303, 318, 335
Adult education, 401
Agence de presse libre du Québec, 360
Agriculteurs, 315
Agricultural colleges, 116, 125, 369, 379
Agricultural credit, 630, 683
Agriculture, 51, 72, 115, 221, 346, 493, 687, 709, 724
Agriculture, Department of, 87
Aird, John, Jr., 196
Alberni, 480
Albert County, 30
Alberta and Great Waterways Railway Company, 625
Alberta Housing Corporation, 678
Algoma University College, 275
Aluminium wiring, 277
Amalgamated Society of Carpenters and Joiners, 154
Amalgamation of Border Cities, 209
Amiante, 358
Andrews, W.R., 146
Annapolis Valley, 73
Apple industry, 56, 73
Arbitration, 242, 552
Architecture, 331
Armstrong, W.G., 453
Arts plastiques, 350
Asiles d'aliénés, 295
Assessment, 135, 483, 592
Assessment Act (1903), 468
Assiniboia, Municipality of, 385
Assurance automobile, 355
Assurance sociale, 309
Atlantic Acceptance Corporation Limited, 254
Attorney General's Department, 179, 240

Automobile insurance, 71, 100, 192, 355, 579
Automotive transportation, 567
Avocats, 354

B

Baie des Chaleurs Railway Company, 297
Baker, Dr. Albert Richard, 512
Bankruptcies, 339
Bannon, Frederick J., 249
Barge, John L., 522
Bathurst, 2
Bathurst Marine Limited, 613
Beauharnois interests, 196
Beban Mine Extension, 531
Beef industry, 370
Belle, C.E., 289
Belleville, 112, 233
Belyea, Arthur Louis, 446
Bennett-Atlin Commission Act (1899), 458
Bible Hill, 87
Bien-être social, 345
Bishop, H.F., 476
Blackhead Road Urban Renewal Scheme, 743
Blind, 144, 155, 392, 585
Boissons alcooliques, 312, 351
Book publishing, 262
Books, 132, 145, 472
Border Cities Amalgamation, 209
Bow River, 655
Bowers, John, 184
Boxing, 427
Bracken, John, 391
Brandon, 424, 425
Brandon Hospital for Mental Diseases, 389
Brandon Packers Limited, 413
Brantford School for the Blind, 144
Brazeau Collieries Limited, 651
Brazil, 677
Bribery, 117, 366, 439, 594
Bridges, 38, 563
Bridgewater Police Department, 98
British Columbia Civil Service Act, 565
The British Columbia Electric Railway Company, 504

Provinces' accession numbers / Numéro d'entrée des provinces

1-36	New Brunswick/Nouveau-Brunswick	437-603	British Columbia/Colombie-Brtitannique
37-110	Nova Scotia/Nouvelle-Écosse	604-622	Prince Edward Island/Île-du-Prince-Édouard
111-288	Ontario	623-680	Alberta
289-362	Québec	681-720	Saskatchewan
363-436	Manitoba	721-767	Newfoundland/Terre-Neuve

Subject Index — Index des Sujets

British Columbia Hydro and Power Authority, 568
British Columbia Power Commission, 554, 568, 573
British Columbia Prohibition Act, 502, 508
British Columbia Railway, 598
Brockville, 168
Building Department (Toronto Board of Education), 161
Building industry, 264
Building safety, 219
Bull semen, 677
Burns, P. & Company, 532
Burwash, 159

C

Calbick, G.A., 453
Calgary, 656, 670
Calgary College, 627
Calgary Correctional Institute, 674
Cameron, Agnes Deans, 472
Campaign funds, 505, 514, 517, 518
Campbell River and District General Hospital, 583
Canada Car and Manufacturing Company Limited, 113
Canada Permanent Trust Company, 108
Canadian Manufacturer's Association, 154
Canadian Northern Railway Company, 488, 505
Cancer, 399
Cape Breton Hospital, 74
Cape Breton Island, 108
Carlow, Frank, 514
Carpenters, 154
Catholic schools, 304
Cattle, 123
Central Prison, 113, 118
Central Prison Labour Commission, 113
Central Railway Company, 6
Centre Huron, 149
Chafe's Nursing Home Fire, 761
Charlottetown Police Force, 619
Chatham, 173
Chemins à barrières, 290
Chemins de fer, 294, 297
Child welfare, 390, 652

Children, 587
Chiropody Act, 541
Chiropraxie, 340
Chiropraxy, 340, 528
Church Missionary Society, 440
Church properties, 636
Churches, 515, 636
Churchill River, 433
Circonscriptions électorales, 35
City of St. John's Act, 740
City of Winnipeg Act, 430
Civic taxation, 3
Civil rights, 231, 238, 250, 260, 578
Civil Service, 565
Clubs, 469
Cluff Lake, 720
Coal miners, 506
Coal mining industry, 12, 23, 52, 57, 64, 70, 79, 464, 495, 496, 498,509, 530, 531, 623, 629, 633, 637, 644, 698, 707
Coastal Industries Limited, 30
Cobourg, 180
Cochrane, District of, 212
Coffin, Wilbert, 332
Cole Harbour, 93
Collective bargaining, 97, 388, 565, 582, 589
Colleges, 116, 125, 275, 369, 379, 590, 627, 672
Collingwood, 213
Colonisation, 299
Colonisation, Département de la, 329
Colonization, 299
Colonization, Department of, 329
Commerce du livre, 326
Commissaires d'écoles, 334
Commission des écoles catholiques de la Cité de Jacques-Cartier, 334
Commission des écoles catholiques de Verdun, 334
Communications industry, 271
The Comox Logging and Railway Company, 558
Compagnie de chemin de fer de la Baie des Chaleurs, 297
Compagnie de chemin de fer Québec, Montréal, Ottawa et Occidental, 294
Compulsory retirement, 436
Concord, 187
Confederation, 725
Conflict of interest, 667
Congregational Churches, 636

Provinces' accession numbers / Numéro d'entrée des provinces

1-36	New Brunswick/Nouveau-Brunswick	437-603	British Columbia/Colombie-Brtitannique
37-110	Nova Scotia/Nouvelle-Écosse	604-622	Prince Edward Island/Île-du-Prince-Édouard
111-288	Ontario	623-680	Alberta
289-362	Québec	681-720	Saskatchewan
363-436	Manitoba	721-767	Newfoundland/Terre-Neuve

Subject Index — Index des Sujets

Consommateurs, 315
Constitution, 316
Constitutional law, 316
Construction, 239, 356
Consumers, 666
Cooper, Fannie, 383
Coopérative de déménagement du 1er mai, 360
Corner Brook, 723
Coroners, 176, 252, 675
Corporal punishment, 538
Corporation de gaz naturel du Québec, 324
Corrigan, P., 520
Corruption, 391
Cosmopolitan Life Assurance Company, 676
Cost of living, 721
Cour municipale de Québec, 337
Courtenay, 490
Courts, 675
Cowper, John Sedgwick, 505
Credit, 90
Crime, 240, 255
Crime organisé, 347
Criminal investigation, 762
Criminal justice, 347
Crop insurance, 404
Crown and Public Lands, Department of, 606
Crown Land Department, 1
Crown lands, 475, 489
Crown Timber Act, 177
Crown timber lands, 1
Crow's Nest Pass Company, 496
Cumberland Railway and Coal Company, 79

D

Dairy industry, 34, 61, 91, 147, 225, 487, 521, 555, 612, 616, 647, 697
Dams, 148, 554
Dartmouth, 78
Davidson, J.R., Dr., 399
Davie, Theodore, 449
Deacon, C.R., 168
Deaf and Dumb Institute, 143
Death benefit, 545
Debtor and creditor, 90
De Cosmos, Amor, 438
Dehorning cattle, 123
Dentistry, 158, 256
Dick, Archibald, 465

Digby, County of, 39
Dimanche, loi du, 343
Dimensional Investments Limited, 235
Dionne, J.A., Docteur, 322
Disposal Services Limited, 280
Dominion Coal Workers'Relief Association, 108
Dominion Power and Transmission Company Limited, 196
Dominion Steel and Coal Corporation Limited, 752
Don Jail, 230
Dorland, Albert, 198
DOSCO, 752
Doukhobors, 486, 547, 556, 572
Drainage, 127, 386, 396
Drawing books, 472
Droit constitutionnel, 316
Droits linguistiques, 353
Drought, 631
Drug prices, 737
Drug raid, 266
Drugless healing, 528
Dry docks, 441
Duckworth, Thomas Richard, 696
Duke, George Clinton, 255
Dump Truck Owners' Association, 232
Duncan, James Lewis, 218
Duncan, William, 440
Dundas, County of, 142
Dunn, Township of, 248
Dunnville, 170

E

East Elgin, 146
East Windsor Health Association, 229
Eastern Irrigation District, 649
École normale Jacques-Cartier de Montréal, 321
Écoles catholiques, 304
Écoles d'architecture, 331
Economic conditions, 60, 67, 519, 631, 634, 658, 736, 754
Édition, 326
Edmonton, 648, 656, 668
Edmonton Real Estate Board Co-operative Listing Bureau Limited, 669
Education\Éducation, 25, 69, 158, 228, 320, 374, 388, 401, 407, 539, 571, 584, 585, 597, 607, 608, 609, 611, 660, 671, 687, 735, 757

Provinces' accession numbers / Numéro d'entrée des provinces			
1-36	New Brunswick/Nouveau-Brunswick	437-603	British Columbia/Colombie-Brtitannique
37-110	Nova Scotia/Nouvelle-Écosse	604-622	Prince Edward Island/Île-du-Prince-Édouard
111-288	Ontario	623-680	Alberta
289-362	Québec	681-720	Saskatchewan
363-436	Manitoba	721-767	Newfoundland/Terre-Neuve

Subject Index — Index des Sujets

Education, Department of, 114, 472, 663
Éducation des adultes, 362
Egg industry, 259
Eight-Hour Day Commission, 42
Election districts, 35, 59, 497, 575, 588, 599
Elections\Élections, 35, 59, 81, 96, 136, 189, 205, 293, 363, 439, 501, 503, 505, 517, 603, 610, 657
Electric power, 268, 731
Electric railways, 504
Electric utilities, 568, 622
Electrical Development Company of Ontario, 157
Electrical energy, 691
Electrical industry, 564
Électricité, 310
Electricity, 310
Electronic eavesdropping, 578
Elevators, 393, 682
Elizabeth Towers Apartments, 762
Elliott, A.C., 439
Embezzlement, 365
Eminent domain, 574
Empire Mills Limited, 566
Employer-employee relations, 31, 239, 242, 251, 582, 701
Energy policy, 268
Enquêtes publiques, 298
Enseignement, 330, 331, 350
Enseignement supérieur, 25
Enseignement technique et professionel, 320
Environment, 281
The Environmental Assessment Act, 281
Environnement, 281
Epidemics, 448
Esquimalt, 441
Esquimalt and Nanaimo Railway Company, 460, 488
Exhibition scholarships, 138
Expropriation, 574
Extortion, 149

F

F.B. McNamee & Company, 441
Factory Act, 4
Faillites, 339
FAME Inquiry, 243
Family, 587

Family Relations Act, 587
Farm machinery, 686
Farmers' Allied Meat Enterprises Co-operatives Limited, 243
Farming, 689
Farr, Michael, 149
Federal-provincial relations, 60, 316, 725
Feeble minded, 47, 160
Fees Commission, 129
Female offenders, 600
Fertilizers, 428
Filmer, A.E., 594
Finance, 60, 316, 368
Finance companies, 254
Finances municipales, 27
Finances publiques, 316
Fire insurance, 479
Firearms safety, 415
Fires, 65, 181, 456
Fiscalité, 341
Fish, 124
Fish conservation, 573
Fisheries, 54, 150, 621, 705, 764
Fishing industry, 394
Fitzstubbs, N., Captain, 452
Flood, Charles H., 467
Floods, 265, 409, 655
Fluoridation, 236
Fluorspar, 741
Food industry, 286
Food prices, 737
Forest fires, 181
Forest Industrial Relations, 561
Forest management, 557
Forestry, 29, 89, 128, 131, 224, 429, 477, 540, 560, 589, 593, 704, 722, 742, 767
Fort Erie, 266
Fort Frances, 179
Fort George, 503
Fort Vermillion School Division, 663
Forty-eight hour working week, 635
Fredericton, 32
Freedom of information, 285
French language, 353
Frontenac, County of, 148
Fruit industry, 526, 562
Fruit trees, 113, 562
Fullerton, C.P., 377
Funeral services, 661

Provinces' accession numbers / Numéro d'entrée des provinces			
1-36	New Brunswick/Nouveau-Brunswick	437-603	British Columbia/Colombie-Brtitannique
37-110	Nova Scotia/Nouvelle-Écosse	604-622	Prince Edward Island/Île-du-Prince-Édouard
111-288	Ontario	623-680	Alberta
289-362	Québec	681-720	Saskatchewan
363-436	Manitoba	721-767	Newfoundland/Terre-Neuve

Subject Index — Index des Sujets

G

Game, 124, 150
Game Conservation Board, 512
Gamey, R.R., 137
Gardhouse, George W., 249
Gasoline prices, 94, 186, 577
Gastown, 581
Gauthier, John A, 518
Gaz naturel, 324, 338
Gendarmerie royale du Canada, 36, 360
Georgetown Industries, 613
Georgetown Shipyard, 617
Gertler, Leonard, 258
Glace Bay, 104
Glenelg, Township of, 184, 194
Globe and Mail, 218
Gloucester County, 2
Gold River, 82
Good Roads Commission, 153
Goodwin, John, 171
Gouvernement provincial, 298, 300
Govan, Philip, 601
Government administration, 713
Government information, 285
Government liability, 574
Government Purchasing Service, 329
Government telephones, 375
Grahame, T.L., 455
Grain, 693
Grain elevators, 393, 682
Grain marketing, 684
Grand Rapids Hydro Electric Project, 419
Grand River, 265
Grande Cache, 673
Greenway, Thomas, 366
Greer, Samuel, 442
Grey, County of, 184, 194
Griffin, Michael, 231
Grizzly Valley Natural Gas Pipeline, 596
Gros Morne National Park, 760
Gulf Garden Foods Limited, 613

H

Haldimand, County of, 248
Half-breed population, 645
Halifax, 78

Halifax and South Western Railway Company, 44
Halifax County Hospital, 93
Halifax, County of, 80
Hallett, Isaac H, 445
Hamilton, 167
Hamilton-Wentworth Region, 279
Hanging, 11
Harbours, 745
Hastings, David, 170
Healing arts, 256
Health, 345, 732
Health and Public Welfare, Department of, 390
Health care, 256
Health information, 284
Health insurance, 507, 525
Health Insurance Commission, 511
Health services, 702
Heavy water plants, 104
Hébert, Jacques, 332
Herbicides, 591
Herd Law, 685
Higher education, 25, 611
Highways, 75, 153, 648
Hill, James, 473
Hillcrest Coal Mines, 626
Hinman, Edgar W., 667
Hollinger Consolidated Gold Mines Limited, 191
Home of the Friendless, 534
Hooke, Albert J., 667
Hôpital Charles Lemoyne, 352
Hôpital général Fleury Inc., 322, 325
Hôpital Jean-Talon de Montréal, 319
Hôpital Saint-Louis de Windsor Inc., 348
Hôpital St. Michel, 323
Hôpitaux, 295, 333
Hospital insurance, 551
Hospitalization, 403, 423
Hospitals, 17, 37, 74, 84, 93, 167, 193, 206, 215, 242, 389, 459, 481, 516, 549, 583, 595, 605, 638, 639, 712
House construction, 385, 739
House of Assembly, 101, 107, 110
Housing, 729
Housing, Ministry of, 272
Hunter, Hugh, 470
Huston, Orville, 179
Hydro development, 573
Hydro-electric energy, 82, 402
Hydro-electric power, 419, 433

Provinces' accession numbers / Numéro d'entrée des provinces

1-36	New Brunswick/Nouveau-Brunswick	437-603	British Columbia/Colombie-Brtitannique
37-110	Nova Scotia/Nouvelle-Écosse	604-622	Prince Edward Island/Île-du-Prince-Édouard
111-288	Ontario	623-680	Alberta
289-362	Québec	681-720	Saskatchewan
363-436	Manitoba	721-767	Newfoundland/Terre-Neuve

Subject Index — Index des Sujets

Hydro-Electric Power Commission of Ontario, 157, 166, 183, 196, 204, 235, 261
Hydro-electric railways, 169
Hydro-Québec, 324

I

Immeubles, 344
Immigration, 289, 695
Impôt, 316
Impôt municipal, 313
Impôt scolaire, 313
Incendies, 308, 357
Indemnisation des travailleurs, 306
Indian land claims, 440, 442
Indian Lands, 235
Indians, 443
Industrial Conciliation and Arbitration Act, 552
Industrial farms, 159, 187
Industrial sabotage, 148
Industrial safety, 237, 270, 763
Industrie de la construction, 356
Industrie des communications, 271
Industrie laitière, 34
Inflation, 666
Inga, 641
Innisfail Municipal Hospital, 638
Institut Albert Prévost, 333
Insulators, 104
Insurance, 71, 92, 100, 162, 192, 241, 355, 404, 479, 507, 510, 511, 525, 544, 545, 551, 579
International Woodworkers of America, 561
Iron Ore Company of Canada, 763
Irrigation, 474, 519, 540, 542, 646, 649

J

Jasper, 648
Jericho Hill School, 585
Jeux olympiques (Montréal, 1976), 359
Joiners, 154
Joliffe, Edward B., 222
Judges, 601
Judicial boundaries, 414
Judiciary, 249, 253, 278, 601
Justice, 291, 337, 642, 675
Justice criminelle, 347

Justice, Department of, 36
Justice, Ministère de la, 36
Juvenile delinquency, 570, 664

K

Kapuskasing Colony, 164
Keays, J.E., 226
Kelowna Police Department, 520
Kildonan, 363
Kingston, Township of, 263
Kootenay, 439, 475
Kootenay Institute for Post Secondary Studies, 584
Kosygin visit, 260
Kurata, Lucien Coe, 253

L

Labour, 42, 48, 151, 239, 494
Labour accidents, 301, 306
Labour disputes, 251, 413, 532, 561, 564, 589, 748
Labour legislation, 85, 744
Labrador, 754
Labrador economy, 736
Lac Abitibi, 300
Laing, George, 171
Lake St. John Power & Paper Company Limited, 311
Land assembly, 99, 680
Land claims, 442, 475
The Land Drainage Act, 386, 396
Land fill sites, 280
Land grants, 460
Land patents, 184, 194
Land prices, 432
Land purchases, 344, 615
Land sales, 30, 272, 499
Land speculation tax, 274
Land tenure, 574, 614
Land titles, 176
Land use, 435
Lands, 1, 44, 235, 440, 442, 475, 489, 524, 614
Lands and Forests, Department of, 202
Lands and Works, Department of, 452, 455, 471
Landslides, 554

Provinces' accession numbers / Numéro d'entrée des provinces

1-36	New Brunswick/Nouveau-Brunswick	437-603	British Columbia/Colombie-Brtitannique
37-110	Nova Scotia/Nouvelle-Écosse	604-622	Prince Edward Island/Île-du-Prince-Édouard
111-288	Ontario	623-680	Alberta
289-362	Québec	681-720	Saskatchewan
363-436	Manitoba	721-767	Newfoundland/Terre-Neuve

Subject Index — Index des Sujets

Langstaff, 187
Language rights, 353
Langue française, 353
Laurel Point, 471
Laurier Palace, 308
Lavallée, V.P., 296
Legislative Assembly, 117, 137, 518, 610, 696
Leiner, Norbert, Rabbi, 238
Lennox, 261
Lethbridge Central Feeder's Association Limited, 662
Lethbridge Gaol Inquiry, 632
Lewis, A.C., 179
Liability of employers, 151
Library service, 717
Licences, 305
Liquidations, 339
Liquor, 24, 83, 165, 405, 473, 508, 517, 553, 580, 696
Liquor Control Board of Ontario, 208
Liquor Licence Act (1900), 463
Liquor License Board of Centre Huron, 149
Liquor license inspectors, 146, 149, 168, 173
Little Manitou Lake, 703
Livestock industry, 685
Livestock marketing, 431, 688
Livre, 326
Local government, 105, 279, 283, 416, 424
Logement, 314
Logging, 558
Logging industry, 726
London Gaol Inquiry, 190
Lotteries, 434
Lumber industry, 13, 54
Lumber trade, 429
Lunatic asylums, 295, 451

M

McCaughrin, Daniel, 201
Macdonald, John A., Sir, 438
Macdonald, M.A., 501, 505
McGillivray Greek Coal and Coke Company, 637
MacInnis, Donald Ross, Dr., 106
McKinnon, G.D., 594
Magistrates, 445, 751
Malden, Township of, 273
Manitoba Agricultural College, 379

Manitoba Central Railway Company, 366
Manitoba Free Press, 366
Manitoba Hydro, 433
Manitoba Hydro-Electric Board, 419
Manitoba Pool Elevators Limited, 393
The Manitoba School Question, 367
Margarine, 412
Maritime Electric Company, 622
Marketing boards, 536
Markham, Township of, 185
Marriage Act, 572
Martin, Joseph, 366
Marystown Shipyard Limited, 766
Maternity benefits, 525
Maternity insurance, 510
Meat industry, 370, 431
Mechanics Lien Act, 665, 711
Media, 271
Medical education, 158, 256
Medical Faculty Dalhousie University, 84
Medical insurance, 92, 241
Medical records, 284
Mental Hospitals Act, 215
Mental hygiene, 516
Mental illness, 160
Mental institutions, 638
Mentally deficient, 53
Mesureurs de bois, 307
Methodist Church, 636
Metis, 425, 645
Metlakaltlah, 440
Middlesex, County of, 190
Milk Control Board of Ontario, 225
Mills, 311
Mimico, 206
Mineral industry, 755
Mineral resources, 120, 411
Mineral transactions, 710
Miners' Relief Societies, 41
Mines and mining, 40, 45, 46, 52, 57, 64, 70, 79, 120, 156, 191, 220, 270, 361, 464, 509, 531, 602, 623, 626, 637, 651, 741
Les Mines Belmoral Ltée, 361
Mining laws, 435, 458, 462, 716
Minto Coal Company Ltd., 12
Misconduct in office, 642, 667
Missions, 440
Moncton, 33
Montréal, 303, 312, 318, 357

Provinces' accession numbers / Numéro d'entrée des provinces

1-36	New Brunswick/Nouveau-Brunswick	437-603	British Columbia/Colombie-Brtitannique
37-110	Nova Scotia/Nouvelle-Écosse	604-622	Prince Edward Island/Île-du-Prince-Édouard
111-288	Ontario	623-680	Alberta
289-362	Québec	681-720	Saskatchewan
363-436	Manitoba	721-767	Newfoundland/Terre-Neuve

Moore, Edward, 632
Moores, Frank D., 759
Morell Creamery Co-operative Association Limited, 616
Morley, A.J., 476
Morning Call, 366
Morrisburgh, 142
Mortgages, 418
Mothers' pensions, 16, 49, 507, 511
Motion-picture theatres, 533
Moulton, Township of, 248
Mount Douglas Park, 527
Mount View High School, 538
Mouvement pour la défense des prisonniers politiques au Québec, 360
Mulgrave, 103
Muller, Hans, 289
Municipal affairs, 263, 273, 416, 417, 586, 641
Municipal finance, 112, 122, 178, 180, 185, 213, 233, 234, 397, 746
Municipal government, 28, 80, 86, 209, 244, 276, 318, 397, 447, 482, 485, 491, 670, 681, 740, 756
Municipal institutions, 119
Municipal laws, 364
Municipal taxation, 3, 27, 126, 135, 246, 529, 643, 699
Municipal water supplies, 236
Municipalities, 283, 480, 490, 491, 523

N

Nakusp & Slocan Railway Company, 449
Nanticoke, 261
Napanee River, 148
National parks, 128
National Thrift Corporation, 68
Native people, 675
Natural gas, 324, 408, 596, 654
Natural Products Marketing (British Columbia) Act, 536
Nelson, Jean Clyne, 664
Nelson Public School, 484
Nelson River, 433
New Brunswick Power Company, 9
New Westminster, 459, 461, 489, 499, 535
New Westminster Fire Department, 456
New Westminster Water Department, 456

Newfoundland economy, 736
Newfoundland Liquor Commission, 747
Niagara escarpment, 258
Niagara Falls, 111
Niagara Parks Commission, 203
Nickel industry, 156
Nordegg, 651
Norquay, John, 365
North Pacific Lumber Company, 489
North Pickering, 272
North Shore, 290
Northern Alberta, 658
Northern Development, Department of, 212
Northern Ontario, 181, 281
Northern Pacific and Manitoba Railway Company, 366
The Nova Scotia Elections Act, 59
Nova Scotia Housing Commission, 99
Nova Scotia Light and Power Company Limited, 82
Nova Scotia Teachers' Union Sydney Local, 97
Nuclear energy, 268
Nurses, 595
Nursing, 757
Nursing homes, 761

O

Oakalla Prison Farm, 548
Oakalla Women's Correctional Centre, 600
Occupational Training Council, 597
Oil companies, 94, 186
Oil prices, 94, 186, 269
Old age homes, 466, 534, 761
Old age pensions, 15, 41, 55
Olympic games (Montreal, 1976), 359
Ontario Agricultural College, 116, 125
Ontario Athletic Commission, 207
Ontario Hospital, 167, 206
Ontario Nord, 281
Ontario Northland Transportation Commission, 210
Ontario Power Service Corporation, 204
Ontario Prison Reform Commission, 121
Ontario Provincial Police Force, 222, 226, 255
Ontario Reformatory, 214
Ontario School for the Blind, 155
Ontario Securities Commission, 245

Provinces' accession numbers / Numéro d'entrée des provinces

1-36	New Brunswick/Nouveau-Brunswick	437-603	British Columbia/Colombie-Brtitannique
37-110	Nova Scotia/Nouvelle-Écosse	604-622	Prince Edward Island/Île-du-Prince-Édouard
111-288	Ontario	623-680	Alberta
289-362	Québec	681-720	Saskatchewan
363-436	Manitoba	721-767	Newfoundland/Terre-Neuve

Subject Index — Index des Sujets

Ontario Temperance Act, 165, 168, 170
Organized crime, 240, 347
Orillia, 201
Osgoode Hall, 176
Oshawa, 178, 261
Ostéopathie, 340
Osteopathy, 340
Ottawa Collegiate Institute, 188
Ottawa South, 189

P

Pacific Great Eastern Railway, 513
Palais législatif, 292
PAP Holdings Ltd., 676
Parks, 527, 760
Parliament buildings, 376, 377, 457
The Pas, 429
Patterson, William, 149
Penal Commission, 706
Pendray, W.J., 471
Pensions, 15, 16, 41, 49, 55, 141, 287, 507, 511, 727, 733
Perth, 140
Pesticides, 257, 591
Petroleum industry, 530, 650
Petroleum products, 269
Phoenix, 467
Pickering, 261
Pictou, 40
Pictou County, 46
Pipelines, 596, 716
Planta, J.P., 450
Plugging Case, 501
Plumbing and pipe-fitting industry, 564
Police, 98, 163, 172, 198, 211, 222, 226, 231, 238, 240, 255, 260, 266, 267, 291, 312, 360, 373, 383, 398, 520, 535, 559, 581, 619, 696, 762
Police Commission, 670
Police commissioners, 476
Police magistrates, 170, 171, 176, 201, 446, 450, 467
Pollution, 248
Poor, 39
Porcupine-Chilkat Districts, 462
Pork industry, 624
Post-secondary education, 584

Potato, 10, 26
Power resources, 691
Presbyterian Church, 515, 636
Price Brothers & Company Limited, 311
Prince Edward Island Hospital for the Insane, 605
Prince Edward Island Housing Authority, 615
Prince Edward Island Land Development Corporation, 615
Prison reform, 121
Prisoners, 548
Prisons, 18, 58, 113, 118, 187, 190, 193, 214, 230, 282, 378, 444, 453, 454, 461, 548, 600, 618, 632, 706
Privacy, 284, 285, 578
Prohibition, 502, 508
Project III, 569
Property sales, 420
Prostitution, 373
Protestant School Board of Greater Montreal, 336
Proton, Township of, 122
Provincial air service, 202
The Provincial Electoral Franchise Act (1931), 59
Provincial government, 298
Provincial Highway Board, 50
Provincial Home, 466
Provincial Hospital, 17
Provincial Hospital for the Insane, 37
Provincial Mental Hospital, 639
Provincial Mental Institute, 638
Provincial-municipal relations, 529, 543
Provincial officials, 107, 110, 129, 667
Provincial Party, 513
Provincial taxation, 643, 699
Provincial Training School, 638
Public buildings, 219
Public enquiries, 298
Public finance, 134, 316, 368, 468
Public health nursing, 511
Public Lands Office, 604
Public schools, 69
Public servants, 470
Public service, 67, 565, 582, 694
Public Service Commission, 176
Public services, 31
Public welfare, 193, 345, 392, 750, 752
Public Welfare, Department of, 652
Public Works and Services, Department of, 765
Publishing, 262
Pulp and paper mills, 343

	Provinces' accession numbers / Numéro d'entrée des provinces		
1-36	New Brunswick/Nouveau-Brunswick	437-603	British Columbia/Colombie-Brtitannique
37-110	Nova Scotia/Nouvelle-Écosse	604-622	Prince Edward Island/Île-du-Prince-Édouard
111-288	Ontario	623-680	Alberta
289-362	Québec	681-720	Saskatchewan
363-436	Manitoba	721-767	Newfoundland/Terre-Neuve

Puntledge River, 573

Q

Quebec Liquor Board, 344
Quebec Natural Gas Corporation, 324
Québec (Ville), 335
Queen Hotel, 65
Queen's University, 175
Queens County Jail, 618

R

Radial Railway Commission, 169
Radium, 197
Railways, 7, 139, 169, 210, 297, 449, 488, 513, 598, 625
Railwest Railcar Manufacturing Plant, 598
Ranch Ehrlo Society, 719
Rates and Taxes Act, 19
Real estate, 336
Real property, 418, 546, 574, 592
Realtors, 669
Rebates, 286
Reclamation of land, 475, 524
Red Deer College, 672
Redistribution, 575, 599
Reformatories, 121, 214, 674
Régie des alcools du Québec, 344
Registrars of deeds, 140, 142
Registry offices, 176
Relations employeurs-employs, 31
Relations fédérales-provinciales, 316
Remuneration of officials, 101, 110, 129, 176
Rentals Act, 78
Research, 223
Restigouche Boom Company, 5
Retail stores, 620
Retirement, 436
Richmond County, 75
Riots, 506, 581
Ritchie, Donald, Mrs., 549
Rive nord, 290
Rive sud, 290
Road-user charges, 567
Roads, 20, 38, 50, 153, 380, 558, 648
Ronto Development Company, 274

Royal American Shows Inc., 679
Royal Canadian Mounted Police, 36, 360, 679
Royalties, 132
Rural credit, 72
The Rural Credits Act, 387
Rural life, 709

S

Saanich, 523
Sackville, 99, 105
Saint John, 28
Saint John and Quebec Railway Company, 7
St. John's, 729, 740, 745, 746, 753
St. Lawrence, 741
St. Regis Paper Company (Canada) Ltd., 30
Salaires, 342
Salaries, 659
Samson, Robert, 360
San Jose Scale Act, 133
Sanatorium Bégin de Sainte-Germaine de Dorchester, 327
Sanatorium Ross de Gaspé, 328
Sandwich, 209
Sanger, Daniel LeRoy, 548
Santé, 345
Santé au travail, 358
Sargent, R.A., 578
Sarnia, 235
Sauvetage minier, 361
Scholarships, 138
School boards, 97, 103, 336, 484, 485, 492
School books, 132
School taxation, 546, 723
School trustees, 663
Schools, 2, 22, 69, 174, 188, 228, 304, 374, 585, 638, 758
Scott, John T., 501
Second Narrows Bridge, 563
Separate schools, 228, 367
Service des achats du gouvernement, 329
Services publics, 31
Settell, E.C., 183
Settlers, 460
Seven Sisters Falls' Power Agreement, 391
Sewage disposal, 758
Shaughnessy Heights, 491
Shearer, J.G., Rev., 373

Provinces' accession numbers / Numéro d'entrée des provinces

1-36	New Brunswick/Nouveau-Brunswick	437-603	British Columbia/Colombie-Brtitannique
37-110	Nova Scotia/Nouvelle-Écosse	604-622	Prince Edward Island/Île-du-Prince-Édouard
111-288	Ontario	623-680	Alberta
289-362	Québec	681-720	Saskatchewan
363-436	Manitoba	721-767	Newfoundland/Terre-Neuve

Subject Index — Index des Sujets

Sherbrooke, Township of, 248
Sherriffs, 129, 176
Shipyards, 617, 766
Shopping centres, 620
Shulman, Morton, 252, 255
Silicosis, 21
Small-pox, 448
Social insurance, 309
Social Services and Rehabilitation, Department of, 752
Soldiers' aid, 500
Soldiers' Settlement Colony, 164
Songhees Indian Reserve, 488
South Park School, 472
South Shore, 290
Southern Alberta, 631
Spalding, Warner Reeve, 437
Spinks, J.M.M., 442
Sports, 207
Springhill, 70, 79
Standard Forms Commission, 700
Strikes, 384, 413, 506
Sturgeon Falls, 200
Sumas, 524
Sumas Dyking District Relief Act, 524
Sunday legislation, 343
Sûreté du Québec, 360
Sûreté provinciale, 312
Surface rights, 435, 716
Surrey, 586
Swim, Bennie, 11
Sydney School Board, 97
Syndicalisme, 356

T

Taber, F.B., 168
Tait, Leonard, 476
Taxation, 3, 14, 19, 27, 126, 135, 139, 246, 316, 341, 483, 529, 546, 592, 643, 653, 699, 714
Taxi Owners Reciprocal Insurance Association, 317
Taylor, F.G., 391
Teachers, 97, 659
Teaching, 43
Teamsters Union, 232
Technical and vocational education, 320, 597
Technical education, 374, 687

Telephones, 375
Temiskaming and Northern Ontario Railway, 210
Temperance, 165, 168, 170, 173
Terrains, 300
Texada Island, 438
Textbooks, 145
Thomas, Robert William, 520
Thompson, Frederick, 750
Thompson, Harry, Mrs., 453
Thompson, Robert, 484
Thompson, Ruth, 750
Tilley East Area, 634
Timber, 8, 177, 489, 566, 569
Timber licences, 557, 560
Timber resources, 477
Timmins, 191
Toohey, William, 198
Toronto, 244, 276
Toronto Board of Education, 161
Toronto Island, 257, 288
Toronto Jail, 282
Toronto Police Court, 172, 176
Toronto Police Force, 163, 211, 231, 238, 260, 267
Toronto Stock Exchange, 245
The Totogan Farms Limited, 420
Tourist industry, 111
Trade-unions, 356, 564
Transients, 668
Transport, 342
Transport scolaire, 349
Transportation, 62, 216, 422, 567, 728, 734
Travail, 306
Travail du dimanche, 343
Tree farm licences, 566, 569
Trucking industry, 728
Truro, 87
Trust funds, 395
Tuberculose, 302
Tuberculosis, 302, 690
Turnpike trusts, 290

U

Unemployment, 154
Unemployment relief, 199, 200, 218
United Church of Canada, 515, 636
United Packinghouse Workers of America, 413

Provinces' accession numbers / Numéro d'entrée des provinces

1-36	New Brunswick/Nouveau-Brunswick	437-603	British Columbia/Colombie-Brtitannique
37-110	Nova Scotia/Nouvelle-Écosse	604-622	Prince Edward Island/Île-du-Prince-Édouard
111-288	Ontario	623-680	Alberta
289-362	Québec	681-720	Saskatchewan
363-436	Manitoba	721-767	Newfoundland/Terre-Neuve

Subject Index — Index des Sujets

Universities, 718
University finance, 175
University of British Columbia, 478
University of Manitoba, 372, 388, 395
University of Toronto, 130, 138, 141, 175
Upper Gullies Elementary School, 758
Uranium industry, 720
Uranium mining, 602
Urban renewal, 743
Usines, 311
Usines de pâtes et papiers, 343

V

Vale Colliery Commission, 46
Vancouver, 485, 492, 501
Vancouver Community College, 590
Vancouver General Hospital, 481
Vancouver Island riots, 506
Vancouver Police Force, 559
Vegetable marketing, 421
Venereal diseases, 160, 400
Veterans, 164
Vice, 373, 383
Victoria, 447
Victoria General Hospital, 84
Victoria Industrial School for Boys, 174
Victoria Police Commission, 476
Violence, 271
Vocational education, 320, 597
Vogel, Richard, 601
Voting, 152

W

Wages, 48, 166, 738
Walkem, George A., 438
Walkerville, 209
Waste Management Inc., 280
Water haulage services, 419
Water power developments, 402
Water works regulations, 157
Waterfowl, 257
Waterloo Region, 283
Watt, W.J., 211
Welland, 152, 171
West Elgin, 136
Westaskiwin, 648
Western University of London, 175
Whatshan Dam Inquiry, 554
Whelihan, Charles Edward, 140
Wilderness challenge camps, 719
Williams, Harry J., 278
Windfall Oils and Mines Limited, 245
Windsor, 209
Winnipeg, 397, 408, 410, 417, 427, 430, 432
Winnipeg Electric Company, 391
Winnipeg General Strike, 384
Winnipeg Police Force, 373, 383, 398
Women, 48
Women's farms, 187
Working week, 635
Workmen's compensation, 63, 77, 95, 151, 306, 371, 494, 628, 692, 741
Workmen's Compensation Act, 13, 195, 227, 247, 406, 576
Workmen's Compensation Board, 54, 382, 537, 550, 749
Wright, Robert, 231

X - Y - Z

X-rays, 197
York, Township of, 199, 234
Youth, 735

Provinces' accession numbers / Numéro d'entrée des provinces

1-36	New Brunswick/Nouveau-Brunswick	437-603	British Columbia/Colombie-Brtitannique
37-110	Nova Scotia/Nouvelle-Écosse	604-622	Prince Edward Island/Île-du-Prince-Édouard
111-288	Ontario	623-680	Alberta
289-362	Québec	681-720	Saskatchewan
363-436	Manitoba	721-767	Newfoundland/Terre-Neuve